MORNING
Meditations

365 Daily Devotions

MARK AGAN

Introduction

I started writing a daily devotional for our church members, hoping to give them a daily encouragement from God's Word. I never intended to write a book, I just wanted to give them something each morning to challenge them in their walk with God.

I began posting them to my blog and also to Facebook. I was very encouraged from the responses I would get from people who were blessed by them and some who even began to share them with others.

After doing this for over a year, it occurred to me that I should compile these daily devotionals into a book and make it available to anyone else who might find them helpful.

It is my desire that these will encourage and strengthen you in your daily walk with the Lord! –Mark Agan

About The Author

Mark Agan has been in the ministry for over thirty years. He has pastored churches in Georgia, Florida, and now in North Carolina, where he currently pastors. He is also the Chaplain for the Chatham County Sheriff's Office in Chatham County, North Carolina.

To learn more about the author, visit his web site at: **www.MarkAgan.com**

Other Books By Mark Agan

RESTORATION: There's Life After The Locust

The Deceptive Side Of Suicide

A Home Built God's Way

911: What's Your Emergency?

The Power of Meditating On Scripture

What Are You Thinking? Winning the Battle Of Your Mind

Keeping It All Together When It's All Falling Apart

Church Membership Matters

How To Make Your Prayer Time Fresh & Exciting!

...and others are available on **www.Amazon.com.**

A New Beginning

"In the beginning was the Word, and the Word was with God, and the Word was God." (John 1:1)

Every January we have the opportunity to look back and reflect over the past year. What made us happy? What did we enjoy? What did we regret?

Well, the Bible has a lot to say about beginnings. Genesis 1:1 reminds us that *"In the **beginning** God created the heaven and the earth."* But in the Book of John we see another beginning. John says, *"In the **beginning** was the Word, and the Word was with God, and the Word was God."* Since we know that the *"Word"* is Jesus, John is telling us that Jesus was at the beginning. What a thought… that before there was anything, there was Jesus!

There is a lesson for us in this truth. The lesson is that no matter what you are wanting to do, make sure Jesus is a part of the beginning. If you want it to be a success, make sure to start with Jesus. Start with the Word! Sadly, few people start with Jesus then they wonder what went wrong. If what you are doing doesn't start with Jesus, it is doomed to fail!

Many marriages have failed because they didn't begin their marriage with Jesus. Many homes have become divided because they were not built upon Jesus.

Start this year off with Jesus. Determine to put Him first place in your life. Make Him the foundation of your life, your marriage, and your home. If you will do that, you can have a brand new beginning!

The Battle Is The Lord's

"And all this assembly shall know that the LORD saveth
not with sword and spear: for the battle is the LORD'S..."
(I Sam. 17:47)

Picture this: young shepherd boy, David, has just seen Goliath curse and defy the God of Israel. Every Israelite soldier is shaking in his boots, too scared to face Goliath. Suddenly young David runs out of nowhere to face Goliath, himself. Now...the Philistines, the Israelites, Goliath, and even Israel's King Saul mistakenly think this is just a battle between the Philistine army and the Israelite army.

They think that the winner is yet to be determined, but David sets the record straight. The winner has already been declared BEFORE the battle even begins! While everyone is holding their breath to see what the outcome will be, little David runs toward Goliath and reminds everyone there that *"the battle is the LORD's."*

May I remind you this morning that although your faith may be under attack by Satan, the battle doesn't belong to Satan. Although the world seems to be winning against Christianity at every turn and even though the wicked seem to be getting away with their ungodliness, we must remember that the battle doesn't belong to the world or to the wicked. The battle is the LORD'S!

You may feel you are all alone at your school or at your job. But the truth about the matter is, just as David didn't face Goliath alone, you are not fighting this battle alone, either! Just remember *"the battle is the LORD's."*

Dirty Hands!

"Wherefore come out from among them, and be ye separate, saith the Lord, and touch not the unclean thing; and I will receive you," (2Cor. 6:7)

One of Susannah Wesley's daughters wanted to do something she wasn't completely sure was right. Her mother said she should not do it if she wasn't sure it was the right thing to do, but her daughter was not convinced.

Later, that evening, Susannah and her daughter were sitting beside a fire that had gone out. The coals were now cold. Susannah said, "Pick up that bit of coal."

"I don't want to," said the girl.

"Go on," said her mother. "The fire is out, it won't burn you."

"I know it will not burn me, but it will blacken my hands," she replied.

"Exactly," said her mother. "That thing you wanted to do, may not have burned you, but it would blacken you. Leave it alone!"

Satan often brings temptation into our lives by saying to us, "Go ahead, touch it. It won't burn you. It's not so bad." But the Bible says not to even "touch" the unclean thing.

The question to ask, when faced with a decision is not, "What's wrong with it?", but "What's right with it?" We should avoid those things which might even blacken our lives before the Lord.

How To Deal With A Difficult Employer (Part 1)

"Servants, be obedient to them that are your masters…"
(Eph. 6:5)

After David killed Goliath, and the women began singing his praises, it caused King Saul to be jealous of David. And because of his jealously, he was out to kill David. David had done nothing wrong, yet he was being targeted unfairly by the king.

So, what do you do when your employer begins treating you unfairly? Let's look at David's actions toward Saul and learn from him.

1. David maintained a good SPIRIT. 1Samuel 18:14 says, *"And David behaved himself wisely in all his ways; and the LORD was with him."* No matter what Saul's actions were toward David, the Bible says that *"David behaved himself wisely."* He didn't let his anger get the best of him and cause him to retaliate because then he would have been acting as badly as Saul.

You cannot change someone else's actions, but you can control *your* actions. Ask God to help you maintain a good spirit today so that you can act, not react to your circumstances.

Tomorrow, we will look at the second way to deal with a difficult employer.

How To Deal With A Difficult Employer (Part 2)

"Servants, be obedient to them that are your masters..."
(Eph. 6:5)

Yesterday, we saw the first way David responded to his leader, Saul. **First, David maintained a good SPIRIT.** Today let's look at the second way.

2. David maintained a good TESTIMONY. First of all, David maintained a good testimony before King Saul. (v.15) says, *"Wherefore when Saul saw that he behaved himself very wisely..."* Saul could plainly see that David was acting better than he was. Treat your employer right, even when they are not treating YOU right.

Secondly, David maintained a good testimony before the other people. In (v.23) David spoke humbly and honored the king's position before the other people. Then (v.24) says, *"And the servants of Saul told him, saying, On this manner spake David."* Word got back to the king what David had said! Be careful how you speak of your employer to the other employees because word WILL get back to them.

Notice one last thing. (v.15) says, *"Wherefore when Saul saw that he behaved himself very wisely, he was afraid of him."* If your employer has been treating you badly, just determine to maintain your testimony by keeping a good spirit.

Fighting For The Faith (Part 1)

"..it was needful for me to write unto you, and exhort you that ye should earnestly contend for the faith..."
(Jude 1:3)

Each Book of the Bible was written in a different time to different people for different purposes. Jude says, "I have written this book to challenge you to contend for the faith." And Jude doesn't just challenge his readers to *"contend for the faith"* but to *"**earnestly** contend for the faith."*

The word *"contend"* means to struggle as in combat. When a soldier is in combat, he gives everything he's got. His very life, and the lives of others, are at stake. The word here means to contend to the point of exhaustion. What Jude is talking about is spiritual warfare.

What do you want us to fight for, Jude? He says, *"For the faith."* Not just faith, but for THE faith. He is talking about a body of truth. He's talking about *"the faith that was once delivered to the saints."* What is the faith? It's the basic doctrines, the basic truths of the faith. There are some truths that are absolutely essential to the Christian faith and if you take away any of them, then you don't have the Christian faith. For example: the virgin birth, the resurrection of Jesus Christ, and the inspiration of the Bible. These are precious truths that we must be willing to stand for, and to fight for!

Tomorrow, I will give four specific ways in which we can *"earnestly contend for the faith."*

Fighting For The Faith (Part 2)

"..it was needful for me to write unto you, and exhort you that ye should earnestly contend for the faith..." (Jude 1:3)

Here are four ways we can contend for the faith:

FIRST—We Must STUDY the faith. Before we can *"earnestly contend for the faith"* we must know what the faith is. We must know what the basic doctrines (or teachings) of the Bible are. The average believer spends very little time actually studying the Bible for themselves. If we are going to *"earnestly contend for the faith"* we must, first, study the faith.

SECOND—We Must SHOW the faith. One of the best defenses of the faith is a strong, consistent testimony in front of the world. It will be difficult to fight for the faith when you miss church half the time and live like the world. So, there is no better way to *"earnestly contend for the faith"* than when others see you constantly living and standing for what is right.

THIRD—We Must SHARE the faith. Sharing the faith means telling others about Jesus and what He has done in your life. Part of *"the faith"* we are contending for is that Jesus died for our sins; He was buried and rose again the third day. And if we will repent and put our faith in Him, He will forgive our sin and take us to heaven when we die. That is the gospel message and that is the faith we should be sharing.

FOURTH—We Must STAND for the faith. To contend for the faith doesn't mean that you have to be contentious. But we must be firm and not give in to those who want to water down what the Bible teaches.

Ask God to give you the courage, today, to *"earnestly contend for the faith."* The world is looking for something that is real. Will they see that in you?

Are You Holding A Harp Or A Javelin?

"Saul...sat in his house with his javelin in his hand: and David played with his hand. (1Sam. 19:9)

David and King Saul were in the same room, but they were very different people.

SAUL held a JAVELIN. It says Saul *"sat in his house with his javelin in his hand."* He was jealous of David and was looking for a way to harm him. The javelin wasn't leaning against the wall, it was in his hand. He wanted quick access to it. When you hold on to jealousy it will affect you.

Jealously will consume your mind. Saul couldn't hold anything else while his hands were holding the javelin. He constantly thought David was out to get him. Jealously will consume your mind and make you paranoid of others.

Jealousy will destroy your spirit. A person who is jealous isn't thinking rationally. They will interpret everything you do and say through the filter of that jealousy. They are constantly holding on to that feeling so that it is within easy reach to use against you.

DAVID held a HARP. David had a different spirit than Saul because it says *"and David played with his hand."* David held a harp because his motive was to please the king and be a help to him. He didn't need a javelin because he wasn't trying to hurt anyone.

There's a big difference between a javelin and a harp! A javelin is used to spear someone; a harp is used to soothe someone. While Saul was trying to hurt David, David as trying help Saul. Which person are YOU most like? Are you holding a javelin or a harp?

Getting Some Rest

*"Come unto me, all ye that labour and are heavy laden,
and I will give you rest." (Matt. 11:28)*

Today the average person has so many irons in the fire they end up getting burned! What we need is rest. So what can we do to get this rest we so desperately need?

FIRST—We must go to Jesus. Jesus said, *"Come unto me, all ye that labour and are heavy laden."* People try everything from energy drinks to the latest memory foam mattress and STILL cannot find the rest they need.

That is because, if your spirit is not at rest, your body will never really be at rest. A troubled spirit troubles the body as well. You can lay down at night, but if your spirit is not at rest, it will hinder your body from resting, too.

SECOND—We must fully surrender to Him. In (v.29) Jesus said, *"Take my yoke upon you..."* When an animal is yoked it is controlled by the master. So it is with Jesus. The soul has but to yield to Him; to be still and rest in Him in order to find the rest He promises. See, it is not the yoke, but resistance to the yoke that causes difficulty.

THIRDLY—Jesus said, *"Learn of me."* It is when we learn more about Jesus, and His care for us, that we begin to find rest for our souls. There are so many lies we hear from Satan every day, and many of those lies are about our Lord. "He doesn't love you;" "He doesn't care about you;" are just a couple.

2 Peter 1:2 says, *"Grace and peace be multiplied unto you through the knowledge of God, and of Jesus our Lord,"* So, stay in the Word every day because it is the knowledge of God that multiples His *"Grace and peace"* in our hearts, and therefore provides the very rest our soul needs.

9

The Eyes Of The Lord

"The eyes of the LORD are in every place, beholding the evil and the good." (Prov. 15:3)

You are being watched! There is no place to hide without being seen. No, you are not being watched by a stalker; you are being watched by the Lord!

It would be a scary thing to know you were being watched by a stalker, but what a comforting thought to know you are always being watched by the eyes of a loving God.

God sees everything you and I do because *"The eyes of the LORD are in every place."* There is no trouble, no distress, no temptation, and no trial that we face but what God doesn't see and take notice of. What a thought!

FIRST—*"The eyes of the LORD are...beholding the evil."* God sees that boss, or co-worker, or person who is treating you unfairly. He sees the evil others are doing to you while you are trying to do right. Be encouraged because their evil actions are not going unnoticed.

BUT, that means the Lord also sees the evil YOU do as well! Just as the ungodly cannot hide their evil from God, you and I cannot hide our evil from God's all-seeing eye, either.

SECOND—*"The eyes of the LORD are...beholding ...the good."* Many times we feel that our faithfulness is not being rewarded. Cheer up, God sees your good; He sees your faithfulness. God sees the times you didn't feel like praying but you prayed anyway. He sees the times you were discouraged and didn't feel like going to church but you went on anyway.

So, keep on doing right. The Bible says that not even a cup of water given in Jesus' name will go unrewarded, because *"The eyes of the LORD are in every place..."*

Are You Gathering Or Scattering?

"He that is not with me is against me; and he that gathereth not with me scattereth abroad." (Matt. 12:30)

Everyone can be put into one of two categories; we are either **with** Jesus, or **against** Jesus. We are either **gathering for** Jesus, or we are **scattering from** Jesus.

First of all, Jesus said, *"He that is not with me is against me."* What many do not realize is that the greatest harm to Christianity doesn't come from the atheists; it comes from lukewarm believers. How? Because a lukewarm believer isn't really living FOR the Lord. That's why they're lukewarm. And because they aren't actively living FOR Jesus, He says their lives actually begin to work AGAINST Him.

A lukewarm believer lives and acts like the world does, which goes against the very message of the gospel that says Christ came to save us from the very sin in which they are living! And because they claim to be a Christian, yet are living like those who are not Christians, they are seen as hypocrites which actually turns people away from Christ.

Next, He says, *"he that gathereth not with me scattereth abroad."* The charge is for us to gather with Him. How can we gather with Him?

We can gather in our WORSHIP. Are you gathering with Him and His people at church, faithfully? When you worship, is your mind, will, and emotions gathered on Jesus alone?

We can gather in our WITNESS. Does your life draw (or gather) others to Jesus? Are you faithfully living and giving the gospel to others which allows the Holy Spirit to gather (or draw) them to Jesus? So, which are you doing today; gathering or scattering?

Are You Slipping? (Part 1)

"Therefore we ought to give the more earnest heed to the things which we have heard, lest at any time we should let them slip." (Heb. 12:1)

Years ago, when I was a teenager, our church youth group went white-water rafting. Although I had never been rafting before, I quickly learned that if you are not diligent, your raft can drift off course and into rocks or on to a sand dune.

There was a designated spot down the river where the instructors said we were to get out of the raft. They said that while the river continued on past that spot, it was too dangerous to keep rafting because it wasn't safe.

Just looking at the river, it didn't seem that bad. But on around the corner, where we couldn't see, were dangerous waterfalls. They told to be extremely careful and get out at the right spot, otherwise we could let our raft drift off course and into dangerous territory.

The same thing can happen to us, spiritually. We can easily just put our spiritual lives on autopilot and become complacent and before we know it we have let things slip until we are much further away from the Lord than we ever realized.

Tomorrow I will give you six dangers that come from rafting that we also need to beware of so that we do not put our spiritual lives in danger.

Today, ask God to help you stay alert, spiritually, to the dangers and temptations around you that might cause you to slip.

Are You Slipping? (Part 2)

"Therefore we ought to give the more earnest heed to the things which we have heard, lest at any time we should let them slip." (Heb. 12:1)

Today, I want to give you six dangers of drifting, while rafting, that also apply to your spiritual life.

First—you always drift downstream. Without paddling, you will never go upstream. Likewise, you will never get closer to God by accident; it must always be intentional.

Second—drifting usually happens without realizing it. If you miss one church service, it is easier to miss the next one...then the next one...and before you know it you are out of church.

Third—drifting take no effort on your part. Going downstream requires you to do nothing but sit back and relax. As soon as you begin to relax in your Christian life, you will find yourself drifting.

Fourth—drifting often puts others in danger. If someone is following your lead, then when you begin to drift, it can lead them into dangerous waters as well!

Fifth—the closer you get to the waterfall, the faster the current. It may seem that you can handle the current right now where you are drifting, but you will not be able to handle it the closer you get to the falls. Suddenly you will find your life out of control, wondering where you went off course.

Sixth—drifting, if not stopped, will end in disaster! Whether you become shipwrecked by hitting a rock, a log, or go over the waterfall, either way you are shipwrecked!

Determine now, to stay on course. Don't let things start slipping in your walk with God, or you just may find yourself past the point of no return!

Peace With God

"Therefore being justified by faith, we have peace with God through our Lord Jesus Christ:" (Rom. 5:1)

Millions of dollars are spent each year on products or services promising to relieve stress and hopefully bring a measure of peace to a person.

The trouble is, man's lack of peace does not stem from things that are **external**. A lack of peace is something that is **internal**. The good news is that the Bible tells us how to have peace no matter how stressful our circumstances are.

But before I tell you how to have the peace OF God, if you are not sure of your salvation you first need to make peace with God. See, an unbeliever is not at **PEACE** with God, he is at **WAR** with Him! John 3:36 says, *"..he that believeth not the Son shall not see life; but the wrath of God abideth on him."*

Notice in our main verse above, the Bible clearly tells us that the peace of God comes only through Jesus Christ after we are justified by our faith in Him. It says, *"Therefore being justified by faith, we have peace with God through our Lord Jesus Christ:"*

You will never find true peace for your heart at the bottom of an alcohol bottle. Peace cannot be inserted into your soul through a drug needle. There is only one place true peace of mind and spirit can be found and that is through Jesus Christ.

Losing In Order To Win

*"I count all things but **loss** for the excellency of the knowledge of Christ Jesus my Lord...and do count them but dung, that I may **win** Christ," (Phil. 3:8)*

In the world's view of things, one must guard against losing in order to win. But with God it is completely opposite. In heaven's economy, things are reversed.

FIRST—we must be willing to LOSE before we can WIN. Paul said, *"I count all things but loss."* There are some things we must be willing to lose (to get rid of) in order to receive fully what God has for us. As long as our hands are holding on to the things of this world, they will never be able to hold the true riches God has for us.

SECOND—we must become EMPTY in order to be FILLED. Eph. 5:18 says, *"And be not drunk with wine, wherein is excess; but be filled with the Spirit;"* The reason many are not *"**filled** with the Spirit"* is because they are too full of this world!

THIRD—we must become THIRSTY in order to be SATISFIED. Isa. 44:3 says, *"For I will pour water upon him that is thirsty, and floods upon the dry ground:"* Andrew Murray said, "It is only into the thirst of an empty soul that the streams of living water flow. Ever thirsting is the secret of never thirsting." Only a thirsty man will seek water to quench that thirst. Only a man who is thirsty for God to fill him will be satisfied with what God has to offer him.

Have you counted *"all things but loss"* for Christ? Are you empty? Are you thirsty for what God has for you, today?

The Power Of Being Purged

"..every branch that beareth fruit, he purgeth it, that it may bring forth more fruit." (John 15:2)

In a couple of months, it will be that time of year when women begin their spring cleaning. Our houses have been closed up all winter and when spring arrives it is a great time to open up the windows and let the fresh air in. It is also a time to clean the house from top to bottom (as my mother would say).

Just as a house can get cluttered with dust, dirt, and a multitude of other things, our lives can also become cluttered with things of this life. Those things eventually need to be purged, or cleaned up. Likewise, our lives must also experience a purging from time to time.

Jesus said that a branch which produces fruit must be purged in order to produce MORE fruit. This purging process isn't a bad thing, although it can feel like it sometimes.

When a branch is purged, everything is removed from the branch which would divert the vital nutrients from producing fruit. Likewise, God has to purge our lives, from time to time, of anything which may hinder Him from producing in us the fruit we could be producing.

A gardener only purges the branches that he cares about. This morning, take a moment to thank the Lord for caring enough for you to purge you of things which may hinder you from becoming the man or woman you were created to be.

16

They Found The Colt

"And they went their way, and found the colt tied by the door without in a place where two ways met;" (Mark 11:4)

This little colt interests me because many times in life WE are like this little colt was.

1. This colt was tied up. Many times it seems as if we've been "tied up" or limited by our circumstances in life. We feel as if we are going nowhere; we are not making any progress. It can be a difficult place to be!

2. This colt was at a crossroads. He was *"in a place where two ways met."* You will come to many crossroads in life where you will need to make a decision about which way to go. This little colt had no choice but to wait on Jesus!

He might have felt as if no one knew where he was...BUT JESUS DID! If you are at a crossroads today, do what this colt did... just wait on the Lord.

3. This colt was tied by the door. Jesus is the door! The best place you can be while you are waiting is *"tied by the door."* Stay faithful in your prayer time, Bible reading, and church attendance. Eventually that door will open. You need to be there when it does.

4. This colt was loosed. He was eventually loosed from what had him bound, BUT....he was loosed in God's time, not his!

In (v.3) Jesus said, *"The Lord hath need of him."* Be encouraged! The Lord has need of you! He wants to use you, but He needs you to be patient and wait upon Him. In the meantime, God may want to use your attitude of patience to be a blessing to someone else who is also bound by something.

Not Liberty, But Love

"..use not liberty for an occasion to the flesh, but by love serve one another." (Gal. 5:13)

When God saved us, He freed us from the bondage of sin that we were enslaved to. He set us free! Notice three things about this liberty we now have in Christ.

FIRST—the CALL to Liberty. Paul said, *"ye have been called unto liberty;"* We once were under the Law, but not now! The Law has no claim upon us anymore. Aren't you thankful for the day when the Holy Spirit of God called you *"unto liberty"?* Aren't you thankful the Lord didn't leave you in bondage to your sin, with no hope of ever being set free?

SECOND—the CAUTION of Liberty. *"..only use not liberty for an occasion to the flesh."* Though we are now free, we still cannot do certain things. You see, our love for the Lord will make us draw the line for ourselves at certain things. Liberty doesn't mean freedom to do as we please, but rather freedom to do as HE pleases. Liberty does not mean license. We do not have a license to sin. Having liberty in Christ does not mean we are free TO sin but that we are free FROM sin. Sin no longer holds us hostage.

THIRDLY—the CAUSE of Liberty. *"..but by love serve one another."* Now our life is not about law but about love! We no longer have to serve sin; we now get to serve the Saviour. Paul says here that God didn't save us to sin, He saved us to serve...to serve one another in love.

Strength From Weakness

"And he said unto me, My grace is sufficient for thee: for my strength is made perfect in weakness..." (2Cor. 12:9)

There is a misunderstood truth among Christians regarding strength and weakness. We often try to forget our weakness, but God wants us to remember it. Many self-help books have been written to help us "conquer" our weakness and be freed from it, but God wants us to rest and even rejoice in it.

When we think of our weakness, we want to shrink from it and cover it up. Yet Christ taught His servants to say, like Paul, *"Most gladly...will I...glory in my infirmities...I take pleasure in infirmities..."* We have been led to believe that our weakness is our greatest hindrance in life and in serving God, but God tells us that it is our weakness that is the secret of strength and success. Paul realized this and that is why he could say, *"my strength is made perfect in weakness."*

See, God isn't looking for Christians who have no weaknesses; He isn't looking for believers who already have the strength to live the Christian life on their own. To the contrary. God is looking for those who realize that it is because of their weakness that they must rely on HIS strength to make it.

So, don't look at another believer and say, "I wish I were as strong as they are." No! Look to Jesus and say, "I know I am weak, but I also know that YOU are strong and I come to you with my weakness and rely upon YOUR strength.

Then, like Paul, you can say, *"for when I am weak, then am I strong."*

A Daily Choice

"..choose you this day whom ye will serve...but as for me and my house, we will serve the LORD." (Josh. 24:15)

Every day we get up, we have many choices to make like "What will I wear?" or "What will I eat?" But we also have another choice, will we serve the LORD?

We must choose to serve the SAVIOUR. Joshua said, *"we will serve the LORD."* Without realizing it, we can actually become a slave to other things in life. Some are a slave to money. Others are a slave to their calendar, feeling they must do everything that comes their way. Sometimes it can be hard to know what to choose, but Joshua said, "The choice is easy. My house will serve the LORD and no one else."

We must choose to serve Him SINCERELY. In (v.14), Joshua said, *"Now therefore fear the LORD, and serve him in sincerity and in truth..."* In other words, we must serve Him from our heart, sincerely, not just with our lips. Anyone can "say" they are serving the LORD, but He wants us to serve Him *"in sincerity and truth."*

We must choose to serve Him SOLELY. Next, in (v.14) he said, *"and put away the gods which your fathers served on the other side of the flood, and in Egypt; and serve ye the LORD."* God won't share the spotlight with anyone! We cannot serve many gods. We are to put away all other things in our life which compete for our worship and service. God wants us to worship and serve Him solely.

So today, and every day, we have a choice to make. Will we serve the gods of this world, or serve the one, true, LORD!

Where Is God?

"And ye shall seek me, and find me, when ye shall search for me with all your heart." (Jer. 29:13)

Have you ever been so discouraged that you felt God had left you all alone. Well, that will never happen because He has promised us in Heb. 13:5, *"I will never leave thee, nor forsake thee."*

FIRST—God wants us to SEEK Him. He said, *"And ye shall seek me..."* The most precious things in life are those things which we must seek after. Diamonds and gold do not grow on trees, just waiting for someone to pluck them off. No, finding them requires a lot of effort. We must *"seek"* after them.

The same is true about God. Sure, even a new believer can read the Bible and find God on a surface level. But to learn the deeper truths God has awaiting us require that we *"seek"* for them.

SECOND—God wants us to FIND Him. He said, *"ye shall seek me, and find me,"* There are those, like atheists, who say God cannot be found. But an atheist cannot find God for the same reason a thief cannot find a police officer...they aren't really LOOKING for Him! No, my friend, if God had not wanted to be found, mankind would still be in spiritual darkness to this day. But praise God, He made a way for us to find Him!

The key to finding God is in that last phrase, *"when ye shall search for me with all your heart."* Seek him, today. Give Him your undivided attention and you might be surprised what you find!

Another Spirit

"But my servant Caleb, because he had another spirit with him, and hath followed me fully, him will I bring into the land..." (Num. 14:24)

What made Caleb different than everyone else? What gave him FAITH when everyone else had FEAR? God said *"he had another spirit."*

He had a SERVANT'S spirit. *"But my servant Caleb..."* Caleb wasn't trying to be something he wasn't. He knew his place as God's servant. One thing that will help keep you from a complaining spirit is to have a *servant's* spirit.

He had a SACRIFICIAL spirit. *"my servant Caleb...hath followed me fully."* He sacrificed everything else in order to follow God fully. Usually, a person murmurs and complains because they feel they deserve better than what they have. Not Caleb. He said, "I will gladly sacrifice other things in order to follow God completely.

He had a SUCCESSFUL spirit. In other words, having a servant's spirit and a sacrificial spirit paid off! It was a success! How do we know? Because the last part of the verse says, *"him will I bring into the land whereinto he went; and his seed shall possess it."* Not only did HE get blessed by God for having the right kind of spirit, but God also blessed his seed. Future generations reaped the benefits of his right spirit. Your children and grandchildren will reap with the blessings or the curse of the type of spirit YOU have.

Today, ask God to give you *"another spirit,"* a spirit that will glorify the Lord.

The Cancer Of Covetousness

"And he said unto them, Take heed, and beware of covetousness:" (Luke 12:15)

Covetousness is something that can affect us all. And, if left untreated, can spread like a spiritual cancer! There are four things covetousness will do in a person's life.

Covetousness will keep you from seeing God's blessings. (v.16) says this rich man had already *"brought forth plentifully."* Did he thank God for what he had? No. He only complained about what more he still wanted. If you find yourself complaining about what God HASN'T given you, you may be covetous.

Covetousness makes you unthankful for what you already have. The rich man said, *"I have no room..."* Was that true? No. The Bible says he had enough room to store the blessing God had already given to him, but evidently that wasn't enough. Don't allow Satan to make you think that what you already have is not enough. There are many people who would gladly trade what little they have for what you are unthankful for!

Covetousness will create a desire for things that will never fully satisfy. Even the new barn this man built would not make him happy for long. When you become covetous, you will always be longing for something you don't have and therefore will perpetually be unhappy.

Covetousness will make you blind to the needs of others. This rich man evidently had more blessings than he could possibly use for himself. Instead of building greater barns, why didn't he empty one of the barns and give those blessings to those in need? Covetousness had blinded him to the needs of others.

Examine your heart and see if you have been infected with the cancer of covetousness!

Are You Imagining Things?

"Casting down imaginations, and every high thing that exalteth itself against the knowledge of God," (2Cor. 10:5)

Satan works non-stop trying to build up strongholds in our mind. He does this through imaginations.

FIRST—an imagination must be CAST DOWN. He said, *"Casting down imaginations."* Why? Because an imagination isn't true; it is simply...imagined. When I was a child, lying in my bed in the dark I "imagined" there might be a Boogeyman under my bed. Now, there was no such thing. In fact, with all the toys I had under my bed, there was no room for a Boogeyman under there! It was all an imagination.

Likewise, Satan specializes in creating false imaginations in our minds that can lead us into sinful actions.

SECOND—our thoughts must be taken CAPTIVE. *"and bringing into captivity every thought to the obedience of Christ."* The only way police officers can stay safe when arresting someone is by keeping the criminal under control. Likewise, the only way we can keep our mind safe from Satan's attacks is to keep our thoughts under control. We do this by *"bringing into captivity every thought to the obedience of Christ;"* which simply means choosing to obey God when a thought comes into our mind that runs contrary to what God has clearly said in His Word. By doing this, we block Satan from building a stronghold of imaginations in our mind.

Examine your thoughts, today, and see if there are any strongholds Satan may be trying to build up.

Getting A Vision

"Where there is no vision, the people perish..."
(Prov. 29:18)

Yesterday, we talked about imaginations. There is a difference between imaginations and having a vision.

Imaginations come from SATAN; a vision comes from GOD. God's purpose and plan for your life isn't an imagination, it's a vision! The biblical word *vision* refers to a revealed mental picture. When God places a vision in your heart, it's not an imagination that may or may not be true. If God gave it, IT IS TRUE!

Imaginations are MAN-CENTERED; a vision is GOD-CENTERED. Imaginations flows from feelings and emotions, based on man. Therefore, they are subject to change. God's vision flows from His Word and therefore never changes!

Imaginations come from a SINFUL HEART; vision comes from a PURE HEART. In Matt. 5:8, Jesus said, *"Blessed are the pure in heart: for they shall **see** God."* Those who are *"pure in heart"* will *"see"* (or get their vision from) God.

Imaginations are to be CAST DOWN; vision from God is to be OBEYED. Paul said in Acts 26:19, *"Whereupon, O king Agrippa, I was not disobedient unto the heavenly vision:"* Satan's imaginations are built on lies, but a vision from God is based on reality and should therefore be followed and obeyed.

You can follow your imaginations if you want, but it is a dead-end road. On the other hand, if you will follow God's Word, and the vision He has put in your heart, you will find blessings you never dreamed!

Fight The Good Fight

"Fight the good fight of faith, lay hold on eternal life,"
(1Tim. 6:12)

Too often, God's people are engaged in the wrong kind of fight; they are fighting the pastor or other church members. But that isn't the fight God has called us to. Paul told Timothy to *"Fight the good fight of faith..."*

Your spouse is not your enemy. Another church member is not your enemy. Your employer is not your enemy. So, who IS our enemy? SATAN! The Bible says, *"For we wrestle not against flesh and blood, but against principalities, against powers, against the rulers of the darkness of this world, against spiritual wickedness in high places" (Eph. 6:12)*.

We are in a fight to the finish. It is not a physical warfare; it is a spiritual warfare. Satan is our eternal foe and he will not stop until he has defeated us. Thankfully, the Bible also says, *"Ye are of God, little children, and have overcome them: because greater is he that is in you, than he that is in the world" (1John 4:4)*.

As you go about your day, today, remember to stand for truth; stand for right. You have a faith worth defending, so fight for right, today!

God's Will Or God's Won't?

"And he that searcheth the hearts knoweth what is the mind of the Spirit, because he maketh intercession for the saints according to the will of God." (Rom. 8:27)

It is clear from the Word of God that a Christian, if left to himself, does not know how to pray. We are too weak, in and of ourselves, to connect with the Father through prayer. That is why Paul says in (v.26), *"the Spirit also helpeth our infirmities: for we know not what we should pray for as we ought:"*

But thankfully that is one of the ministries of the Holy Spirit...He helps us to pray! (v.26) goes on to say, *"but the Spirit itself maketh intercession for us with groanings which cannot be uttered."* In other words, the Holy Spirit says to the Father what we **should** say but don't know how to say.

Not only that, (v.27) says, *"he [the Spirit] maketh intercession for the saints according to the will of God."* When we are surrendered and submitted to the Holy Spirit, He will intercede on our behalf and pray through us *"according to the will of God."*

Fleshly prayers are NOT prayed *"according to the will of God."* God will not hear a fleshly prayer. Therefore, it is imperative that you surrender yourself right now to the filling and leading of the Holy Spirit so that when you pray, you will be praying according to God's WILL, and not God's WON'T!

One Sat On The Throne

*"And immediately I was in the spirit: and, behold, a throne
was set in heaven, and one sat on the throne."*
(Rev. 4:2)

When John was caught up by the Spirit into Heaven, he saw amazing sights. One thing he saw was a throne. Notice three things:

FIRST—there is a throne in Heaven. John said, *"behold, a throne was set in heaven..."* There is a place where the God of glory dwells and watches over His creation. Aren't you thankful that life isn't just a series of random circumstances but rather a divine plan controlled from the throne room of God?

SECOND—there is someone ON that throne. Notice John said he saw *"one...on the throne."* There is not two, or five, or ten sitting on the throne in Heaven. There is only ONE! No false god has a right to sit on the throne in Heaven. But can I say this...neither do you and I have a right to sit on the throne of our lives, either. There is only ONE who is in charge; it isn't you and it isn't me. It is the LORD!

THIRD—he saw this when in the Spirit. John said, *"And immediately I was in the spirit..."* Notice that he didn't see the throne, or God sitting on the throne, until he was first in the Spirit. You'll never see God in His rightful place while you are living in the flesh. You'll never see the God who has all power and who is in control of all things until you first start walking in the Spirit.

Whatever trial you may be going through, just remember this...GOD IS STILL ON THE THRONE!

Jellyfish Christians

"But let him ask in faith, nothing wavering. For he that wavereth is like a wave of the sea driven with the wind and tossed." (James 1:6)

The Jellyfish is a slimy looking creature with long, stringy legs called tentacles. Its head is shaped like an umbrella and the body is so clear you can almost see through it. Come to think of it, there are several characteristics that some Christians share with the Jellyfish.

Jellyfish have no clear direction. A Jellyfish, more or less, just moves wherever the current takes it. They aren't strong or fast swimmers. Likewise, many Christians are weak, spiritually. They aren't strong enough to stand against temptation or peer pressure so they just go with the flow.

Jellyfish can hurt themselves. Because a Jellyfish just goes wherever the current takes it, it is often injured or killed when the waves push it into a human, or an object. When we just go with the flow, it will more than likely end up injuring, or possibly killing, us spiritually.

Jellyfish can be harmful to others. With their many tentacles and stingers, they are a threat to anyone who comes near them. Some Christians are the same way! You never know what kind of mood or spirit they will be in when you are around them. The attitude they have and the words they say often hurt other people.

Don't let those around you determine who you are, spiritually. Don't let the waves of circumstance push you. Don't be a Jellyfish Christian.

Waiting On The Lord

"Lead me in thy truth, and teach me: for thou art the God of my salvation; on thee do I wait all the day."
(Ps. 25:5)

One reason God was able to use Joshua greatly was because Joshua was a patient man. He had learned how to wait on the Lord and wait on the man of God. The Psalmist also had learned the lesson of waiting on God.

Let's look at this verse backwards, taking the last phrase first.

THIRD—We see the PRIORITY mentioned. *"on thee do I wait all the day."* Waiting on God is to be our number one priority. Why? Because if we rush ahead of God we can get ourselves into all kinds of trouble.

SECOND—We see the PERSON mentioned. *"for thou art the God of my salvation..."* We are not just waiting on anyone, we are to be waiting on God. Why? Because He is our salvation (or our deliverance). If we will wait on Him, He will deliver us in His timing.

FIRST—We see the PRINCIPLE mentioned. *"Lead me in thy truth, and teach me..."* The whole purpose of us waiting on the Lord *"all the day"* and trusting His timing for our deliverance is so that He can teach us the truth (or lessons) we need to learn. The lessons God wants us to learn only come as we patiently wait on Him and allow His timing to be accomplished in our lives.

Psalm 27:14 simply says it this way: *"Wait on the LORD: be of good courage, and he shall strengthen thine heart: wait, I say, on the LORD."*

None Of These Things Move Me

"But none of these things move me, neither count I my life dear unto myself, so that I might finish my course with joy..." (Acts 20:24)

We live in an ever-changing culture. Technology changes so quickly that something your purchased brand new just a few months ago is already outdated! It is in this ever-changing world that I am thankful for an un-changing God! Malachi 3:6 says, *"For I am the Lord, I change not."*

In (v.22) Paul said, *"And now, behold, I go bound in the spirit unto Jerusalem, not knowing the things that shall befall me there:"* In other words, Paul said, I am following the Holy Spirit into Jerusalem, even though I do not know what may happen to me there. Even when it came to unknown circumstances, Paul said, *"none of these things move me."* Paul had determined to not let his circumstances move (or deter) him from God's plan for his life.

Let me ask you this question: what does it take to move you? What would it take for Satan to be able to stop you from serving God? What does it take for him to keep you out of church? Paul said, "There are many unknown circumstances and many things that could happen to me while serving God, but none of the things will move or deter me from accomplishing God's purpose in my life."

That is why Paul could say, *"I have fought a good fight, I have **finished my course**..." (2Tim. 4:7).* He had determined that nothing would stop him from reaching the finish line and complete the race God had given him to run.

Determine, today, that nothing will move you from what God wants to do **in** and **through** your life.

31

How To Survive Dark Times

"Jonathan told David, saying, Saul my father seeketh to kill thee: now therefore, I pray thee, take heed to thyself until the morning, and abide in a secret place, and hide thyself:"
(1Sam. 19:2)

King Saul was out to kill David because of his jealousy of David. As a result, David had to run for his life! It was a dark time for David because Jonathan said to David, *"take heed to thyself until the morning."* Sometimes it seems as if Satan has us on the run. We find ourselves all alone, in a very dark time of our life.

How can we survive those dark times of life? What can we do to make sure we make it *"until the morning"*?

FIRST—David kept doing right even when others were doing wrong. Verse 1 says that king Saul had told his son and all of his servants to kill David. I'm sure it seemed to David like everyone was out to get him. Often you may find that you are the only one not doing wrong, but if you are going to make it through the dark times, keep doing right.

SECOND—Jonathan said to David, *"take heed to thyself until the morning, and abide in a secret place."* There is no better secret place, than abiding with the Lord! Psalm 91:1 says, *"He that dwelleth in the secret place of the most High shall abide under the shadow of the Almighty."* When you are in someone's shadow, you are VERY close to them! To *"abide under the shadow of the Almighty"* means to be so close to Him that His very shadow covers you! You can't get much closer than that!

So, if you are in a dark time of your life, determine to get as close to God as you can. It's the safest place you can be!

32

Whose Friend Are You?

"And from thenceforth Pilate sought to release him: but the Jews cried out, saying, If thou let this man go, thou art not Caesar's friend..." (John 19:12)

When Jesus was brought before Pilate, the Bible says Pilate wanted to release Him. He didn't want to have Him crucified, but the Jews cried out and said, *"If thou let this man go, thou art not **Caesar's friend.**"*

Being a friend requires a CHOICE. Pilate had a choice to make, would he be a friend to Caesar or would he be a friend to Jesus? We have the same choice, today—will we be a friend to the world, or will we be a friend to Jesus? You cannot have it both ways. The Bible says, *"No man can serve two masters" (Matt. 6:24).* James said, *"know ye not that the friendship of the world is enmity with God? whosoever therefore will be a friend of the world is the enemy of God."*

Being a friend requires ACTION. A true friend is not a friend in word only. A true friend is one who will show his friendship when it really counts.

By our actions, we show whether we are a friend to this world, or a friend to Jesus. Every day the world is watching our actions to see where our loyalty lies. When we are angry and we speak hateful words, our actions are showing whose friend we are. When we choose to lie instead of telling the truth, our actions are showing whose friend we are. When it is church time but we choose to do something else instead of being at church, our actions are showing whose friend we are.

Joshua said, *"choose you this day whom ye will serve...but as for me and my house, we will serve the LORD."* Today, you have a choice to make—whose friend will YOU be?

Our Daily Bread

"Man shall not live by bread alone, but by every word that proceedeth out of the mouth of God." (Matt. 4:4)

In comparing the Word of God to our daily bread, Jesus taught us a great lesson. Bread is a very important part of life. No matter how strong a man may be, if he does not get nourishment on a regular basis he will grow weaker until he eventually dies.

FIRST—bread must be eaten. I may know all about bread. I may have several loaves in my house. I may have enough bread to give to others who are hungry and malnourished, but that bread will not help me unless I eat some myself.

Likewise, having a surface knowledge of the Bible, or even knowing enough to preach to others will not benefit me unless I choose to feed on it myself. The Bible does not provide the spiritual nutrition I need unless I take it into my heart and life and obey it.

SECOND—bread must be eaten daily. We cannot eat one meal a week and expect to stay healthy. The same is true, spiritually. The only Bible some people read is when they come to church once a week. Yet, they wonder why they seem to be so weak, spiritually. We are to partake of the bread (God's Word) every day if we expect to be strong in the Lord. The Psalmist understood this when he wrote, *"O how love I thy law! it is my meditation all the day"* (Ps. 119:97).

If you want to have fellowship with Christ, you will find Him in His Word. Take some time every day to partake of this daily bread.

How Long Halt Ye Between Two Opinions?

"And Elijah came unto all the people, and said, How long halt ye between two opinions? if the LORD be God, follow him: but if Baal, then follow him. And the people answered him not a word." (1Kings 18:21)

Elijah is standing before the false prophets of Baal and a showdown has begun. Whichever god answered by fire would be the true God. So Elijah gathers all the false prophets together and says to them, *"How long halt ye between two opinions?"*

FIRST—UNBELIEVERS are halting between two opinions. For many, the choice is between "There is a God" or "There is no God." They will not take Him at His Word and accept Him by faith; they must SEE it to believe it.

SECOND—BELIEVERS are halting between two opinions. Many believers KNOW there is a God; they have that one settled. But their choice is between "Will I completely surrender my life to God" or "Will I live my life for myself?" They are halting between "Will I walk, completely yielded to the Spirit" or "Will I walk in the flesh?"

Some are halting between tithing or not tithing. Others are halting between attending church faithfully or only coming on Sunday mornings.

The truth about the matter is—for a believer, there really is no choice. Elijah said, *"If the Lord be God, follow Him."* That makes the choice clear, doesn't it? What are you waiting for? Why are you halting between two decisions? *"If the Lord be God, follow Him."*

Bigger Than God

"And...he [Elijah]...arose, and went for his life...and he requested for himself that he might die; and said, It is enough; now, O LORD, take away my life..."
(1Kings 19:3-4)

In 1 Kings 18, Elijah stood up against 450 prophets of Baal and called down fire out of heaven! I can't even imagine the boldness and courage he must have displayed that day on Mount Carmel.

Fast-forward one chapter and we see where Queen Jezebel found out that Elijah had killed all her false prophets. She sends Elijah a message that she is going to have him killed, and we read the following and he is praying for God to take away his life!

What happened to this man of God who was so bold in chapter 18 that caused him to run for his life and even ask to die in chapter 19? In chapter 18, he was full of courage and boldness, but in chapter 19 he was full of fear. What changed?

Here's what happened. In chapter 18, he compared the 450 false prophets to God, and saw God was bigger than them. That gave him courage. But in chapter 19, he was so afraid of Jezebel that she became bigger than God in his eyes!

When fear is the biggest thing in your life, God isn't! Satan wants you dwelling on your circumstances so that they become bigger than your God. David didn't compare Goliath to HIMSELF. Rather, he compared Goliath to GOD, and Goliath was no match for Him!

Keep your eyes on Jesus and you will see there is nothing bigger than God!

Meditating On His Precepts

"I will meditate in thy precepts..." (Ps. 119:15)

Some people love to be in a crowd. They love to be surrounded by other people. But a lot can be said for being alone, at times. Charles Spurgeon said, "There are times when solitude is better than society, and silence is wiser than speech." While fellowship is good, our real growth as a Christian happens when we get alone with God and *"meditate in [His] precepts."*

We meditate on the truths of God's Word in order to get the spiritual nutrition from it. Truth is like an orange; in order to get a nice glass of orange juice, that orange must be pressed and squeezed many times. If the orange isn't squeezed, the juice will not flow, and the precious nutritional value will be wasted. You see where I'm going with this, don't you?

Through meditation, we squeeze and press the truths of God's Word thereby extracting every bit of spiritual nutrition possible that we might benefit from it.

You can squeeze that orange and extract a glass full of juice, but that juice will be of no benefit to you as long as it stays in the glass. At some point, you must turn the glass up and drink it! You must **ingest** it so you can **digest** it.

The same is true for God's Word. Reading the Bible is the first step, but it is not the final step. Reading the Bible is like pouring it into a glass. You have extracted the truth. But meditating on what you read is like drinking it and gaining the full nutritional value it has to give you.

Spend some time today meditating on God's precepts.

His Day Will Come

""David said furthermore, As the LORD liveth, the LORD
shall smite him; or his day shall come to die..."
(1Sam. 26:10)

Have you ever had someone that seemed to be against you no matter how good you treated them? David knew exactly what that was like. King Saul was jealous of David and wanted to kill him. David had done everything to honor the king, yet King Saul wanted him dead.

David teaches us a couple of lessons about how to treat those who mistreat us.

FIRST—David did right even when he was done wrong. One night while King Saul and his men were asleep, David and Abishai snuck into camp where the king was and took his spear and water. Abishai asked David if he could kill King Saul, but David said, *"Destroy him not: for who can stretch forth his hand against the LORD'S anointed, and be guiltless?"*

When we retaliate against our enemy, we are sinking to their level and are just as guilty as they are. David could have easily gotten revenge on Saul, but he took the higher ground. As Christians, our testimony is more important than getting back at someone. We must do right, even when we've been done wrong.

SECOND—David realized God would take care of King Saul. David said, *"his day shall come to die.."* David said, "I am going to let God fight this battle. His day will come. God will take care of him in His timing."

It can be difficult, but the best thing we can do when that person comes against us is to let God fight our battle and realize *"his day will come."* God knows how to deal them far better than we ever could!

You'll Understand Later

"..the commandment of the LORD is pure, enlightening the eyes." (Ps. 19:8)

Notice that the Bible says that *"the commandment of the LORD is pure, **enlightening** the eyes."* The word "commandment" is an authoritative order; it is something to obey. So, how does a commandment open one's eyes?

There is a recurring principle in the Bible which says that obedience to Scripture brings greater understanding of Scripture. When we obey God's Word it opens our eyes, giving us a greater understanding of its truths. In other words, the Bible teaches us that if we will OBEY, first, we will UNDERSTAND later.

*"a good **understanding** have all they that **do** his commandments..."(Ps. 111:10)*

*"I **understand** more than the ancients [my elders], because I **keep** thy precepts." (Ps. 119:100)*

So, there is a correlation between obeying and knowing, or obeying then understanding. Even Jesus said in John 7:17, *"If any man will **do** his will, he shall **know** of the doctrine, whether it be of God, or whether I speak of myself."* Very simply, Jesus said that if you will first DO (obey), then you will KNOW, later.

The doing comes first, the knowing comes later. The obeying comes first, the understanding comes afterwards. If you are at a place where you are waiting for God to give you more understanding of what He wants you to do, begin by being obedient to what you ALREADY understand. Light obeyed bring greater light, but light ignored bring darkness! So, obey now and you will understand later!

Responding To Personal Attacks
(Part 1)

"Let mine enemy be as the wicked, and he that riseth up against me as the unrighteous." (Job 27:7)

There is nothing more hurtful than to have someone personally attacking you. The sad fact is that this also happens in the church, too!

If anyone knew about personal attacks it was Job. Those who were supposed to be his "friends" were the very ones launching personal attacks against his actions and his character. Even though the attacks had no merit, they nonetheless hurt. So, how are we to respond when we have been attacked?

FIRST—HOLD your TONGUE. Job said in (v.4) *"My lips shall not speak wickedness, nor my tongue utter deceit."* Though his attackers outright lied about Job, Job refused to stoop to their level and lie about them. So, the first thing to do is hold your tongue.

SECOND—PROTECT your INTEGRITY. Next, Job said in (v.5), *"God forbid that I should justify you: till I die I will not remove mine integrity from me."* Job was not going to admit to their false accusations simply to stop their attacks. If Job had done that, he would have been deceitful, himself. All he had left was his integrity, and he wasn't about to jeopardize that!

When you are being attacked, hold your tongue and keep your integrity so that you will know you are doing right even when you have been done wrong. Tomorrow, we will see the last two ways Job responded to personal attacks.

Responding To Personal Attacks (Part 2)

"Let mine enemy be as the wicked, and he that riseth up against me as the unrighteous." (Job 27:7)

There is nothing more hurtful than to have someone personally attacking you. Job was no stranger to personal attacks, especially by those whom he thought were his "friends." Yesterday we saw the first two ways Job responded, and how we too should respond, when attacked. This morning, we will see the last two ways we are to respond.

THIRD—KEEP doing RIGHT. Job said in (v.6a), *"My righteousness I hold fast, and will not let it go..."* Job determined he would still do right even when he was being done wrong. Don't let the wrong actions of others cause YOU to do wrong. Don't allow the sinful attitudes of others keep YOU from having the right attitude.

FOURTH—GUARD against BITTERNESS. Job said in (v.6b) *"..my heart shall not reproach me so long as I live."* Bitterness can easily grow in your heart when you are under attack. You can easily become angry and bitter at your attacker. You must guard your heart from allowing hate and bitterness to destroy your spirit. Remember, they are simply allowing Satan to use them to get to you. Don't let them!

When you are being attacked, determine to keep on doing right and pleasing God. Let God handle the attacker. You are the one who has to be able to lay your head on your pillow at night, knowing you did right when others did you wrong.

Jesus Drew Near

"And it came to pass, that, while they communed together and reasoned, Jesus himself drew near, and went with them." (Luke 24:15)

In Luke 24, we see two disciples of Christ who are leaving Jerusalem headed to Emmaus. They were discouraged and were headed back home. They were perplexed because this man, Jesus, whom they had given their lives for and were looking to Him to deliver Israel was now dead. The hope of the new kingdom Jesus promised seemed all but lost. No doubt they wondered to themselves, "What do we do now that our hope is gone?"

But as they are walking down that road, discouraged and sad, the Bible says, *"Jesus himself drew near."* Jesus knew their discouragement and took time to be with them. What a thought! That of all the things Jesus could have busied Himself with, after His resurrection, He took time to encourage two discouraged disciples!

Listen, Jesus is not too busy for you, either! He's not too busy to help you in YOUR discouragement. Notice it specifically says, *"Jesus...drew near."* He was already close to them, but this seems to indicate that He got even closer! Here's a great thought:

When you are at your LOWEST, Jesus is at His NEAREST!

Psalm 34:18 says, *"The LORD is nigh unto them that are of a broken heart..."* What a promise!

If you are discouraged this morning, just remember that Jesus is closer than you think!

42

Their Eyes Were Holden

"But their eyes were holden that they should not know him." (Luke 24:16)

As these two discouraged disciples were walking together on the road back to Emmaus, Jesus drew near to them and engaged them in conversation. What is interesting is the fact that these were followers of Jesus, yet they didn't recognize Jesus. To them, he appeared to be a stranger.

The Bible says that *"their eyes were holden that they should not know him."* Evidently God chose to temporarily hide His identity from them. Why did He do this? Well, for one reason, had they recognized Him, they may not have heard anything else He said! They would have been so shocked to see Him alive that they would not have heard the message he had for them.

But I believe another reason *"their eyes were holden"* may have been because the world is always looking for the sensational. They are always looking for the miraculous. They want signs instead of taking God's Word, alone. They have to SEE something before they will BELIEVE something.

God wanted them to listen to His Word before they saw anything. God doesn't want us LOOKING for SIGNS, He wants us LISTENING to the SCRIPTURES!

(v.31) says, *"And their eyes were opened, and they knew him..."* At the right time, God opened their eyes to see who Jesus really was.

You may not SEE what all God is doing in your life right now. That's okay. Get in God's Word and He will TELL you something before He SHOWS you something. Just be faithful and in time, like those disciples, God will open your eyes and you will see how God was working all along.

Slow To Believe

"Then he said unto them, O fools, and slow of heart to believe all that the prophets have spoken:" (Luke 24:25)

We are still talking about those two discouraged disciples on the road to Emmaus. When Jesus begins to talk to them He chastens them by calling them foolish. Jesus said they were foolish because they were *"slow of heart to believe."*

We STILL have this problem today! Despite the prayers He has answered for us in the past, we STILL are slow to believe He can meet our current need. We worry, fret, and become anxious. Why? Because we are *"slow of heart to believe."*

People who are slow to believe God are foolish because they never seem to have enough proof to believe. No matter what God does for them, it is not enough.

Jesus also said they were *"slow of heart to believe **all** that the prophets have spoken."* Notice the word *"all."* They believed "some" of what the prophets said, just not *"all"* of it. They believed the GLORY part, just not the SUFFERING part.

Can you relate? Like us, they had selective faith. Aren't we that way, too? In some things we fully trust God and don't seem to waver in that faith. Other times, it seems we struggle to trust God in even the smallest things. What is the answer to a lack of faith?

Rom. 10:17 says, *"So then faith cometh by hearing, and hearing by the word of God."*

Whatever God has brought you TO, He can bring you THROUGH! Don't doubt, don't worry, don't fret. Take God at His Word and don't be *"slow of heart to believe."*

44

Loving The Lord

*"O love the LORD, all ye his saints: for the LORD
preserveth the faithful, and plentifully rewardeth the proud
doer." (Ps. 31:23)*

Today is Valentine's Day. This is the day when people
are focused on their "true love." There will be many cards,
candy, and special gifts give today as a way to show that
special someone that they are loved.

Have you noticed how often we use the word "love"?
tend to use that word very loosely nowadays. We says, "I
love my car," "I **love** my house," or "I **love** Krispy Kreme
doughnuts." You saw that one coming, didn't you? ☐

Notice the Psalmist said, *"O love the LORD."* How
does our love for the Lord measure up to our love for the
things of this world? Do we tend to show more love and
affection for material things, than for the LORD who died
to pay for our sins?

FIRST—we should love the LORD because this verse
says, *"the LORD preserveth the faithful."* That word
"preserveth" means He guards and keeps us. What a
reason to love Him!

SECOND—we should love the LORD because next it
says *"the LORD...plentifully rewardeth the proud
doer."* We should love Him because of His plentiful
blessings in our life when we obey Him.

As you go about your day, today, think about how
great God's love is for you, and about how many reasons
you have to also love Him!

Always With Us!

"Lo, I am with you alway..." (Matt. 28:20)

What a difference it will make in our life when we realize the Lord is always with us. The Bible teaches God is omnipresent (everywhere at once), and we say we believe it. Yet, aren't there times when we live as though He is not present with us?

Satan would have us believe there are times when our Lord has forsaken us and left us all alone. He says that when our friends and family have left us, God walked out, too. But the Bible says differently.

He is with us when no one else CAN be with us. Consider the Old Testament prophet, Jonah. He was on the run from God and, as a result, was swallowed by a whale God had prepared for him. No one could get to him if they tried. No one knew where he was. Ah...but God did! He never left God's sight for a moment. What a blessing it was for Jonah to realize that even his underwater whale submarine could not shut him off from God's presence!

He is with us when no one else WANTS TO be with us. The apostle Paul sat in prison awaiting his trial before Nero. No one wanted to be in prison with him. In fact, Paul said, *"no man stood with me, but all men forsook me"* (2 Tim. 4:16).

But it was in the loneliness of that prison cell that Paul realized he had an unseen heavenly visitor in there with him! He went on to say, *"all men forsook me...Notwithstanding the Lord stood with me, and strengthened me..."*

Hallelujah! No matter if we find ourselves in a place where no one else CAN be with us, or WANTS TO be with us, our Lord is always there! You are not walking through that valley alone, friend. He is with you, today!

The Person God Talks To

"Abraham fell on his face, and God talked with him…"
(Gen. 17:3)

One of the greatest privileges we have as Christians is to have God talk to us. Imagine the Creator of all the universe speaking to us! Wow! But God does not talk to just anyone. There are certain characteristics God looks for in a person to whom He speaks.

FIRST—God speaks to THANKFUL people. (v.1-2) says Abraham was ninety-nine years old when God appeared to him and made him a covenant saying, *"I...will multiply thee exceedingly."* Abraham probably thought that at ninety-nine years old his life and usefulness was coming to an end. "Not so," God said, "I'm just getting started!" Abraham was thankful and grateful that God would do such a thing for him.

SECOND—God speaks to HUMBLE people. When God spoke to him, the Bible says Abraham *"fell on his face."* Abraham was showing humility before God by falling to his face. God will not speak to a proud person; He is looking for someone who will bow themselves before Him in humility.

THIRD—God speaks to ATTENTIVE people. God began speaking to Abraham and for the remainder of the chapter, God did most of the talking and Abraham did most of the listening. As the old saying goes, "God gave us two ears and only one mouth because God meant for us to listen more than we speak." One reason most people never hear God speaking is because they won't be quiet long enough to hear Him.

God wants to speak to you. Get into His Word with a thankful, humble, attentive spirit and you will be surprised what God will say to you!

Your Thoughts Affect You

"For as he thinketh in his heart, so is he..."
(Prov. 23:7)

Meet Nick. Nick was a big, strong man who worked for many years in a railroad yard, repairing rail cars. Nick was a dependable, hard worker but he had a problem... Nick was negative. He never seemed to see the positive because he was always thinking the negative.

One day, when quitting time had come and everyone was leaving, Nick accidentally locked himself inside one of the refrigerated boxcars. The boxcar was empty and not connected to any train.

Knowing he was in a refrigerated boxcar, Nick imagined the temperature was well below freezing and therefore feared the worst. He did what he could to try and stay warm, but the longer he was in there the colder he got.

The next morning, Nick's coworkers found his lifeless body in the boxcar. The autopsy revealed that his body temperature had lowered enough for him to die, but here's the really strange part. The investigators found that the refrigeration unit on the boxcar was not working that night. In fact, it had not been working for some time.

Furthermore, the temperature inside the boxcar the night Nick froze to death was only 61 degrees! They were shocked to find out Nick had frozen to death in slightly less-than-normal temperature all because in his mind he THOUGHT he was freezing the entire time!

In other words, Nick expected to die, so he did!

The Bible is clear, our thoughts have a tremendous impact on our actions. Make no mistake about it, if you are dwelling on thoughts of bitterness, anger, fear, or anxiety it WILL affect you because *"as he thinketh in his heart, so is he."*

When You're Down In The Pits

"I waited patiently for the LORD...He brought me up also out of an horrible pit, out of the miry clay, and set my feet upon a rock, and established my goings." (Ps. 40:1-2)

Are you facing circumstances so overwhelming it seems as though you are down in a pit? David felt the same way. So, what do you do when you're thrown into a pit of circumstances that you cannot control?

FIRST—Wait patiently. That doesn't sound like fun, but David said, *"I waited patiently..."* Sometimes God puts us into circumstances to test our faith by teaching us to wait on Him. What is He doing? He is trying to teach us to have PATIENCE in the PIT!

While you wait, focus on any areas in your life God may be trying to change in you. It could be your attitude God is trying to work on. He may want to change your heart before He changes your circumstances.

SECOND—Keep your focus on the Lord. Notice David said, *"I waited patiently for the LORD;"* The next thing to do is to focus on the LORD in your pit. Just like He was with Daniel in the den of lions and with the 3 Hebrew children in the furnace, God is with YOU in your pit! Don't get so focused on your pit that you lose sight of God IN your pit.

THIRD—Refocus spiritually. God sometimes puts us into a pit to slow us down because we've been running ahead of Him. God has you there for a reason. So take this pit experience as sort of a "Time Out" with God. Use this "Time Out" to rest and refocus spiritually and learn whatever it is God is trying to work out in your life.

Take heart! Your pit won't last forever. Just keep your eyes on Jesus!

Called To Be Saints

"To all that be in Rome, beloved of God, called to be saints..." (Rom. 1:7)

We never know how really **bad** we are until we try to be really **good**. We never know how really **selfish** we are until we try to be **sacrificial**. We never know how many **vices** we truly have until we try to practice all the **virtues**. And we never know what **sinners** we are until we really try to be **saints**. Yet, the Bible says we are *"called to be saints."*

FIRST—There is an EXPECTATION of being a Saint. There are no two ways about it, God has *"called"* us to be saints. And with this calling, there is an expectation to fulfill that calling. You would think, looking at the way some Christians are living, that they think they were called to be devils, rather than *"called to be saints."*

While we are not saved by good works, our salvation should clearly be evidenced by good works and a clean life. Christianity puts its first emphasis on character, not on service. In other words, we are called to BE something before we try to DO something. So, there is an expectation that if God has *"called"* us *"to be saints"* we are to LIVE like saints.

SECOND—There is an ENABLING to be a Saint. Living up to sainthood can be a tall order! Especially since the world's view of sainthood is perfection. But though it may seem difficult, it is possible. Whom God calls, He equips for that calling. The good news is God has already equipped you! When God saved you, He put His Spirit inside you which will enable you to be the saint He has *"called"* you to be!

So, today, live like the saint that God says you are!

Bringing Joy To The Angels

"Likewise, I say unto you, there is joy in the presence of the angels of God over one sinner that repenteth."
(Luke 15:10)

There is so much we do not know about the activity that is going on in Heaven. But this verse gives us a glimpse into the spiritual realm and teaches us a few things.

The EXISTENCE of angels is CONFIRMED. To speak of angels in the office or work place today is to invite sarcasm or ridicule. The world sees angels as a myth or fairytale. But all throughout the Bible the existence of angels is confirmed. In fact, the Bible describes them as, *"ministering spirits, sent forth to minister for them who shall be heirs of salvation"* (Heb. 1:14).

The EXAMINATION of angels is CONCLUSIVE. Not only do angels exist, but they are aware of what is going on here on earth. How can there be *"joy in the presence of the angels of God over one sinner that repenteth"* if they do not know that a sinner has repented? They DO know! They are watching; they are observing!

The EXCITEMENT of angels is CONVICTING. What an atmosphere of complete peace and happiness there must be in Heaven right now. No devil to contend with; no lies, no heartache, no death, no sinful activity at all! Yet the Bible says that when one sinner repents and turns to Christ, the perfect peace and joy of Heaven is somehow made even better! For it adds one more reason and cause for rejoicing around the Throne of God!

Today, and every day, we have an opportunity to increase the joy of Heaven by sharing the Gospel and seeing people saved. Don't neglect an opportunity that God may give you today to bring joy to the angels!

Protection Against A Snake Bite

Some years ago a man was hunting in South America when he heard the cries of a bird fluttering, seemingly agitated, over its nest where a baby bird was sitting. As he walked closer, he saw why. Creeping slowly toward the tree was one of the most venomous snakes in South America. The snake's forked tongue darted in and out as though anticipating his prey.

Just as the hunter raise his gun to shoot the snake, he saw something strange happen. The mother bird flew away, fluttering here and there as though it was looking for something. A minute later, it returned with a small leaf-covered twig which it laid carefully over the nest. It then perched at a higher branch, calmly watching the approach of the enemy.

The snake twisted and turned up the tree, then slowly slithered down the branch, preparing to strike its prey. All of the sudden the snake's head snapped backward, as if receiving a deadly blow! Then it slithered away as quickly as possible.

The hunter later learned from the natives that the twig the bird had placed over its nest came from a bush which contains a deadly poison to the snakes. The very sight and odor of it causes them to flee! The bird knew about this bush and had used it as a defense when the enemy approached.

This story reminds us of ANOTHER SERPENT (Satan), even more deadly. It also reminds us of ANOTHER TREE (the Cross), which has the power to drive away the enemy! The twig we can use to protect ourselves from the serpent is the Word of God. So, if Satan comes slithering up to you with some temptation today, just run to the tree, grab a verse and cover yourself!

Ye Shall Receive Power

"But ye shall receive power, after that the Holy Ghost is come upon you: and ye shall be witnesses unto me both in Jerusalem, and in all Judaea, and in Samaria, and unto the uttermost part of the earth." (Acts 1:8)

Acts 1 records the days of Christ after His resurrection but before He ascended back to Heaven. Verse three says He spent 40 days *"being seen of them...and speaking of the things pertaining to the kingdom of God:"*

He is about to give them the Great Commission. But before He commands them to go into all the world with the Gospel, He says, *"But ye shall receive power, after that the Holy Ghost is come upon you..."* So before He gives them a job to do, He promises them power to do that job.

God never intended for them to do what He commanded, alone; He promised them help! The most frustrated Christians are those trying to do the work of the ministry on their own. God never intended for us to minister through OUR power, but through the power of the Holy Ghost.

But here's the best part...while they were told to wait until the Holy Ghost came UPON them *(this was in the days before the indwelling of the Holy Spirit),* today, we have the Holy Spirit, not UPON US, but INSIDE US!

We have access to that very same power they had back then because we have access to the very same Holy Ghost and He is living within us!

Don't try to live the Christian life through your own power. Surrender yourself to the leading and filling of the Holy Ghost this morning and you, too, *"shall receive power."*

Clean The Inside, First

"Thou blind Pharisee, cleanse first that which is within the cup and platter, that the outside of them may be clean also." (Matt. 23:26)

Have you ever been in a restaurant, about to take a sip of your drink, only to notice the glass was not clean? There's nothing like turning up your glass and seeing food stuck to the bottom! When a glass is dirty on the inside, you don't want to use it. That is what Jesus was saying about the Pharisees. The Pharisees were more interested in the external, than the internal.

FIRST—The outside is important. Just because Jesus rebuked their flawed thinking doesn't mean the outside isn't important. Some say, "Well, what I look like on the outside isn't important because the Bible says *'the LORD looketh on the heart.'"* That is true. But that same verse also says, *"man looketh on the outward appearance."* Since man can ONLY see the outside, and not our heart, our outside is important.

SECOND—The inside is most important. God is interested in the outside being clean, but a clean OUTSIDE with a dirty INSIDE is nothing but a hypocrite! Over and over, the Bible teaches that it's what's in your heart that reveals the real you. If your heart is not right with God, all the outward show in the world is worthless!

THIRD—It takes both a clean outside and clean inside to produce the right testimony. The reason many lost people want nothing to do with Christianity is because they have seen past the phony outside of some Christians and have seen the real dirt on the inside. Don't be a hypocrite. Sure, you need to show the world a clean, pure, outward appearance. But, for goodness sake, clean the INSIDE first!

Earthen Vessels

"For God, who commanded the light to shine out of darkness, hath shined in our hearts...But we have this treasure in earthen vessels..." (2Cor. 4:6-7)

Sometimes we put people up on a pedestal. We lift them up as if they are super-spiritual and somehow untouchable by Satan. But Paul reminds us that the best of us are still but *"earthen vessels."*

What makes us special isn't so much the earthen vessel itself (our outward beauty or appearance), because even the world has that. What makes us special is the CONTENTS of our earthen vessel. Paul said, *"we have this **treasure** in earthen vessels."* What is this *"treasure"*? (v.6) says it is the *"light"* God has *"shined in our hearts."*

Remember how that God told Gideon and his army to break their pitchers in order to reveal the light within? Sometimes God may have to break us in order for His light to shine out. Don't discount broken people. Sometimes they are the very ones God can use the most to shine His light to others!

God wants to use you, today. Not because your vessel is so important, but because of the treasure you have INSIDE your vessel. Determine to let the light of Jesus shine to those around you, today!

55

I Will Be With Him In Trouble

"He shall call upon me, and I will answer him: I will be with him in trouble:" (Ps. 91:15)

If we had our choice, no one would choose to have troubles or trials in their life. But God knows that a grounded and growing Christian is not made from a trouble-free life. It is often the struggle that provides us with strength.

FIRST—Troubles are PERMITTED. Make no mistake about it, if you live long enough, you WILL experience troubles. But the troubles we experience do not come of their own will. Because they are *permitted* it means they must have *permission*. That should encourage you and I. If our troubles must have God's permission to come into our life, then that means God is in complete control over them.

SECOND—Troubles have a PURPOSE. It may seem hard to understand, but troubles have a ministry in our lives. God uses troubles to turn us into stronger believers. It is the weights in a gym that help build our physical muscles, and it is the troubles we face that help develop our spiritual muscles as well.

Another purpose of our troubles is to allow us to sense the nearness of our Lord. Psalm 46:1 says that *"God is our refuge and strength, a very **present** help in trouble."*

Whatever trouble you are facing today, allow God to work its purpose in your life. Pray and ask Him to let you sense His presence and help in your time of need.

Prepare To Meet Thy God

"..prepare to meet thy God." (Amos 4:12)

Israel had the same problem a lot of people have today. No matter how good God was to them, they seemed always wander away from Him. He sent all manner of trials into their lives hoping to draw them back to Him, so eventually He said, *"..prepare to meet thy God."*

It is also a sobering reminder to us, as well. Jesus could return at any moment and we will stand before Him to give account of our lives. Are you prepared to meet Him?

UNBELIEVERS need to be prepared. Every unbeliever, who dies in their sin, will be judged at the Great White Throne Judgment. There is no more terrifying thought in all the world than the thought of standing before God, knowing you were not prepared to meet Him.

BELIEVERS also need to be prepared. I'm afraid that many believers see salvation only as "fire insurance." Because they have been saved, they see no further need for preparation. As believers, we will not be judged at the Great White Throne Judgment. We will give account of our lives at The Judgment Seat of Christ. While our sin has already been judged, this will be a judgment of rewards.

While every believer will live with Christ for eternity, not every believer will have the same rewards in eternity. 1 Cor. 3:13-15 clearly says that God will put the works (or lack of works) we did for Him down here, to the test. He will judge them with fire. (v.14) says, *"If any man's work abide which he hath built thereupon, he shall receive a reward."* But (v.15) says, *"If any man's work shall be burned, he shall suffer loss: but he himself shall be saved; yet so as by fire."*

Are you prepared to meet God?

Stepping Out Of The Boat (Part 1)

"And when Peter was come down out of the ship, he walked on the water, to go to Jesus." (Matt. 14:28-29)

While sitting in a boat, Peter had already seen Jesus perform miracle after miracle. He had seen Jesus calm the storms. He had seen Him walk on water, and he had seen Him produce a multitude of fish after having fished all night and not catching anything.

Now, Peter is once again in a boat when Jesus comes walking on the water. At some point, Peter must have said to himself, "There's got to be more for me than just sitting in a boat. I want to walk on the water to Jesus." So, at Christ's invitation, he stepped out of the boat and onto the water.

If you are going to get closer to Jesus, you must be willing to step out of the boat.

FIRST—Peter was not content with where he was. You will never move forward in your Christian life until you become discontent with where you are, spiritually. Being in the boat was good. By being in the boat, Peter was already closer to Jesus than anyone still on the shore, but now just being in the boat wasn't good enough; he wanted to be even closer to Jesus.

How long have you been where you are, spiritually? How long have you been riding in the same boat? Ask the Lord to give you a fresh vision of where you COULD be, spiritually. Ask the Lord to give you a hunger for something more than what you have right now.

What is it you need? Maybe you need a greater love for God's Word. Maybe you need a deeper prayer life. Whatever it is, don't settle for sitting in the boat. There is a whole new level of your walk with God that He wants you to get to. Don't settle for anything less!

Stepping Out Of The Boat (Part 2)

"And when Peter was come down out of the ship, he walked on the water, to go to Jesus." (Matt. 14:28-29)

Yesterday, we saw that, like Peter, there is a whole new level to our walk with God than just sitting in the boat. Before Peter could walk on the water, some things had to happen. Today, we will see the last two things Peter had to do, in order to step out of the boat.

SECOND—Peter was willing to leave where he WAS for where God wanted him TO BE. It's interesting that Peter didn't ask Jesus to get into the boat, rather he got out and walked on water to get to Jesus. The Christian life isn't about Jesus becoming more like us, but about us becoming more like Him!

The reason some are still sitting in the same spiritual boat they have been in for years is because they are not willing to leave where they ARE for where God wants them TO BE.

THIRD—Peter was willing to leave some people behind who didn't want to go with him. You may find that you are the only one in your boat who wants to walk closer to Jesus. Not everyone is going to rejoice in your desire for a closer walk with the Lord. But, like Peter, you must be willing to say, "Though no one join me, still I will follow!"

Don't let what others say, deter you from stepping out of the boat. In fact, it could be that by YOU stepping out, it will encourage others to step out, too! (v.33) indicates that Peter's step of faith affected the rest of the disciples still in the boat.

So, decide today that you are willing to leave the boat and the brethren behind if necessary in order to step out and walk on the water to Jesus!

A One-Eyed Christian

"The light of the body is the eye: if therefore thine eye be single, thy whole body shall be full of light."
(Matt. 6:22)

Jesus said that the eye is *"The light of the body."* In other words, the eye is the gateway to the soul; it is a gateway that gives entrance to the mind of man. What man looks at is what he thinks about and what he thinks about is what he actually becomes (Prov. 23:7).

It is a powerful truth that whatever our eye focuses upon affects us. In fact, the condition of our eyes can affect our entire body!

BLINDED EYES can affect us. If you had no sight, it would drastically alter the way you moved around. Spiritually speaking, how often are we "blinded" to things in our own life? We are blinded to the SIN in our lives. We see the sin in other people's lives, but fail to see it in our own life. We are also blinded to the blessing of God in our lives. Those who have their sight often take that sight for granted. When was the last time you thanked God for the ability to see?

BLURRY EYES can affect us. Those who have sight can still be affected by blurry vision. I wear contact lenses. There have been times when one of my contacts got shifted in my eye and it impaired my ability to drive until I got it corrected.

Likewise, double vision also affects a person as well. Spiritually speaking, when we get our eyes on everything else in this world, it affects our desires; it affects our heart.

What we need as Christians is a *"single"* eye for the Lord. We need an eye that is solely focused on God. After all, the Bible says, *"No man can serve two masters"* (Matt. 6:24). Are you a one-eyed Christian?

The Lord Hath Need Of Him

"And if any man say unto you, Why do ye this? say ye that the Lord hath need of him..." (Mark 11:3)

Just before Jesus was about to make His triumphal entry into Jerusalem, He sent two of His disciples on a mission to get a colt for Him to ride upon. He told them exactly what kind of colt to look for and where it would be. He also told them that if anyone asked why they were taking it they were to say, *"the Lord hath need of him."*

See, it's not the size of the gift you give the Lord that is important. It's what God wants to DO with your gift to Him that is important. This man gave his colt and Jesus used it for His triumphal entry. At another time a young boy gave his lunch and Jesus used it to feed 5,000 people!

The question isn't "How big is your gift?" The question is "Will you give whatever He needs that you have?"

The Lord Hath Need of Your TIME. We get so busy, today, that we seldom take time to just be with Jesus. We have no time for prayer and Bible reading. We have no time for church. We seem to have little time to give our Lord, but the Lord hath need of your time.

The Lord Hath Need of Your TALENTS. Many talented people are sitting in the church pew week after week covering up the talent God has given to them. What is even more of a shame is that some will gladly use their abilities for the world, but not for God. If anyone deserves your talent it is the Lord.

What is it that the Lord hath need of in YOUR life? What is it you have been holding back from the Lord? Surrender it, today. Give it to Him freely, because the Lord hath need of it!

Make Thee An Ark

"Make thee an ark of gopher wood; rooms shalt thou make in the ark, and shalt pitch it within and without with pitch."
(Gen. 6:14)

The story of Noah and the Ark is one of the most amazing stories in all the Bible. There are many lessons we can learn from Noah.

FIRST—Noah had to BUILD an ARK. God said to him, *"Make thee an ark..."* What a job God gave to him! No one would have blamed him for feeling overwhelmed.

Building an ark to house that many animals and people was nothing short of a monumental undertaking. Yet, somehow, he rose to the challenge. God gave him the skill, the tools, and the help he needed to do what He had commanded Noah to do.

SECOND—Noah had to PREACH a MESSAGE. 2Peter 2:5 said Noah was a *"preacher of righteousness."* If he had been like some preachers, today, he would have toned down the message in order to be popular with the crowd. But he didn't do that. How do we know? Because you will NEVER become popular with the world while preaching on *"righteousness"* and living right.

THIRD—Noah had to PREPARE a FAMILY. Next, God said to Noah, *"rooms shalt thou make in the ark..."* Noah was to prepare rooms for his entire family to get into the Ark. And it worked because (Gen. 7:7) says, *"And Noah went in, and his sons, and his wife, and his sons' wives with him, into the ark..."* Because of Noah's faithfulness and testimony, he was able to save his entire family from God's judgment!

Mom and dad, how much room are you making for the Lord in your home? Are you preparing your children to get into the ark?

I Heard Him, Myself

"And many more believed because of his own word; And said..we have heard him ourselves..." (John 4:41-42)

The Bible says that many of the Samaritans believed on Jesus because they heard Him, themselves. It is one thing to hear ABOUT someone else; it is another thing to hear from them, yourself.

Week after week, believers go to church and hear the pastor get up and share what he got from the Lord during his study time that week. What a blessing it is to have a pastor who prays and studies in order to feed something fresh to his people. Don't ever take that for granted.

But there is nothing like hearing from God, yourself! That's right! Your pastor isn't the only one who can hear from God. Every time you open God's Word and begin to read and study it, God will give YOU a fresh word, as well.

Some Samaritans in John 4 believed on Jesus because of the testimony of the woman at the well. But it says, *"many more believed because of his own word."* Many times my faith has been increased because of a message I heard from another preacher. But the greatest times of growth in my spiritual life has been those times I got a message from God, myself; when God spoke to ME through His Word.

Faithfully hearing your pastor preach God's Word each week will do so much for your Christian growth, but don't let that be ALL you get from God all week. If you will take time daily to read and study God's Word, then you will begin to hear God speaking to you, too. Then, like the Samaritans you can say, "I heard Him myself!"

Do You Please Him?

"..I do always those things that please him."
(John 8:29)

What a powerful statement Jesus made when He said, *"I do always those things that please him,"* referring to the Father. Can you say that God is always pleased with what you do? I must confess that I cannot say that. There are many things I have done in my life, of which I am ashamed. I do not always do things that please the Lord, but I sure WANT to please Him.

Do the THOUGHTS YOU THINK please Him? Man sees your actions but God sees your heart. He knows the very thoughts you and I think. Can you say that your thoughts always please the Lord, or do you dwell on thoughts of anger, bitterness, or lust?

Do the WORDS YOU SPEAK please Him? The psalmist said, *"Let the words of my mouth, and the meditation of my heart, be acceptable in thy sight, O LORD, my strength, and my redeemer" (Ps. 19:14).* Does the way you talk to your spouse, your children, your parents, or your employer, please the Lord?

Does YOUR CHOICE OF FRIENDS please Him? We are known by the company we keep, and our choice of friends will either influence us for good or for evil. The Bible says, *"Be not deceived: evil communications corrupt good manners" (1Cor. 15:33).* Do the friends you have encourage you to live a godly, holy, life that pleases God? Or do you find that they tend to lead you away from what you know is right?

Examine yourself and ask God to help you today to *"..do always those things that please him."*

Working Out What God Works In

"..work out your own salvation with fear and trembling.
For it is God which worketh in you both to will and to do of
his good pleasure." (Phil. 2:12-13)

Many people have misinterpreted this verse to mean that we are saved by our works. They think it is saying that we are to work for our salvation. But notice it doesn't say to work FOR your own salvation; it says, *"work OUT your own salvation."* We are to work OUT, what God has worked IN.

FIRST—We Must Let God Work IN US. (v.13) says, *"For it is God which worketh IN you..."* Salvation is the "first" thing God wants to work in us. Until you have been born again, God cannot work anything else in you. Once you are saved, you then must allow God to work in you daily so that you will walk in the Spirit and not in the flesh. God works in us when we read and meditate on His Word.

SECOND—We Must Let God Work THROUGH US. (v.12) says, *"work out your own salvation..."* Working out your salvation simply means to live out what God has put inside you. As the Holy Spirit works in your heart, you live that out for others to see. As you learn truths from God's Word, you put those into practice on a daily basis. You see, you aren't working FOR something. You are working OUT something.

Today, ask the Lord to help you "work out" your salvation, so that others may see what God has been working in you!

Like A Watered Garden

"And the LORD shall guide thee continually...and thou shalt be like a watered garden..." (Isa. 58:11)

There are all kinds of gardens. There are big gardens and little gardens. There are gardens in the city and gardens in the country. Gardens come in many different shapes and sizes and are cultivated for different purposes, such as flower gardens and vegetable gardens.

FIRST—The WORK of a Garden. In order to have a beautiful garden that will produce the best crop possible, it will take a lot of work! A successful garden does not happen by accident. Likewise, you will not become a thriving, fruitful Christian by accident. It takes effort on your part to grow into the Christian God wants you to be.

SECOND—The WEEDS in a Garden. Even the most beautiful gardens in the world are not free from the possibility of weeds. You may never "see" weeds in a particular garden, but that is only because the gardener constantly keeps a lookout for them. If left unattended, weeds will take over a garden, because they spread. If sin is left unattended in our lives, sin will inevitably take over! Sin will spread! Therefore, we must be vigilant and watch for sin so that we may keep it from taking over our life.

THIRD—The WEALTH of a Garden. A garden has the potential of producing a wealth of flowers, fruits, or vegetables, depending on what was planted. A successful garden is often not only a blessing to the gardener, but also to others. The botanical gardens, for instance, are often a great attraction that many visitors enjoy seeing, even though they had no part in working the garden themselves.

Likewise, the fruit of our lives should be a blessing to everyone we come in contact with. They should be able to see the Holy Spirit at work in us *"like a watered garden."*

Say Something

"Let the redeemed of the LORD say so..." (Ps. 107:2)

There is a lot to be said for how we as Christians are to live our lives as an example before unbelievers. There is no doubt that God expects us to do so. But, at some point, we must be ready and willing to speak up and speak out about our faith and how it has changed our life.

FIRST—The DIFFICULTY of Speaking Out. The thought of speaking out about their faith makes some people as nervous as a long-tail cat in a room full of rocking chairs! For some it comes naturally, but for others the thought of speaking out almost causes a panic attack. But the Bible says in 2 Tim. 1:7, *"For God hath not given us the spirit of fear; but of power, and of love, and of a sound mind."*

SECOND—The DUTY of Speaking Out. It is not always easy being a witness, but at some point a witness must get on the witness stand and tell their story. Listen, we as believers have a duty to speak out. The world is shouting their perverted messages out every day. We have the truth and the truth needs to be heard.

Paul said in Rom 10:14, *"How then shall they call on him in whom they have not believed? and how shall they believe in him of whom they have not **heard**? and how shall they hear without a preacher?"* God may not have called you to stand behind a pulpit and preach, but He HAS commanded you as a believer to spread the Gospel whenever and wherever God gives you the opportunity.

Ask God, today, to give you the boldness you need to take any opportunity you have to share the Gospel with someone.

It Shall Be Well

"And he said, Wherefore wilt thou go to him to day? it is neither new moon, nor sabbath. And she said, It shall be well." (2Kings 4:23)

2 Kings, chapter 4, tells the story of a woman whose son had died and she told her husband she needed to get him to the man of God (Elisha) for help. What is interesting is that even though her son was already dead, and things looked hopeless, she said to her husband, *"It shall be well."* It didn't look well right then, but she knew if she could just get him to the man of God, everything would be alright!

FIRST—The THINGS OF GOD Were Already Familiar to Her. She didn't wait until this emergency to get to the man of God. She was already familiar with the things of God BEFORE tragedy struck. Don't wait until something bad happens, be faithful to church and God right now.

SECOND—The MAN OF GOD Was Already Familiar to Her. She had already been feeding Elisha and had even built a Prophet's Chamber onto their house just for him. Sadly, many can't go to the man of God in a crisis because they have already spent so much time tearing him down at home! Honor your pastor and pray for him because in a crisis he will be the best friend you have!

Elisha ended up raising her son from the dead. I guarantee you, that for the rest of that boy's life he knew that no matter what problem he faced, as long as he could take it to God, it would be alright.

Whatever you are facing this morning, take it to Jesus. Trust Him with it and then you can say, *"It shall be well."*

Before I Formed Thee

"Before I formed thee in the belly I knew thee; and before thou camest forth out of the womb I sanctified thee, and I ordained thee a prophet unto the nations." (Jer. 1:5)

The birth of a child is always a miracle from God. How special it is to see that new life come into the world. When God spoke these words to Jeremiah, it gave us a glimpse of three great truths about God:

FIRST—God created you. He said, *"Before I formed thee in the belly..."* Despite what the world may teach, we are not a product of millions of years of evolution. No! We are the loving creation of an all-powerful God! God clearly said that Jeremiah was a person in *"the belly."* It wasn't just some unformed tissue, it was a person—it was Jeremiah! And he had been *"formed"* by God.

SECOND—God knows you. Next, God said, *"I knew thee..."* There are some things I already knew about my grandson, before he was even born. I knew it would be a boy. I knew his name would be Isaac James Agan. I also knew he would be a beautiful baby who will grow up to be a strikingly handsome man because....after all, he is my grandson! But God's knowledge of us goes so much deeper. He knows every cell in our body and even the DNA of those cells. WOW! That is the God we serve.

THIRD—God has a plan for you. Last, God said, *"I ordained thee a prophet unto the nations."* Before Jeremiah was even born, God had a plan for his life. long before Jeremiah knew who God was, God knew who Jeremiah was and that He would call him to be His prophet. Isn't that amazing?

Just remember, this morning, that you are no different than Jeremiah. God created you, too! God knows you too! And God has a wonderful plan for your life, too!

The Blessing Of Your Burden

"My grace is sufficient for thee: for my strength is made perfect in weakness..." (2Cor. 12:9)

No one likes burdens, yet we all have our burdens to bear. Often we look at others and think, "If only I had no burdens like them." But the truth is, they no doubt are bearing burdens you know nothing about.

Burdens are no fun, but there is a blessing that often accompanies our burdens. Some flowers, such as a rose, must be crushed before it can release its full fragrance. Some fruit must be bruised before it will attain its full ripeness and sweetness. Some metals, such as gold, must be put through the fire before it reaches its full value and purity.

So it is with a child of God. J. Sidlow Baxter said, "It is true with many of us that we must be laid low before we will look high. We must know God's smiting before we can appreciate God's smiling."

But the blessing of our burdens is this...whenever God sends a trial with one hand, He gives us grace with the other hand! Therefore our trials become our triumphs. The very things which seem to break us are the things God uses to make us. Satan may give us a pathway of thorns, but God can turn it into a blanket of roses!

Yes, there is a blessing to your burden...it is God's grace IN your burden! And He promised that His grace would be sufficient. In fact, God said to Paul in the next part of this verse, *"My strength is made perfect in weakness."*

Maybe you are going through a trial, this morning. Don't resist it; rest in it. Allow God to perfect His strength in you through your trial. Allow His grace to do its work in you and then you will see the blessing of your burden!

Strength From Your Weakness

"..out of weakness were made strong." (Heb. 11:34)

Few biographies have influenced young Christians more than that of Hudson Taylor, missionary to China. When asked his secret for being so greatly used of God, he replied, "The Lord was looking for a man weak enough to use, and he found me."

There are no more powerful forces in nature than wind, water, and lightning. They are so powerful because they take the path of least resistance. Spiritually speaking, the Holy Spirit always seeks the path of least resistance to the will of God. That is why Paul wrote, *"God hath chosen...the weak things of the world to confound the mighty..."*

It's not weakness but resistance that hinders God. In other words, if you are not being used of God, it is not because you are weak, rather it is because of your resistance toward Him.

All through the Bible, we see those whom God greatly used, but it was only AFTER they yielded their weakness to Him. When our resistance to God's will is broken down, God can do great things through us.

MOSES, what is that in your hand—a little shepherd's rod? Yet God used that rod to divide a sea and deliver the Children of Israel. SHAMGAR, what is that in thine hand—a little ox goad? Yet God used that little ox goad to allow him to slay 600 Philistines! GIDEON, what is that in thine hand—a simple earthen pitcher? DAVID, what is that in thine hand—a sling and five smooth stones?

Listen, friend, God NEVER uses the unclean, but He DOES us the weak, the foolish, and those despised of man. That means He can even use YOU and your weakness!

Walking Worthy (Part 1)

"That ye might walk worthy of the Lord unto all pleasing, being fruitful in every good work, and increasing in the knowledge of God;" (Col. 1:10)

Notice three things Paul says in this verse about how to walk worthy of the Lord.

FIRST—*"That ye might walk..."* The Christian life is a walk; it is a journey. God did not save us to SIT, He saved us to SERVE. He saved us to progress in our walk with Him. We are to have a daily walk (fellowship) with Jesus.

Are you sitting in neutral or are you growing and moving forward in your walk with God?

SECOND—*"That ye might walk worthy..."* This does not mean we are to walk in a way that makes us worthy to be saved. Rather it means to walk in a way that is befitting of your conversion. It means to walk as one should walk who professes to be a Christian; it means a walk becoming to your faith.

THIRD—*"unto all pleasing..."* This means we are to live in a way that pleases the Lord. Our conduct, our conversation, and even our companions should please the Lord. Notice it says, *"unto **all** pleasing."* This means it is not a once-in-a-while thing. It is pleasing the Lord in "ALL" areas of our life.

It IS possible to *"walk worthy of the Lord."* Ask God to help you live a life befitting your conversion. Ask Him to help you have an attitude that pleases Him, today!

Walking Worthy (Part 2)

"That ye might walk worthy of the Lord unto all pleasing, being fruitful in every good work, and increasing in the knowledge of God;" (Col. 1:10)

Yesterday, we looked at the first three parts of this verse which tells us how to walk worthy of the Lord. Today, we will look at the last two parts.

FOURTH—*"being fruitful in every good work..."* A fruit tree that bears no fruit is not worthy to even be called a fruit tree. Why? Because it is no different than every other tree that bears no fruit. Likewise, a believer who bears no spiritual fruit is not walking *"worthy"* of the name Christian because his life is no different than every other unbeliever who bears no spiritual fruit. A true Christian will bear fruit.

FIFTH—*"and increasing in the knowledge of God."* A believer who is walking *"worthy of the Lord"* is one who is ever learning and ever growing in their walk with God. When you got saved, you may have been ignorant of spiritual truths in the Bible, but after being saved for years, you shouldn't STILL be ignorant of spiritual truths. You should be able to see growth in your Christian walk. You should have more knowledge of God and His Word, now, than you did this time last year.

Are you walking *"worthy of the Lord"*? Is your life bearing fruit that evidences that walk? Are you *"increasing in the knowledge of God"*? If not, determine, today, that you want to begin walking worthy of the name Christian.

He'll Give You More

"And he said unto them, Take heed what ye hear: with what measure ye mete, it shall be measured to you: and unto you that hear shall more be given." (Mark 4:24)

There is nothing more important in the life of a believer than hearing, learning, and applying the truths of God's Word to our lives. Notice three things in this verse.

FIRST—There Must Be ATTENTION to the Truth. Jesus said, *"Take heed what ye hear."* First, we must *"hear"* the truth. It is our responsibility to put ourselves, and our family, in a church where the truth is being preached. So many choose a church based on the facilities, the music, the youth, or something else. First, and foremost, make sure you are in a church where you will hear the truth of God's Word thundered from the pulpit every week.

SECOND—There Must Be SUBMISSION to the Truth. Jesus said, *"Take heed..."* Hearing the truth of God's Word preached every week will not do much for you if you are not going to *"Take heed"* to it. Before God will ever give you more truth, you must obey what He has already given you.

THIRD—There Will Be An ILLUMINATION of the Truth. Lastly, Jesus said, *"and unto you that hear shall more be given."* There is a promise here that when you obey what you already know, God will illuminate MORE truth to you. In other words, the reason many in our churches have not grown more in God's Word than they already have is because they have not been obeying what God has already given them!

God wants to open up more truth to you. Start obeying the truth God has already given to you, and then you find He will give you more!

Mountain-View Living

"He carried me away...to a great and high mountain.
(Rev. 21:10)

Drones are amazing! You can fly a drone high into the air and see much further away than simply standing on the ground. John didn't have a drone; he had something better—the Spirit! John was carried away by the Spirit *"to a great and high mountain."* From this mountain view, he saw things he never saw at ground level.

Sadly, the average Christian never sees further than where they are right now. They never seem to see the BIG picture of what God wants to do in their lives. They are content with ground-level living, when God wants them to experience mountain-view living!

FIRST—we must be willing to leave where we are. The only way John was able to see what he had never seen before was because the Spirit carried him away. He was willing to leave where he was so he could see what he had never seen.

SECOND—we must be willing to go higher. The Spirit didn't take John from where he was to another place on the ground. He went *"to a great and high mountain."* If we are going to experience mountain-view living, we must leave where we are for higher ground.

God wants us to have the mountain view; He wants us to see the BIG picture of the world around us as it relates to God's plan. Don't keep your eyes down here, get a mountain view!

As long as you are content with low-level living, you will never experience what God has for you up on the mountain. Surrender yourself, today, and let God give you a glimpse of mountain-view living!

Filled With The Spirit (Part 1)

"And be not drunk with wine, wherein is excess; but be
filled with the Spirit;" (Eph. 5:18)

When we got saved, the Holy Spirit came to dwell
within us (John 14:7). When the Holy Spirit came, He
didn't come in doses; a little here and a little there. No, at
salvation, we received ALL there was to receive of the
Holy Spirit. The Bible is clear that either you have the Holy
Spirit or you do not have the Holy Spirit.

So, when the Bible says we are to *"be filled with the*
Spirit" it doesn't mean we get MORE of the Spirit. Rather,
it means the Holy Spirit has more of us! Meaning, the more
of our life we yield to the Holy Spirit the more He is able to
fill and control.

When Paul said, *"Be not drunk with wine...but be*
filled with the Spirit" he likens a SPIRIT-filled person to an
ALCOHOL-filled person; both are controlled by what they
are filled with. In other words, if you are not *"filled with*
the Spirit" it is because you are *"filled"* with something
else! And what FILLS you CONTROLS you!

Some people lash out in anger toward others because
they are *"filled"* with bitterness. Others brag on themselves
and lift themselves up because they are *"filled"* with pride.
Still others commit immoral acts because they are *"filled"*
with lust. Why? Because what FILLS us CONTROLS us.

What is filling you, today? What is controlling you?
Tomorrow, we will look at how you can KNOW you are
filled with the Spirit.

Filled With The Spirit (Part 2)

*"And be not drunk with wine, wherein is excess; but be
filled with the Spirit;" (Eph. 5:18)*

How Can You Experience the Spirit-Filled Life?

FIRST—Recognize that you are empty, spiritually.
Sadly, many are so used to walking in the flesh that they do
not even know what it is like to walk in the Spirit! The first
step to being *"filled with the Spirit"* is recognizing your
need and dependence upon the Holy Spirit.

SECOND—Confess and forsake all known sin. The
Holy Spirit will not fill a dirty vessel. You cannot live in
sin AND be filled with the Holy Spirit at the same time.

THIRD—You must walk by faith, not by feelings.
Your flesh will crave sin like a drug addict craves his next
hit. Therefore, walking in the Spirit means there must be a
moment-by-moment reliance upon Him, no matter how you
feel (Gal. 5:16-17).

**FOURTH—You must dwell in God's Word and let
God's Word dwell in you**. Since what FILLS you
CONTROLS you, it is important to fill your mind with the
Word of God. You cannot expect to be *"filled with
the Spirit"* while filling your mind with the garbage of this
world.

As you live this way, confessing and turning from sin,
relying on the indwelling Spirit for His power, and being
obedient to His Word, you will begin seeing how the Holy
Spirit will control your thoughts, your emotions, your
words, your attitudes, and all of your life!

If you have not done so, surrender every area of your
life to the control of the Holy Spirit, today! Then, you can
be *"filled with the Spirit."*

A Word For The Worrywart

"Take no thought for your life, what ye shall eat, or what ye shall drink; nor yet for your body, what ye shall put on."
(Matt. 6:25)

The dictionary defines "Worrywart" as a person who tends to worry habitually and often needlessly. Are YOU a worrywart? Do you worry about everything? Well, the good news is that God has got a word for you!

He Reminds Us of the FOWLS of the AIR. In (v.26) He says, *"Behold the fowls of the air: for they sow not, neither do they reap, nor gather into barns; yet your heavenly Father feedeth them. Are ye not much better than they?"* Have you ever heard a bird fretting over not being able to pay rent for its bird nest? Have you ever heard them worrying over where the next worm is coming from to feed their babies?

Of course not! And Jesus said that if the Father meets their needs, will He not even MORE meet the needs of His children?

He Reminds Us of the FLOWERS of the FIELD. In (v.28-29) He says, *"And why take ye thought for raiment? Consider the lilies of the field, how they grow; they toil not, neither do they spin: And yet I say unto you, That even Solomon in all his glory was not arrayed like one of these."* Jesus said that if He cares enough for a simple flower that grows wildly in a field, how much MORE does He care for you?

Do you know what God's word is to you, this morning? Don't be such a WORRYWART!!! There is no problem too big for our God to handle, and there is nothing As long as you are living for Him and seeking to please Him with your life, you have absolutely nothing to worry about! Isn't that a blessing!

Ordinary, Yet Extraordinary

*"Now when they saw the boldness of Peter and John, and perceived that they were **unlearned** and **ignorant** men, they marvelled; and they took knowledge of them, that they had been with Jesus." (Acts 4:13)*

In the Bible, God always seemed to use the ordinary.

- He used an ordinary rod in the hand of Moses.
- He used five ordinary loaves and two ordinary fishes to feed 5,000 people.
- He used an ordinary jawbone of an ordinary donkey in the hand of Samson to slay 1,000 Philistines.
- He used an ordinary rock in an ordinary sling to defeat Goliath!

Even the twelve apostles were just ordinary people like the rest of us.

Why does God delight in using ordinary, everyday people in his service? Because when the world sees God's power at work through an ordinary person they realize it wasn't the person, but God IN the person that made the difference! When everyone saw the miracles those *"unlearned and ignorant"* disciples were doing they *"marvelled..and..took knowledge of them, that they had been with Jesus."*

"But there's nothing special or spectacular about me. Surely God could never use me," you might say. If that's what you think, be encouraged—worthless nobodies are just the kind of people God uses! In fact, if you think about it, that's all He has to work with! After all, even the most powerful prophets like Elijah and Elisha were worthless nobodies without God.

You may not have much to offer God. Well, the great thing is...all He wants you to offer Him is YOURSELF! He will take care of the rest.

Do What He Says

"His mother saith unto the servants, Whatsoever he saith unto you, do it." (John 2:5)

What great advice Mary, the mother of Jesus, gave to those at the marriage in Cana. She said, "Whatever Jesus says to do, do it!" I can't think of any better advice to give anyone. In fact, that is basically what Christianity is in a nutshell...doing whatever Jesus tells us to do.

FIRST—Obedience to Christ proves that you "KNOW" Him. Jesus said in (John 10:27) *"My sheep hear my voice, and I know them, and they follow me:"* Only those who truly "know" Jesus can hear His voice. The word *"hear"* is more than just hearing with your ear, it is acting upon what you heard. Disobedience comes when we **hear** what Jesus says, yet we choose not to **do** what Jesus says.

SECOND—Obedience to Christ proves that you "LOVE" Him. Jesus said in (John 14:15) *"If ye love me, keep my commandments."* You cannot convince me that a person who has no desire to obey what the Bible teaches really loves Jesus. If you love Jesus, you will love His Word. And if you love His Word, you will **obey** His Word.

Week after week, people go to church and sing, "Oh, how I love Jesus..." yet Monday through Saturday they are not even **reading** God's Word, much less **obeying** God's Word. Does that person *really* love Jesus? According to Jesus, they don't.

Do you want to prove that you really know Jesus and love Jesus? Get in His Word today. Read it, then *"Whatsoever he saith unto you, do it."*

Your Reward Is Great

"Rejoice ye in that day, and leap for joy: for, behold, your reward is great in heaven..." (Luke 6:23)

Some of the most hated people in all the Bible were those who took a stand for truth and right. Noah was a preacher of righteousness and was mocked and ridiculed. Joseph took a stand for purity and was thrown into prison. John the Baptist took a stand and was beheaded. In Luke 6, Jesus tells us four things about those who do right:

FIRST—Prepare to be LONELY. If you stand for right, sometimes you will stand alone! Those who stand for right will not be the popular ones. They will be the first ones people will separate from. When you choose to stand for right, be ready to stand against the crowd.

SECOND—Prepare to be LIED ABOUT. If you stand for right, the wicked crowd will not hesitate to spread things about you that just aren't true. Joseph was lied about because he refused the sexual advances of his employer's wife. She falsely accused him of attacking him. Satan is a liar, so he will use his lies against you when you stand for right.

THIRD—Prepare to be HATED. Jesus clearly taught that the world will hate those who oppose it. He said in *(John 15:19) "I have chosen you out of the world, therefore the world hateth you."*

FOURTH—Prepare to be REWARDED. "Preacher, you are not exactly encouraging me to stand for right! Why should I stand for right if all these bad things will happen?" It's simple. You should stand for what is right because Jesus said that when you do, *"your reward is great in heaven."* He is keeping a record of it all and will reward you for taking a stand in spite of the opposition you face.

A House Divided (Part 1)

"..every city or house divided against itself shall not stand:" (Matt. 12:25)

Sin and Satan are always the culprits whenever a house is divided. And it doesn't take much to divide a house or a church because if Satan is given one inch, he will take a mile!

FIRST: The SOURCE of a Divided House. There are some specific sins that will always cause division in a house or a church.

IMMATURITY causes division. Paul said to the church at Corinth, *"And I, brethren, could not speak unto you as unto spiritual, but as unto carnal, even as unto babes in Christ"* (1 Cor. 3:1). I have never heard of a church that split because everyone was growing too much in the Lord; they are usually split because of spiritual immaturity.

JEALOUSY causes division. Immaturity often produces jealousy. The immaturity and jealously in the church at Corinth was evident because they were arguing over which apostle they were saved and baptized under! Jealousy is sure sign of immaturity.

PRIDE causes division. It was the sin of pride which divided Satan from God to begin with. He thought he deserved a position higher than what God had given to him. As soon as pride comes into a house or church, right after it will come contention (Prov. 13:10).

GOSSIP causes division. Gossip doesn't bring people together; it tears people apart! (Prov. 17:9) says, *"..he that repeateth a matter separateth very friends."* When one Christians throws mud at another Christian, Jesus is the one who gets hit! Has your house or your church become divided? If so, see if any of these sins are in your life.

A House Divided (Part 2)

"..every city or house divided against itself shall not stand:" (Matt. 12:25)

Yesterday, we saw the "SOURCE" of a divided house. Today, I want us to see **The "SERIOUSNESS" of a divided house.**

In this verse Jesus isn't talking about HIS house being divided. He's talking about SATAN'S house being divided. Because in (v.26) He said, *"And if SATAN cast out SATAN, he is divided against himself; how shall then HIS KINDOM stand?"*

Jesus says that if Satan were to rise up against himself, his kingdom would not be able to stand. But Satan rising up against himself sounds good, doesn't it? Yes, but there's one problem...Jesus is telling us that Satan's house is NOT divided.

Satan would never drive out his own demons. He wouldn't divide against himself. Satan's house isn't divided, IT'S STRONG! As much as God loves you, that's how much Satan hates you and is hell-bent on destroying you. He and his demons are like an underground terrorist network. Only, they are more **sinister**, more **subtle**, and more **successful** than Al-Qaeda or ISIS will ever be.

That is why a divided house is so serious! If you let your HOME become divided; or if you allow your CHURCH to become divided...THE CAUSE OF CHRIST is what will suffer! Don't allow Satan to cause division in your heart, your home, or your church because Satan wins when you do.

If there is division in your home, or church...repent, seek forgiveness, and let God bring restoration so that you can have God's love, joy, and peace in your life once again.

Stressed Out!

"But Martha was cumbered about much serving..."
(Luke 10:40)

Stress is something that we face every day. Even children aren't immune to stress nowadays. In Luke 10, we see a woman who was stressed out and we learn a few lessons about stress from her experience.

LESSON #1: Stress will ACTIVATE your FRETTING. Stress will cause us to fret and worry. And many times we are worried over things we have absolutely no control over. More than not, we bring stress on ourselves unnecessarily. For example, when we fail to adequately prepare it can cause us stress. Martha did not feel adequately prepared for Jesus to visit and as a result she got stressed out.

LESSON #2: Stress will AFFECT your FOCUS. Because Martha was stressed out, she was no longer focused on Jesus, the guest of honor. Rather, she was focused on all the work that had to be done. The Bible says she was *"cumbered about much serving."* Stress comes when we become more focused on our WORK FOR God, than on our WORSHIP OF God.

LESSON #3: Stress will ALTAR your FELLOWSHIP. Martha's stress got her focus on Mary because she said, *"Lord, dost thou not care that my sister hath left me to serve alone? bid her therefore that she help me."* Not only will stress get your focus off of the Lord; it will also get your focus on others you feel aren't doing as much as you. Her stress caused her to be angry with her sister.

Don't let the circumstances of life get you stressed out. If you do, it will activate your fretting, affect your focus, and altar your fellowship.

The Master Is Come

"And when she had so said, she went her way, and called Mary her sister secretly, saying, The Master is come, and calleth for thee." (John 11:28)

It had been four days since Lazarus had died and Jesus was not there. Have you ever gone through a trial and it seemed as if Jesus was far away? Mary and Martha had lost their brother, Lazarus. I'm sure they wondered where Jesus was and why He was not there to prevent Lazarus from dying in the first place. Then, right in the middle of their grief, Martha runs to Mary and says, *"The Master is come!"*

Oh, what a glad day when the Master came into this world! For thousands of years the Messiah had been prophesied; a deliverer had been promised. But century after century passed by with no Messiah in sight. Where is He? Does He not see the death, sorrow, pain, and grief sin has brought? Does He not see that sin and wickedness is running rampant?

Then one quiet night in a little stable at Bethlehem a baby is born. So miraculous was His birth that wise men came on a long journey just to see Him. As they stood around the manger beholding the very Son of God, maybe one of the onlookers turned to another and said, "The Master is come! The Messiah is finally here!"

Maybe you are going through a difficult trial right now and you are feeling all alone. Maybe Satan has whispered in your ear that Jesus is nowhere to be found. May I encourage you by reminding you that the Master is come! He's right there with you and has promised to never leave nor forsake you.

It's Jesus Calling!

"And when she had so said, she went her way, and called Mary her sister secretly, saying, The Master is come, and calleth for thee." (John 11:28)

Yesterday, we looked at the first part of this verse, where Mary said, *"The Master is come."* Today I want to focus on the next phrase, *"and calleth for thee."*

Can you imagine what Martha must have felt like when she heard the words *"The Master...calleth for thee"*? Here was the Creator of the world, God incarnate in the flesh and He was calling for Martha! Wow! What an honor. But guess what; He's calling for you, too!

FIRST—Jesus Is Calling You For SALVATION.

If you have never trusted in Jesus Christ as your Savior, He is calling you! The creation around you speaks of a CREATOR, but He wants to be so much more than the Creator, He wants to be your SAVIOUR! When Jesus died on the cross, He was dying to pay for your sin and He is calling you to repent and put your trust in Him as your Saviour.

FIRST—Jesus Is Calling You For SERVICE. Once you have been saved, God's next call to you is for service. God didn't save us to SIT; He saved us to SERVE! Sadly, there are believers who have been saved for years, but they are still sitting, instead of serving. Jesus is calling you to use your gifts and abilities for Him.

God has a plan for your life. He has something you can do for the Kingdom of God. If you are not involved in some area of service for Him, *"The Master...calleth for thee."*

Show And Tell

"Come, see a man, which told me all things that ever I did: is not this the Christ?" (John 4:29)

I always enjoyed "Show and Tell" when I was in school. You never knew what object a classmate would bring to school to tell about.

John, chapter 4, tells of a woman that Jesus met at Jacob's well. It didn't take very long after their encounter for her to realize Jesus wasn't an ordinary man. He told her things about her past that a stranger wouldn't have known. In fact, the things He said about her were so amazing that she said to Him, *"Sir, I perceive that thou art a prophet."*

Jesus finally told her that He was more than a prophet; He was the Messiah. She was so excited about her encounter with Jesus that she ran into the city saying to everyone she met, *"Come, see a man, which told me all things that ever I did: is not this the Christ?" (v.29)*

You may not have a lot of talent and you may not feel you have a lot of ability, but you know what you CAN do? You can "Show and Tell" people about Jesus! It didn't require any talent for this woman to tell others about Jesus. She had not been to Bible college; she hadn't learned a lot of deep Bible theology. She only knew that she had met the Messiah and wanted everyone she knew to meet Him, too!

You may not still be in school, but don't miss an opportunity to "Show and Tell" others about Jesus, today!

What Really Matters In Life (Part 1)

"The Spirit of the Lord is upon me, because he hath anointed me to preach the gospel to the poor; he hath sent me to heal the brokenhearted, to preach deliverance to the captives, and recovering of sight to the blind, to set at liberty them that are bruised," (Luke 4:18)

The Bible clearly reveals what was important to the Lord and the things that were important to Him should also be important to us. But that is not the case for some folks.

There is a story of two paddle boats which left Memphis about the same time traveling down the Mississippi River to New Orleans. As they traveled side by side, sailors from one vessel made a few remarks about the snail's pace of the other vessel. Words were exchanged. Challenges were made and the race began. Competition became vicious as the two boats roared through the deep South.

One boat began falling behind because they didn't have enough fuel. There had been plenty of coal for the trip, but not enough for a race. As the boat dropped back, an enterprising young sailor took some of the ship's cargo and tossed it into the ovens. When the sailors saw that the supplies burned as well as the coal, they fueled their boat with the material they had been assigned to transport. They ended up winning the race, but they burned their cargo!

A lot of folks have done the same thing with their life. They have taken the one life God has given them and consumed it on the wrong things. As far as the world is concerned they might have won the race, but in the sight of God they have burned their cargo.

What Really Matters In Life (Part 2)

"The Spirit of the Lord is upon me, because he hath anointed me to preach the gospel to the poor; he hath sent me to heal the brokenhearted, to preach deliverance to the captives, and recovering of sight to the blind, to set at liberty them that are bruised," (Luke 4:18)

Yesterday, we saw that what mattered most to Jesus, while He was on this earth, was ministering to hurting and hopeless people. What are some things that should matter to us in life?

FIRST—Your HEART Matters. You cannot adequately minister to others until you have allowed the Lord to first minster to you. If your heart is not right with God, you will not be able to effectively minister to others.

SECOND—Your HOME Matters. Satan is launching an all-out attack on our homes. He is attacking husbands and wives, as well as our children. What good is it to have a thriving career if your home is a mess? All the toys and gifts in the world cannot make up for time not spent with your children and spouse. I've never heard of a man, on his deathbed, who said, "I wish I had spent more time at work." Invest in your family. Why? Because your home matters.

THIRD—Your HARVEST Matters. One of the main responsibilities of us as Christians is to lead others to a saving knowledge of Jesus Christ. We have been given the task and command to *"preach the gospel to every creature" (Mark 16:15).* What good has the life God has given to us been if we die and never point anyone to Jesus?

Stop living your life for things that have no eternal significance. Start investing, today, in what *really* matters in life: your HEART, your HOME, and your HARVEST!

Dealing With Disappointment

"My tears have been my meat day and night, while they continually say unto me, Where is thy God?"(Ps. 42:3)

If you live for very long, you will face disappointment. The Psalmist, in Psalm 42, sure was discouraged. He was so down that he cried *"day and night."* Have you ever been that low? Have you ever been so disappointed with life that you just wept constantly? The Psalmist was discouraged because:

His PLANS had not been FULFILLED. Evidently, circumstances were preventing him from going into Jerusalem on the annual trip to the Temple for worship. Something prevented his plans and it discouraged him. When our plans in life get derailed by unforeseen circumstances, it can disappoint us and leave us discouraged.

His FEELINGS had not been RELIEVED. He was so depressed that he had lost all of his appetite. He said, *"My tears have been my meat day and night."* He literally went to bed with a tear-soaked pillow and woke up with a tear-soaked pillow!

And to make matters worse, his enemy was taunting him, too. He was saying to this Psalmist, *"Where is thy God?"* In other words, if your God really loved you, where is He at in all of this? So, not only was he struggling with EMOTIONS on the inside, but he was also battling an ENEMY on the outside.

His QUESTIONS had not been ANSWERED. Ten times the psalmist asked God "Why?" and we have no record that God ever gave him an answer. God has all the answers bur He's not obligated to share them with us. David stopped looking at his circumstances and started looking for God in his circumstances!

An April Fool's Prank Gone Wrong!

"Wise men lay up knowledge: but the mouth of the foolish is near destruction." (Prov. 10:14)

April Fool's Day is usually the one day where people usually alert to suspicious things, knowing they could be the target of an April Fool's joke. However, one Tennessee woman didn't quite get the memo and this prank went south fast.

Susan Hudson decided it would be a great April Fool's joke to call her sister and say, "Helen, I shot my husband. I'm cleaning up the mess. Let's go bury him in Blackwater." Now, if Hudson learned anything in this, it's that her sister is a snitch because after receiving the call, she called the police! Officers showed up to Hudson's home and took her into custody until her husband came home and it was clear that he was safe.

In the end, Hudson's words of wisdom were, "Be careful if you're planning on pranking gullible relatives!" Here are two ways to avoid being a fool on April Fool's.

FIRST—A wise person will THINK before they SPEAK. Prov. 29:11 says, *"A fool uttereth all his mind: but a wise man keepeth it in till afterwards."* Not every thing that comes into your mind should come out of your mouth. Think about the impact your words may have on your hearers.

SECOND—A wise person will REFLECT before they REACT. Prov. 29:20 says, *"Seest thou a man that is hasty in his words? there is more hope of a fool than of him."* When we react out of haste or anger, we will say something foolish and hurtful. Don't be a fool on April fools, today!

Bandits And Brethren (Part 1)

"And it came to pass, when Joseph was come unto his brethren that...they took him, and cast him into a pit..."
(Gen. 37:23-24)

Joseph was a young man of character and, because of that, God blessed him. But because God blessed him, others despised him. The sad part of Joseph's story is that his attacks didn't come from those outside his family; they came from within his family.

It wasn't BANDITS who threw Joseph into the pit, it was his BRETHREN. Sadly, some of most vicious attacks we face come from the brethren! Sometimes, it is other Christians who will come against you more than unbelievers. In fact, Jesus had more trouble with the religious crowd than with anyone else! Sadly, some of the worst attacks preachers get are from other preachers. Why does this happen?

I believe we see in this story of Joseph, what prompted his brethren to attack. The brethren will often attack...

When You Are BLESSED More Than Them. (v.3) says that their father, *"loved Joseph more than all his children,"* His brothers clearly saw he was special and it made them jealous. (v.4) says, *"And when his brethren saw that their father loved him more than all his brethren, they hated him, and could not speak peaceably unto him."*

When some Christians think you are more blessed by God than they are, they will often attack you out of jealousy. They know they are not successful on their own, so the best they can do is try to tear down your work.

Ask the Lord to guard you from jealousy. You may not agree with someone else 100%, but you can pray for them.

Tomorrow, I will give you two more times when the brethren will often attack.

Bandits And Brethren (Part 2)

"And it came to pass, when Joseph was come unto his brethren that...they took him, and cast him into a pit..."
(Gen. 37:23-24)

Today, I want to give you two more times when the brethren will often attack.

When You Have A Greater VISION Than Them. *(v.5) "And Joseph dreamed a dream, and he told it his brethren: and they hated him yet the more."* His brothers couldn't stand the fact that God had given him a vision they didn't have.

Don't be surprised if, when you seem to have a bigger vision for your life, the brethren start attacking you. It is often those who have no vision who attack those that do!

When You Are EXALTED Above Them. You know the rest of the story. Joseph was later promoted by God over all the land. He was exalted far above his brothers. Nothing will bring the attacks of the brethren more than when God exalts you above where they are.

Instead of being happy for Joseph, (v.11) says, *"his brethren envied him."* When you are attacked by those who should be cheering you on, you can be sure there is usually some envy and jealousy that is causing it.

What did Joseph do? How did he handle the attacks from his brethren? Joseph just kept on doing right even when he was done wrong. He stayed right when he was cast in the PIT and even stayed right when he was later cast into PRISON. He didn't lift himself UP by trying to tear them DOWN.

If you are being attacked by "the Brethren," don't sink to their level. Don't get your eyes on the BANDITS (the world) or the BRETHREN. Just keep your eyes on Jesus!

Part Of The Family

*"For this cause I bow my knees unto the Father of our Lord Jesus Christ, Of whom the whole **family** in heaven and earth is named," (Eph. 3:14-15)*

From the very first Book in the Bible, God puts an emphasis on the family. When God created Adam in the Garden of Eden, He didn't leave him alone; He gave him a wife and children. There is no denying the importance of family in God's mind.

But, just as the family unit is important to God, there is another family that is important to Him...the church family. Sadly, many do not see the need or importance of having a good church family that they can be a part of.

Every year our church rents a resort in Gatlinburg, TN. and we have FAMILY CAMP for a whole week together. Now, some churches would not like to spend a week together, but this has become one of the most anticipated events we do all year long!

We look forward each year to getting together and playing games, eating, having s'mores and marshmallow roasts, morning devotionals, evening services, trips into Gatlinburg...and a whole lot more!

One reason it has been so successful is that we genuinely enjoy being with each other. Paul goes on to say in *(v.17)* *"That Christ may dwell in your hearts by faith; that ye, being rooted and grounded in **love**..."* There is nothing like a church family that is *"rooted and grounded in love."*

If you are not a part of a loving church family, I want to encourage you to ask the Lord to lead you to one where you can attend, serve, and grow together. There's nothing like being part of the family!

It's For Your Own Good!

"And the LORD commanded us to do all these statutes, to fear the LORD our God, for our good always, that he might preserve us alive, as it is at this day." (Deut. 6:24)

As a child, when I was sick, my mother used to make me take medicine. Now, I never remember ANY medicine ever tasting good. It usually had a nasty taste to it, but mom would make me take it anyway and she would say that it was for my own good.

God gave Moses some commandments for Israel to keep. When Moses gives the commandments to Israel, he says to them that they are *"for our good always."* Then Moses tells them that they are to keep the commandments of God for their own good.

FIRST—Obeying God Would PROTECT Them. Moses said, *"that he might preserve us alive."* There were commandments given that would literally protect their lives if they would obey them. When we read and obey God's Word, it will protect us from many of the fatal mistakes made by unbelievers.

SECOND—Obeying God Would PURIFY Them. Not only will obeying God's Word protect us physically, it will protect us spiritually, as well. In the next verse, Moses said, *"And it shall be our **righteousness**, if we observe to do all these commandments before the LORD our God, as he hath commanded us."* God's Word has a purifying effect on us. It purifies our spirit, our mind, and our soul.

It is human nature to discredit the value of Divine commands. Our flesh wants to question and say, "Why is this important? Is this really necessary?" But Scripture tells us that God's commandments will always do us good! Obeying God's Word will not only protect us, it will purify us as well

The Unclean Spirits Went Out

"And forthwith Jesus gave them leave. And the unclean spirits went out, and entered into the swine..." (Mark 5:13)

Here we see a case of demon-possession. The world mocks at such a thing, but we see it as all too real. I believe we still see it in our day. What could cause such a murderous spirit we see in our land, today? It is a regular occurrence to see people, even children, going on a shooting rampage. What else can put such a murderous spirit in a person but Satan, himself? The Bible says Satan *"was a murderer from the beginning" (John 8:44)*.

In Mark 5 we see such a demon-possession taking place. This man lived among the tombs, crying and cutting himself. He was living with no hope, and in despair. That, my friend, is how Satan treats his followers. Follow him, if you will, but he will leave you with a life that is hopeless and in despair.

This man was in bad shape, but then JESUS CAME! When Jesus shows up, the story takes a turn for the better. Oh, what a glad day when Jesus showed up in our life, too! Do you remember when He came into your life?

The Bible says that when Jesus came, the demons had to leave. It specifically says that *"the unclean spirits went out."* No soul is big enough to house both Satan and Jesus at the same time. Jesus will not be where Satan is allowed to rule, but Satan can no longer dwell where Christ is in charge.

Have you invited Jesus to be your Savior? Is He ruling and reigning in your life? If so, then Satan has no power over you. Dear friend, cheer up! Satan may be fighting you for all he's worth, but he has no right nor claim over the child of God!

My Name Is Legion

"For he [Jesus] said unto him, Come out of the man, thou unclean spirit. And he asked him, What is thy name? And he answered, saying, My name is Legion: for we are many." (Mark 5:8-9)

Continuing on with the thought from yesterday, we see this demon-possessed man whom Jesus encounters. This man was living among the tombs while crying and cutting himself. It is a stark reminder of the comparison of a person who is filled with the Spirit versus one who is filled by Satan. The fruit of the Spirit is love, joy, and peace, while the fruit of Satan is crying, cutting, and misery!

But notice something unusual about the interaction between this man and Jesus. As Jesus talks to this man, He asks him his name. The demon answers and says, *"My name is Legion: for we are many."* What a strange way to identify yourself. *"**MY** [singular] name is Legion: for **WE** [plural] are many."*

Some commentators say that a legion could represent several thousands of demons...and they were ALL in this one man! So, evidently the demon which spoke to Jesus was the spokesman for them all.

But what I love about this story is we see that even though Jesus was OUTNUMBERED, He was never OVERPOWERED! Jesus had authority and power over every single one of those thousands of demons. And when He commanded them to leave that man's body they had to obey!

Think about it...if Jesus is powerful enough to route a legion of demons, He can certainly route your legion of temptations and subdue your flesh if you will let Him! Thank the Lord that He is more powerful than anything Satan can throw your way, today!

The Swine Must Go!

"And they began to pray him to depart out of their coasts."
(Mark 5:17)

I would like to give you one last thought about this devil-possessed man that Jesus miraculously set free. Notice this man who before was found living among the tombs, was now found *"sitting, and clothed, and in his right mind."*

One would think this would have made everyone happy. I mean, come on...not only had this man's life been saved, but now his family could be restored again. Now, his wife would get her husband back, and his children would get their father back. It seemed like a win-win for everyone...but not so.

Verse 17 says the people began asking Jesus to leave! They were not happy with Jesus at all! Now, they were not angry that the man had been set free. They were angry because Jesus had sent the unclean spirits into a nearby herd of swine and the swine ran into the sea and drowned.

In other words, the people were more angry at losing their swine, than having their friend back. The truth about the matter was they preferred their SWINE to the SAVIOR. When they had to make a choice between their swine or Jesus...Jesus had to go!

Listen, friend, that is the choice we all must make. Will we keep our swine, or do we want Jesus...because we can't have both. When Jesus comes, the unclean things in our lives (the swine) must go!

The greatest hindrance to the spread of the Gospel isn't always Satan, it's us! We don't want to let go of the swine! We cannot have the swine AND Jesus. If we want God's presence in our lives, if we want God's blessings in our lives...the swine must go!

The Blessing Of A Broken Heart

"The LORD is nigh unto them that are of a broken heart; and saveth such as be of a contrite spirit." (Ps. 34:18)

Why is it necessary that we have a broken heart at times? Why doesn't God just keep away all hurt that would break our hearts? Well, I believe there are a couple of reasons God allows a broken heart:

FIRST—Because we fail to appreciate the GOOD if we have not experienced the bad. There are some people who do not appreciate their good health because they have never been real sick. Most of us do not appreciate our eyesight because we have never been without it. God allows us to have a broken heart every now and then so we can fully appreciate the blessings of God in our life.

SECOND—Because we fail to appreciate GOD unless we experience the bad. Be honest, when your car is running well, you never think about the mechanic, do you? But when your car breaks down, the most important person in your life is a mechanic. The same is true for a little child. They think that because they have learned to walk, they no longer need mommy. But as soon as they walk away on their own and they fall and hurt themselves, mommy is the person they run back to for comfort.

How many times have we stubbornly rebelled against God and went our own way, only to run back to Him as soon as we made a royal mess out of our life? God allows us to have a broken heart sometimes because it is the only time that He is really important to us.

God loves all of His children, but the Bible says there is something special to God about those who have a broken heart; those who are hurting and cry out to Him. I believe the reason God is drawn to the brokenhearted is because the brokenhearted are drawn to Him!

And The Brook Dried Up

"And it came to pass after a while, that the brook dried up, because there had been no rain in the land." (1 Kings 17:7)

God told Elijah to prophesy to king Ahab that there would be a famine in the land. After Elijah's prophecy, God led him to go stay by the brook Cherith. It was a place where God would refresh and sustain Elijah during the famine.

Everything was going as planned. Not only was Elijah being taken care of by the brook, but God even sent ravens to bring him bread and flesh to eat each day. Wow! That's what I call full service! But something unexpected happened...just when everything was going as planned, the brook dried up.

I can imagine Elijah saying to God, "Now, Lord, I'm not sure I understand. I obeyed your word and now the very brook you led me to has dried up! Now what am I going to do? Where do I go from here?"

Has that ever happened to you? Has it ever seemed that just when things were going right...you are praying and reading your Bible, you are attending church faithfully...then all of the sudden the bottom falls out? All of the sudden the very brook that was sustaining you has dried up.

Just like God knew where Elijah was, He also knew how long the brook would hold out. Elijah's circumstances did not catch God off guard, and YOUR circumstances haven't caught Him off guard either.

Tomorrow we will see what God did next to provide for Elijah just when he needed it. If your brook has dried up, just be patient and wait on God. He knows where you are and He will come through just when you need Him.

There's Still Oil

"Arise, get thee to Zarephath, which belongeth to Zidon, and dwell there: behold, I have commanded a widow woman there to sustain thee." (1Kings 17:9)

Yesterday, we saw that God had led Elijah to be sustained at the brook Cherith, only to have the brook dry up. It seemed like there was no hope. Ah, but with God there is ALWAYS hope!

What did God do? He sent Elijah to a widow living in Zaraphath. Even though there was a famine, and she only had enough oil to make her son and herself a small meal, she took care of God's man first. As a result, God miraculously kept her supplied with oil until the famine ended!

What is the lesson for us? Even though the brook dried up, there was still oil to supply the need.

See, everyone at one time or another will experience their brook drying up. What you must remember is that when your brook dries up, there is still some oil!

You may feel your resources have run out. You may feel there is no more water in your brook. Just remember, God is not limited to your brook! He NEVER runs out of resources. You just keep on trusting God and when Satan tells you that your brook is dry and there's no hope, just remind Him that God is a miracle-working God and as long as there is a God, there's still oil!

Clean Up Your Own Backyard
(Part 1)

"But the mountain shall be thine; for it is a wood, and thou shalt cut it down: and the outgoings of it shall be thine: for thou shalt drive out the Canaanites, though they have iron chariots, and though they be strong." (Joshua 17:18)

God had given the tribe of Manasseh a piece of land but there were two problems with it. Part of it was covered with trees and there were Canaanites (ungodly people) in the land that God said were to be driven out. Manasseh asked Joshua for MORE land so they wouldn't have to fight the enemy. But, instead of giving them more land, God's said to them, "Before you ask for more, take care of what you already have. Clean up your own backyard, first."

God said, "When you clear the forest, and drive out the giants and the Canaanites—then you'll have plenty of land." You say, "Does that apply to us today?" It sure does!

What would you do with more Bible knowledge when you don't use the Bible knowledge you have? What would you do with more money, when you don't manage wisely the money you already have? The reason some will never have any more money is because they have all that God can trust them with.

The lesson for us today is, if you want bigger and better opportunities, you better start clearing the forest where you are. Manasseh said, "God, give us more land." God said, "You cut down the trees and drive out the giants where you are and you will have all the land you need."

Are you maximizing the potential that God has given you? Are you living to capacity? If not, why not? Ask God to give you the wisdom to use what you already have to the fullest so that He can trust you with more.

Clean Up Your Own Backyard
(Part 2)

"But the mountain shall be thine; for it is a wood, and thou shalt cut it down: and the outgoings of it shall be thine..."
(Joshua 17:18)

The tribe of Manasseh came to Joshua asking for more land because part of the land God gave to them was covered in trees and the other part was inhabited by Canaanites. They couldn't get victory because of the trees and the Canaanites.

So, God answered their request by telling them to do two things which would give them all the land they would need. It is the same two things we are to do if we are going to have complete victory in our Christian life.

FIRST—They were to remove things that were CLUTTERING the land. God said to them, *"the mountain shall be thine; for it is a wood, and thou shalt cut it down:"* The first thing He told them to do was to clear the forest.

Trees are beautiful things; trees are harmless things; and, there is shade in the trees. But, if the trees are cluttering the land, then you have no right to say, "There's not enough room." There's plenty of room, if you cut down the trees. Joshua is saying to them, "Remove the things that are cluttering your life."

Have you done that? I'm not talking about just the sinful things. I'm talking about the trees; things that may not be sinful, but they just clutter your life.

Some say, "I just don't have enough time for church." You would if you would cut down some trees in your life. Ask God to identify the things that may be cluttering your life. It could be a friendship; it could be a love of more money. Whatever it is, ask God to identify it and then remove it so that you can live in victory.

Clean Up Your Own Backyard
(Part 3)

"..thou shalt drive out the Canaanites, though they have iron chariots, and though they be strong." (Joshua 17:18)

Today, we will see that second thing Joshua told Manasseh to do in order to get complete victory.

SECOND—they were to remove things that were CORRUPTING the land. These are the two types of things that keep us from being all we ought to be: the things that *clutter* our lives and the things that *corrupt* our lives.

The Canaanites were ungodly people and because Manasseh was allowing them to stay in the land, they were becoming a corrupting influence on them. That is why God told them to cut down the trees then drive out the Canaanites from the land.

You say, "But, hasn't God gotten it backwards? Shouldn't we drive out the Canaanites, and THEN clean up the woods?" That's not the way God told Joshua to do it. See, before you get ready to go to battle, you'd better clear off a spot to fight from! There might be some Canaanites in those trees!

Christians, today, are not living in complete victory and it is because of things they are allowing to either **clutter** their lives or things that are **corrupting** their lives. Which is it for you?

Ask God to help you identify things that may be cluttering your life; things that are taking up some much of your time you don't have time for God. Ask God to also help you identify anything which may be corrupting your life: a bad friendship, relationship, or sinful desire.

Cut down those trees and drive out those Canaanites, and then you will have the victory God wants for you!

104

Who Are You Walking With?

"He that walketh with wise men shall be wise: but a companion of fools shall be destroyed." (Prov. 13:20)

There is an old saying, "Birds of a feather flock together." Meaning that people tend to hang around with others just like themselves. But this verse isn't so much talking about what IS but what WILL BE. It gives us a glimpse into our future when we decide to walk, or hang around with, certain types of people.

FIRST—It talks about those who are WISE. *"He that walketh with wise men shall be wise..."* If you associate with wise men, you will become wiser, yourself. It is a scriptural principle: if you want to become a better Christian, choose better Christians than yourself to walk with. Find someone who is closer to God than you are and walk with them because *"He that walketh with wise men shall be wise..."*

SECOND—It talks about those who are FOOLISH. *"but a companion of fools shall be destroyed."* Make no mistake about it, we are influenced by those around us, and the Bible says that when you choose to be friends with a foolish person, it will end up destroying you. In other words, just as the positive character traits of a wise man will affect you positively, the negative character traits of a foolish friend will negatively affect you.

Take inventory, this morning, of the types of friends you are walking with. Are they wise or foolish? Does their friendship encourage you to get closer to God, or does it lead you further away from what you know is right?

If your friends are foolish friends, don't keep waking WITH them, you need to walk AWAY from them!

Sunday's Coming!

*"Now upon **the first day of the week**, very early in the morning, they came unto the sepulchre...And they found the stone rolled away from the sepulchre." (Luke 24:1-2)*

When the crucifixion took place, and Jesus hung on the cross, all hope seemed gone for the disciples of Jesus. All of their hopes and dreams for this new "Kingdom" Jesus had talked about and they had preached about suddenly vanished.

It was Saturday night. There was no church service in progress. There was no preaching, singing, or fellowship. There was no joy and no laughter. Why? Because their leader was dead. But in their discouragement and despair, the one thing they failed to realize was—Sunday's coming!

When Sunday came, hope came back! When Sunday came, a new joy and excitement replaced the doom and gloom! It was a new day; a glorious day. This was.... Resurrection Sunday!

Hey, friend...you might be going through the worst trial of your life. You might be facing the most difficult storm you have ever faced. Look up, child of God...SUNDAY'S COMING! Jesus is alive and God is still on His throne! One of these days He will return and, when He does, none of the things we are facing now will bother us one ounce!

This is not the time to hang our head in defeat. Oh, no, friend...Sunday's coming!

Remember How He Spake Unto You

"He is not here, but is risen: remember how he spake unto you when he was yet in Galilee," (Luke 24:6)

When Mary, and the other women, approached the tomb on that first Easter morning, they were in a dilemma. They were expecting to find the body of Jesus so they could anoint it with spices, but when they arrived, Jesus was nowhere to be found!

The problem was that they had forgotten what Jesus had told them earlier; that He must be crucified, buried, and rise again the third day. Therefore, the angels said unto the women, *"remember how he spake unto you."* God's Word had the answer to their dilemma, had they only "remembered" His words.

How many times do circumstances present a dilemma for us? We are at a loss for which direction to go. We are unsure about what decision to make. There's no need to worry and there's no need to be anxious because God's Word has the answers to life's dilemmas!

Sometimes all you need to do is *"remember how he spake unto you."* The more you get into God's Word, the more God's Word will get into you. And the more God's Word gets into you, the more God will speak to you. So when that trial comes, when that dilemma comes, often the answer is as simple as remembering what He has already spoken in His Word.

If you are struggling today, *"remember how he spake unto you."*

Now You See Him, Now You Don't!

"And their eyes were opened, and they knew him; and he vanished out of their sight." (Luke 24:31)

The Bible says that forty days between the resurrection of Jesus and His ascension He *"showed himself alive...by many infallible proofs"* to His disciples. What is interesting is that, instead of remaining visible to them, He communicated to them through sudden appearances followed by times of invisibility.

In our verse above, we see where Jesus "appeared" to two discouraged disciples on the road to Emmaus. He walked with them and then (v.31) says, *"their eyes were opened, and they knew him; and he **vanished** out of their sight."* Here are two truths from this text I hope will encourage you this morning.

TRUTH #1—God is not always VISIBLE, but He is always PRESENT! Jesus was present with these two disciples even though they didn't see Him. (v.17) says that when He appeared to them He said, *"What manner of communications are these that ye have one to another, as ye walk, and are sad?"* How did He know what they had been talking about and that they were sad? Because He was present even though He wasn't visible.

Listen, friend, sometimes you may not FEEL His presence, and you may not SEE Him, but rest assured God is with you!

TRUTH #2—He is God when you see Him, and He is God when you don't! At first, they did not recognize it was Jesus talking to them. Then (v.31) says, *"And their eyes were opened, and they knew him..."* There will be times in your life when it seems God is not present and you are all alone. But keep on believing; keep on trusting. He is God when you see Him, and He is God when you don't!

He Brought Us Out To Bring Us In

*"And **he brought us out** from thence, that he might **bring us in**, to give us the land which he sware unto our fathers."*
(Deut. 6:22-23)

For years, the Children of Israel had been enslaved by Pharaoh in the land of Egypt. But one day God sent Moses to deliver them out of bondage. The Bible says that God brought them OUT, that He might bring them IN. And God wants to do the same with us, too!

FIRST—God wants to bring you FROM something. In the Bible, Egypt is a type of the world. God never intended for His people to make Egypt their permanent dwelling place. He didn't want them serving Pharaoh; He wanted them to serve Him. Aren't you thankful for the day when God delivered you from your bondage to Satan?

SECOND—God wants to bring you TO something. God's plan for Israel was more than just getting them out of Egypt. He didn't want to deliver them from Pharaoh, only to have them homeless afterwards. No, the Bible says He brought them OUT of one place in order to bring them INTO another place. He brought them out of the land of **Pharaoh** in order to bring them into the land of **promise**. He wanted to bring them out of a land of **bondage** in order to bring them into a land of **blessing**!

Canaan (the Promised Land) represents the victorious Christian life. It is God's desire that we leave the world in order to live in victory. But there's a catch! Before we can enter into the land of blessing, we must be willing to leave the land of bondage. We must be willing to LET GO of something before we can TAKE HOLD of something better. If you are still holding on to the things of this world, let go! Let God bring you OUT, so that He can bring you INTO a life of victory, today!

Peace In Perilous Times (Part 1)

"This know also, that in the last days perilous times shall come...evil men and seducers shall wax worse and worse, deceiving, and being deceived." (2 Tim. 3:1, 13)

We are living in troubling times. The Bible says that in the last days *"perilous"* (or dangerous) times would come. We are living in those days right now! These are indeed troubling times that are only going to get worse. The good news is that the Bible tells us how to have peace no matter how difficult our circumstances may become.

FIRST—Peace comes from PRAYING right. (Phil. 4:6-7) says, *"Be careful for nothing; but in every thing by prayer and supplication with thanksgiving let your requests be made known unto God."*

- There must be a **Faithfulness** to pray — *"in every thing."*
- There must be a **Fervency** to pray — *"by prayer AND supplication..."*
- There must be **Faith** when we pray — *"with thanksgiving"* Faith thanks God before the answer comes!

THEN...after you have prayed right, the next verse says, *"the **peace** of God, which passeth all understanding, shall keep your hearts and minds through Christ Jesus."*

In other words, when our prayer life ceases, our peace ceases, too! If you want peace in your life, begin by getting alone with God in your prayer closet, because the first step to peace is spending time with the Prince of Peace!

Peace In Perilous Times (Part 2)

"This know also, that in the last days perilous times shall come...evil men and seducers shall wax worse and worse, deceiving, and being deceived." (2 Tim. 3:1, 13)

The Bible tells us how to have peace no matter how difficult our circumstances may become. Yesterday, we saw that, FIRST—Peace comes from PRAYING right. (Phil. 4:6-7)

SECOND—Peace comes from THINKING right. (Isaiah 26:3) says, *"Thou wilt keep him in perfect peace, whose mind is stayed on thee: because he trusteth in thee."* As one preacher put it, "Much of our lack of peace comes from stinkin' thinkin'." The Bible gives the formula for what we should be thinking about.

*"Finally, brethren, whatsoever things are true, whatsoever things are honest, whatsoever things are just, whatsoever things are pure, whatsoever things are lovely, whatsoever things are of good report; if there be any virtue, and if there be any praise, **think on these things**." (Phil. 4:8)*

If we were honest, we would realize that much of the time we allow our minds to dwell on things which take away our peace.

So basically, if you want to have peace in your life, start thinking about what you're thinking about! In other words, assess what thoughts you allow to occupy your mind. The Bible says that the person whose mind is stayed (or fixed) on God is the person who will have peace in their soul.

Tomorrow, we will look at the third and final way to have peace in perilous times.

Peace In Perilous Times (Part 3)

*"This know also, that in the last days perilous times shall
come...evil men and seducers shall wax worse and worse,
deceiving, and being deceived." (2 Tim. 3:1, 13)*

We are living in troubling times. The Bible says that in
the last days *"perilous"* (or dangerous) times would come.
The Bible tells us how to have peace no matter how
difficult our circumstances may become. So far we've seen
that:
Peace comes from PRAYING right. (Phil. 4:6-7)
Peace comes from THINKING right. (Phil. 4:8)
LASTLY—Peace comes from LIVING right. (Phil.
4:9) says, *"Those things, which ye have both learned, and
received, and heard, and seen in me, do: and the God of
peace shall be with you."* You can't live sinfully and
expect to have the peace of God in your life.

True peace and happiness does not come from living
after the things of this world; they come from walking with
Jesus and obeying His Word. In fact, Jesus told His
disciples this very thing when He said to them, *"If ye know
these things, happy are ye if ye **do** them" (John 13:17).*

A lot of people go to church and hear the Word of God
preached. In other words, they *"know these things,"* Jesus
said. But peace and happiness doesn't come from just
KNOWING what the Bible says. Peace and happiness
comes from DOING what the Bible says. Jesus said,
"happy are ye if ye DO them."

So, if you are lacking peace, this morning, start
praying right, thinking right, and living right....THEN you
can have peace in perilous times.

Living Pure In An Impure World

"For God hath not called us unto uncleanness, but unto holiness." (1Thess. 4:7)

There is no doubt about it, we live in an impure world! It's like we are living in the days of Noah all over again. The day we live in is wicked, yet Paul says, *"God hath not called us unto uncleanness, but unto holiness."* In other words, it IS possible to live a pure life in an impure world.

FIRST—The PURPOSE of Purity. *(v.3a)* *"For this is the will of God..."* God's will is no mystery. It is God's will that you live holy and avoid uncleanness. The word *"uncleanness"* means that which is impure or filthy. You may not feel called to preach, or feel called to be a missionary, but God HAS called you to live holy! God HAS called us to live a pure, holy life.

SECOND—The PROBLEM with Purity. Next, Paul says in *(v.5)* *"not in the lust of concupiscence..."* The word *"concupiscence"* means a desire for that which is unlawful and forbidden. Sadly, sexual immorality is running rampant, not just among unbelievers, but even among professing Christian teenagers! It would shock you to know how many teenagers in good, Bible-believing churches are sexually active. Everywhere they turn, there is a temptation for them to experience that which God has forbidden.

THIRD—The PLAN for Purity. *(v.3b)* *"even your sanctification..."* Sanctification means to be set apart. As believers, we are to be "set apart" from the world and one way we do this, Paul says, is to *"abstain from fornication."*

Parents, Satan is on the warpath and he's coming after our children! It is up to us to teach our children that it is possible to live a pure life in an impure world.

He's Still On The Throne

"In the year that king Uzziah died I saw also the Lord sitting upon a throne, high and lifted up, and his train filled the temple." (Isa. 6:1)

Isaiah saw the Lord in all His greatness and glory. He got a glimpse of God never before seen, but it's interesting that he says this happened *"In the year that king Uzziah died..."*

You have to understand that Uzziah was a great king who was blessed by God. The country was blessed financially and blessed with protection under Uzziah's reign. So, for the king to die, meant there was a lot of uncertainty and insecurity. Everywhere you looked, faces were sad.

Everyone else saw despair and discouragement but you know what Isaiah saw? Isaiah saw the LORD! In other words, Isaiah said, "When things started looking DOWN, I started looking UP!" In the middle of all the despair and discouraging circumstances, Isaiah lifted his eyes and looked past king Uzziah and saw King Jesus! When he did, he was reminded that there was still a king in charge. In verse 1, we see two kings mentioned:

And where exactly did Isaiah see King Jesus? He said, *"I saw also the Lord sitting upon a throne..."* When the bottom fell out of Isaiah's life, he set his eyes on Jesus. And when he did, he didn't see Jesus pacing the floor, wringing His hands worried about the future. Oh, no! He saw *"the Lord sitting upon a throne..."*

Listen, friend, no matter how bad the circumstances are around you, turn your eyes upon Jesus and when you do, you will see that the God of all glory who was on the throne in Isaiah's day is STILL ON THE THRONE in our day, too!!!

114

God's Child-Training Manual

"Then Manoah intreated the LORD, and said, O my Lord, let the man of God which thou didst send come again unto us, and teach us what we shall do unto the child that shall be born." (Judges 13:8)

When my children were born I remember thinking, "I wish children came with an instruction manual!" One of the most rewarding, yet most difficult, jobs in the world is raising children. If only there was a resource we could turn to that would give us the wisdom we need to raise our children right. Ah, but there is!

When God told Samson's parents (Manoah and his wife) that they would have a child, Manoah's response was, *"O my Lord, let the man of God...come...and teach us what we shall do unto the child that shall be born."* Manoah knew what a lot of parents need to realize and that is you need God's help and direction in order to raise your children right. What a great challenge to every parent!

There is no better place to learn how to raise children than in the *house* of God, hearing the *Word* of God from the *man* of God!

Mom and dad, can I challenge you to make sure you have your children in church every time the doors are open? Attending one service here and there will not be sufficient to overcome the constant temptation your child will face in the world on a daily basis. It is foolish to think you can adequately raise your children without God.

So, if you are not already faithfully attending church, get in a Bible-preaching church and take your children every service. Manoah knew that God's man was sent by God to instruct them on how to raise Samson. You have no greater friend than your pastor and no greater child-training manual than the Bible.

The Emptiness Of Sin (Part 1)

"And [Samson] came up, and told his father and his mother, and said, I have seen a woman in Timnath of the daughters of the Philistines...Get her for me; for she pleaseth me well." (Judges 14:2-3)

Most every Christian is familiar with the tragic story of Samson. Every time we read this story, we are reminded of the lure and consequences when one runs after sin. There are two things we learn about sin that I would like to bring to your attention.

FIRST—The POWERFUL PROMISE of Sin. Samson, had a great start in life. He grew up in a godly home, raised by godly parents. But at some point he began living after his flesh. He started going after what his eyes wanted. So, one day when Samson was around an ungodly crowd (the Philistines) he saw a woman that attracted him. He came back and said to his parents, *"Get her for me; for she pleaseth me well.*

Satan will bring your particular taste of temptation wrapped up in the most alluring package possible. Sin promises to bring you fulfillment in your lust. It tells the person who is addicted to porn that they will get the sexual satisfaction they desire. It tells the person addicted to gambling that they will get the big "Pay Day" of wealth they are greedily seeking. It tells the young teen that they will be part of the "in crowd" and finally have the acceptance they seek, if they will only partake of their sin.

Yes, sin promises an awful lot. It promises pleasure without consequences. *"Get her for me* (Samson said)*; for she pleaseth me well.* It's interesting that he could not say she pleased the Lord, only that she pleased his flesh.

Run after sin, if you like, but I promise you will not find the fulfillment it promises.

The Emptiness Of Sin (Part 2)

*"And [Samson] came up, and told his father and his
mother, and said, I have seen a woman in Timnath of the
daughters of the Philistines...Get her for me; for she
pleaseth me well." (Judges 14:2-3)*

Yesterday, we saw **The Powerful Promise of Sin**.
There is a second lesson we learn about sin from the life of
Samson.

SECOND—The AWFUL PROBLEM with Sin.
Only a couple of chapters after he told his parents that this
Philistine woman pleased him well, the Bible says in
chapter 16:1, *"Then went Samson to Gaza, and saw there
an harlot, and went in unto her."* WHAT??? But I thought
you said the first woman pleased you, Samson?

Samson was learning the awful problem with sin...sin
will constantly make promises it cannot keep. It promises
to bring a fulfillment in sin that can only be found in Christ.
The Bible says that there is pleasure in sin, but only for a
season.

I promise you, that the sin you are chasing after today
will leave you empty and lacking pleasure tomorrow. Satan
will show you the pleasure without showing you the
consequences. But here's the really painful part...the
consequences of your sin will last far longer than any
pleasure you got from your sin.

Has Satan began to lure you with some temptation?
Has he already promised you gratification from some sin?
Turn from it, now! Run away as fast as you can! It's not
worth it. It will promise fulfillment, but only leave you
empty.

Are You An Overcomer?

"In the world ye shall have tribulation: but be of good cheer; I have overcome the world." (John 16:33)

When Jesus made the statement that He had overcome the world, at first everyone must have thought He was crazy. I mean, we could imagine someone like Caesar making such a boast, but Jesus? In fact when He made this statement He was about to be betrayed by Judas then carried away to be tried, convicted, and crucified. Doesn't sound much like a person who has *"overcome"* the world.

But Jesus was not saying He had conquered the world like Napoleon had hoped to do. No, the *"world"* He was speaking of is the world system that is presently under the control of Satan whom the Bible calls *"the prince of this world" (John 12:31)*.

The *"world"* is the possessions, powers, and pleasures the earthly life offers. It is organized under the influence of Satan so as to leave God out, and keep man blinded to Christ. Basically, the *"world"* is anything that shuts God out. Because of this, John said we are not to have a love for this world.

It is this *"world"* through which Satan seduces souls away from God. It is just as alluringly attractive as it is deceptively destructive. And because of its allure, millions are overcome by it. But there was One who, though He was tempted by it, overcame it through absolute power and victory! It is He who said, *"I have overcome the world."*

And the wonderful thing is that since we have His Spirit living in us, we can overcome the world, as well, because *"greater is he that is in you, than he that is in the world" (I John 4:4)*.

So, my question for you today is are YOU an overcomer?

It's Coming After You!

"Evil pursueth sinners: but to the righteous good shall be repayed." (Prov. 13:21)

This verse teaches us a biblical principle that is true for everyone, no matter who you are. That principle is you will reap what you sow!

First, it says, ***"Evil pursueth sinners."*** People who live wicked lifestyles cannot escape problems. In other words, because of the company they keep and the places they frequent, they always seem to find themselves caught up in trouble. Trouble follows them. Why? Because *"Evil pursueth sinners."*

Next, it says, ***"but to the righteous good shall be repayed."*** The law of sowing and reaping continually takes effect in people's lives. Sinful people sow to their flesh, therefore they reap corruption. On the other hand, the Bible says that when righteous people sow godliness, they are rewarded by the good that God brings about in their lives. What an incentive to do good and live right!

How you live does have an impact on which you receive in life, evil or good. Why? Because if you choose wickedness, that is what will follow you. But if you choose godliness, that is what will follow you in your life. When you think about it...the choice is pretty clear.

Thank God!

"I thank my God upon every remembrance of you,"
(Phil. 1:3)

When writing to the believers at Philippi, Paul showed how much they meant to him. He said to them that every time they came to his mind, he thanked God for them. What a testimony! They must have really been a blessing in Paul's life for him to say that.

FIRST—Be thankful for those God has put in your life. Paul said, *"I thank my God..."* He didn't take for granted. He realized that God put them in his life for a reason and was thankful for their friendship and fellowship.

SECOND—Realize everyone contributes something to your life. In (v.4) Paul said, *"Always in every prayer of mine for you **all**..."* He was thankful for everyone. He knew that, while he may not be best friends with everyone, God can use everyone to contribute something to our lives...even those who sometimes rub us the wrong way.

THIRD—Be a person others are thankful for. There was something about these believers that blessed Paul and caused him to think of them in a positive light. One thing that Paul appreciated was their faithfulness to him. In (v.5) He said, *"I thank my God...For your fellowship in the gospel from the first day until now;"* Faithful friends are few and far between, so be the kind of friend others will thank God for.

Take a moment, this morning, to thank God for your Christian friends whom God has placed in your life. Thank God for your pastor, your Sunday School teacher, those who encourage you and pray for you. Thank God for them, then ask God to help you be such a friend to others that they will be thankful for you, too!

What Are You Looking At?

"But he, being full of the Holy Ghost, looked up stedfastly into heaven, and saw the glory of God, and Jesus standing on the right hand of God," (Acts 7:55)

After preaching a convicting message, Stephen was attacked physically. Not only did they gnash on him with their teeth, they also began to stone him! I have preached to some tough crowds before, but thankfully that has never happened to me.

Stephen was facing the most intense trial he had faced in his life; so intense that it was literally about to take his life! But what is interesting is how he reacted in this trial. What was it that gave him victory in the midst of his valley?

FIRST—He was FULL of the right thing. The Bible says that before his trial ever started, he was already *"full of the Holy Ghost."* When you are in the middle of your trial is not the time to try and get right with God. You better be walking with God BEFORE your trial if you are going to have the victory.

SECOND—He was FOCUSED on the right thing. Next, it says he *"looked up stedfastly into heaven, and saw the glory of God."* When his circumstances started looking **gloomy**, he got his eyes on God's **glory**! The reason many do not have victory in their trial is because they are more focused on their trial than they are on Jesus.

Stephen *"looked up steadfastly,"* meaning his eyes were fixed, focused, and fixated on Jesus Christ. And when he saw Jesus in His trial, it reminded Him that God was still in control!

Are you facing a trial this morning? If so, what are you looking at? Look up and get a glimpse of Jesus in your trial and then you will realize He is still in control!s

121

When God Forbids You

"..they..were forbidden of the Holy Ghost to preach the word in Asia," (Acts16:6)

Paul and Silas were sent out on a missionary journey in order to preach the gospel. Yet, the Bible says that they were *"forbidden of the Holy Ghost to preach the word in Asia."* The purpose of this devotion is not to discuss WHY the Holy Ghost forbad them; it is simply to remind you that there are times when God forbids us from doing something we are planning to do.

This week, my wife and I have been in Kentucky on a Missions Trip with the teens from our church. It wasn't until the last minute that we realized we would have to go on this trip. To be honest, we had many other things we were planning to accomplish this week back at home. I had three sermons to study for, a Sunday School lesson to prepare, five devotionals to write, a Wednesday night message to preach, and possibly two funerals to take part in. It was shaping up to be a busy week and I needed every minute.

But, as this verse reminds us, God often has OTHER plans! Just as the plans Paul and Silas had were changed by God, I believe my plans were changed this week by God, as well. Not only have I been blessed by this trip, but I know of at least three "Divine Appointments" I believe God had for me!

This week has reminded me once again that when circumstances beyond our control change, then we must trust that God (in His Sovereignty) has a better plan for us than the one we had for ourselves.

So, when God forbids you from accomplishing that nice little plan you have laid out for your life, just remember, He always knows best!

True Praise

"Rejoice in the LORD, O ye righteous: for praise is comely for the upright." (Ps. 33:1)

If anyone deserves our praise, it is the Lord. Notice three things the psalmist tells us about true praise.

FIRST—True praise is PURPOSEFUL. The Psalmist says, *"Rejoice in the LORD..."* There isn't much in this ole' world to praise God for. There is so much sin and wickedness on every hand. Yet the Psalmist says there is ONE thing we can rejoice in; we can *"Rejoice in the LORD."* Our circumstances may change, but our God will NEVER change! What a reason to rejoice!

SECOND—True praise is PERSONAL. *"O ye righteous..."* Next, we see this verse is written to saints, not sinners. It is written to the *"righteous."* Only those who have been saved truly have a reason to rejoice. Sinners cannot rejoice in the Lord because they are still an enemy of His. This verse is also not written to a group but to individual believers. A heart of praise toward the Lord is something EVERY believer should have for the work of grace He has done in our own hearts.

THIRD—True praise is BEAUTIFUL. *"for praise is comely for the upright."* The word *"comely"* means beautiful or attractive. Your attitude and your spirit will either **draw people to Jesus** or **drive people from Jesus**. The more we live with a spirit of praise, the more attractive and beautiful our lives become to those who are lost.

Take a moment and think of all God has done in your life. You just might see you have more to praise the Lord for than you realized!

A Genie In A Bottle

"When the Philistines took the ark of God, they brought it into the house of Dagon, and set it by Dagon." (1 Sam. 5:2)

When I was a kid, there was a TV show called "I Dream of Jeannie." It was about a genie who lived in a bottle. And when that bottle was rubbed she would magically appear out of the bottle ready to grant her master's wishes.

In the Old Testament, the Philistines viewed the Ark of the Covenant as sort of a Genie in a bottle. They had heard of the miraculous things that God had done for Israel because they had possession of the Ark, so they thought that if they possessed the Ark, God would have to do for them what He did for Israel. They mistakenly thought they could manipulate the power and presence of God. Sadly, many have that mistaken notion today, as well.

Many CHRISTIANS believe they can manipulate God. They see God as a Genie in a bottle, thinking that no matter how worldly they live God is supposed to suddenly forget about all their wickedness and bail them out every time they get into trouble. The moment trouble hits their lives they think they can just rub the bottle and God appear at their command.

Many CHURCHES believe they can manipulate God. There are pastors and churches that are also guilty of thinking that because we do things better than someone else, God will automatically bless us more than them. We mistakenly assume that no matter how much like the world our church services are, God will simply overlook that and bless us anyway. Just ask David what happened when he tried carrying the Ark like the Philistines did. A man named Uzzah ended up dead! God doesn't bless things done OUR way; He blesses it when things are done HIS way!

God In Your Living Room

"And the ark of the LORD continued in the house of Obededom the Gittite three months: and the LORD blessed Obededom, and all his household." (2 Sam. 6:11)

King David needed a place to temporarily put the Ark of the Covenant, so they asked a man named Obededom if he would allow them to store it in his house until they could figure out how to move it back to Jerusalem. The Ark of the Covenant represented the presence of God. For three months, Obededom and his family enjoyed the presence of God in their home. Notice some things we learn about having the presence of God in our home.

FIRST—God's presence must be invited in. David didn't force himself into Obededom's home. The only reason the Ark was stored there was because Obededom willingly invited them to put it there. He welcomed the presence of God into his home.

The reason why the presence of God is not felt in many homes...it's not wanted! When sin is permitted to stay in the home, the presence of God cannot remain there.

SECOND—Anyone can have God's presence in their home. Obededom wasn't even an Israelite; he was a Gittite! That goes to show us that anyone who is willing to have the presence of God in their lives can have it.

THIRD—God's presence will bring God's blessings. The last part of the verse says, *"and the LORD blessed Obededom, and all his household."* If you want your home to be blessed; if you want your marriage to be blessed; if you want your children to be blessed, then invite the presence of God to rule in your home. God's presence not only blessed Obededom, but *"all his household."*

If God's presence is not in your home, invite Him in, today!

Getting An Attitude Adjustment

"He that is slow to wrath is of great understanding: but he that is hasty of spirit exalteth folly." (Prov. 14:29)

Many times a person may need a neck adjustment or a back adjustment. But what some people need is an attitude adjustment! The Bible has a lot to say about our temper and how to control it before it controls us.

FIRST—The DESCRIPTION of our temper. Anger is also called "wrath" in the Bible. (James 1:20) says, *"For the wrath of man worketh not the righteousness of God."* Uncontrolled anger is never good; it never helps a situation when a person loses their temper and lashes out in anger. In fact, the opposite is usually true. When a person gets angry, it only causes the tension in the other person to rise as well.

SECOND—The DECISION of our temper. Often, anger comes from pride in our heart. (Prov. 13:10) says, *"Only by pride cometh contention."* You can be sure that when a person stirs up contention, it is coming from a prideful heart. Our temper can get stirred up by anything: the kids, our boss, our neighbors, or uncontrollable circumstances. But ultimately WE make the decision whether or not to be angry.

THIRD—The DEATH of our temper. (Ps. 37:8) says, *"Cease from anger, and forsake wrath: fret not thyself in any wise to do evil."* One way to control our temper is by seeing things from God's perspective. When we see things from God's viewpoint, we realize that He is in control so when things don't go according to OUR plans, they are still going according to HIS plan. That is why our text verse says we need understanding.

Take time to repent of any anger or bitterness that may be in your heart. Your day will go so much better after you've had a good attitude adjustment.

You're Filthy!

"Woe to her that is filthy and polluted, to the oppressing city!" (Zep 3:1)

As a little boy, I was always playing outside. Little boys don't think about how dirty they get when they are playing because the life mission of every little boy is to get dirty and have fun. In fact, to a little boy, you're not having fun UNLESS you're getting dirty!

In our text, God is telling Jerusalem that they are filthy and needed to be cleansed. Many Christians are like Jerusalem, today. They are supposed to be the people of God, but have become filthy! One of the ways in which Jerusalem had become filthy was in their worship.

It was PAGAN worship. *(1:4) "..I will cut off the remnant of Baal from this place..."* Baal was a pagan god. It was the 450 prophets of Baal Elijah encountered. It was what everyone around them was worshipping. They gave into peer pressure! Christians, today, are worshipping the gods of this world because they don't want to be different.

It was PLANET worship. *(1:5a) "And them that worship the host of heaven upon the housetops..."* Astrology is a big thing. Some people have to check their horoscopes every day. If you live more by what your horoscope says than by what your heavenly Father says, you've become filthy in your worship!

It was a PLURALISTIC worship. *(1:5b) "..and them that worship and that swear by the LORD, and that swear by Malcham;"* They were not only swearing by the Lord, but ALSO swearing by a false god as well! Some think they can mix true and false and have a good product but it never works that way.

Get rid of any idols in your life and get back to serving God, and God alone.

Bible Bird Watchers

"Behold the fowls of the air: for they sow not, neither do they reap, nor gather into barns; yet your heavenly Father feedeth them." (Matt. 6:26)

Since God is the Creator of nature, it should be no surprise when He teaches us lessons from nature. For example, God tells us to *"Behold the fowls."* By looking at how God takes care of the birds, we learn how much He cares for us.

FIRST—We see God's divine WORK. Although the birds are not among the biggest of God's creation, He still lovingly provides for them. It says, *"the fowls..sow not, neither do they reap, nor gather into barns; yet your heavenly Father feedeth them."* And although you may not see how, God is able to provide for you, as well.

SECOND—We see God's divine WILL. It is not only God's will, but also His pleasure to take care of both His creation and His children. He delights in doing this because it brings glory to Himself. In fact, He allows us to suffer need at times so that when we pray, He meets our need and then gets the glory for it.

THIRD—We see God's divine WARRANTY. (v.30) says, *"Wherefore, if God so clothe the grass of the field...shall he not much more clothe you..."* What is a warranty? It is a guarantee. We get this with new vehicles and major purchases such as refrigerators, etc. The problem with warranties from man is that they are limited. But God's promises are better because they NEVER expire!

So, become a Bible bird watcher. Realize that the same God who takes care of them, will also take care of you, too!

128

The Value Of An Excellent Spirit

"Then this Daniel was preferred above the presidents and princes, because an excellent spirit was in him..."
(Dan. 6:3)

Daniel stood out from everyone else around him because the Bible says *"an excellent spirit was in him."* There is nothing more valuable than having a good spirit. Because of Daniels spirit...

FIRST—He was PREFERRED. It says, *"Then this Daniel was preferred above the presidents and princes,"* The worlds says, "Climb the corporate ladder anyway you can. Step on as many people as necessary in order to make it to the top." But God has a better way...maintain an excellent spirit. Because he had the right attitude, it endeared him to the king and gave him more favor than those over him.

SECOND—He Was PROMOTED. The last part of (v.3) says, *"the king thought to set him over the whole realm."* Then, (v.28) says, *"So this Daniel **prospered** in the reign of Darius, and in the reign of Cyrus the Persian."* Daniel prospered and was promoted, all because of a good spirit.

THIRD—He Was PROTECTED. Daniel's excellent spirit came from his walk with God and everyone knew it. Even his enemies said in (v.5) *"We shall not find any occasion against this Daniel, except we find it against him concerning the law of his God."* There was no guilt nor guile in the heart of Daniel. Therefore, it protected him from allowing anger and bitterness to grow in his heart.

Determine today to just keep doing right even when you have been done wrong. Don't let your enemies steal your excellent spirit, because in the end you will see there is nothing more valuable.

My Hiding Place

"Thou art my hiding place; thou shalt preserve me from trouble;" (Ps. 32:7)

If anyone knew a thing or two about *forgiveness* it was David because if anyone knew a thing or two about *sinning*, it was also David. You see, David was not only one of the greatest *saints* in the Bible, he was also one of the greatest *sinners* in the Bible, too!

When you think about the fact that among David's many sins, two of them were adultery and murder, it's almost hard to believe this is the same man about whom God said that he was a man after His own heart!

David didn't write about the blessing of being forgiven because he was perfect, but because he knew what it was like to rebel against God and to feel the sting of conviction in his spirit day and night. David also knew what it was like to finally confess his sin to God and feel the sweet relief that only God's forgiveness can bring. That is why he started off the chapter with (v.1) *"Blessed is he whose transgression is forgiven, whose sin is covered."*

After his confession and forgiveness, he says, *"Thou art my hiding place; thou shalt preserve me from trouble;"* A hiding place is for the protection of a person. In other words, confession and forgiveness preserves one from trouble that unconfessed sin would bring.

Examine yourself this morning. Have you lost fellowship with God? Is there any unconfessed sin that could be bringing trouble into your life? If so, confess your sin. Run to God, Who is our hiding place and rest in the peace that only God's forgiveness can bring.

The Word Of The Lord

*"For the word of the LORD is right; and all his works are
done in truth." (Ps. 33:4)*

There is nothing else we have in this world like the
Word of God!

FIRST—God's Word is EDUCATIONAL. *"the
word of the LORD is right."* God's Word is never wrong; it
is always right! No other book can claim that attribute like
the Word of God. The Bible gave details about things, such
as the shape of the earth and things about the way
the human body works, long before scientists and doctors
figured it out. The Bible was used in almost every early
American classroom. Why? Because it is educational.

SECOND—God's Word is EXCEPTIONAL. (v.6)
says, *"By the word of the LORD were the heavens made;
and all the host of them by the breath of his mouth."* No
other book can claim that kind of power! God's Word is
exceptional in that it is alive and is the record of life-giving
words.

THIRD—God's Word is ETERNAL. (v.11) says,
*"The counsel of the LORD standeth for ever, the thoughts
of his heart to all generations."* Good books come and
good books go, but the Bible is unique because it *"standeth
for ever."* That means that what was good for your great,
great, great grandparents is still good for you, today! God's
Word is truth and truth never changes. It was here long
before we were born and will be around long after we are
gone. Matt. 24:35 says, *"Heaven and earth shall pass
away, but my words shall not pass away."*

Take some time this morning to thank God for the
Word of God we have. It is educational, exceptional, and
most of all eternal!

Keeping Company With The Canaanites (Part 1)

"Yet it came to pass, when the children of Israel were waxen strong, that they put the Canaanites to tribute; but did not utterly drive them out." (Josh. 17:13)

God had given the Children of Israel a Promised Land. It was theirs for the taking, but they failed to completely possess the land like God told them to. What happened? They were keeping company with the Canaanites when God said they were to drive them out of the land.

Notice the word *"Yet."* They knew what God had said, *"Yet"* they disobeyed anyway. "So, what's the big deal," you ask? Well, the Canaanites were demon-worshipers and God said they were to be utterly driven out. The Canaanites represent the power of Satan that can keep us from living in complete victory. Do you know what God's plan for Manasseh was? It was complete victory. Do you know what God wants you to have? Complete victory.

"But thanks be to God, which giveth us the victory through our Lord Jesus Christ." (1 Cor. 15:57)

The trouble was, instead of driving them out, they made friends with them! You're always going to be in trouble if you keep company with Canaanites!

Tomorrow, I will give you two specific reasons they had problems with the Canaanites.

132

Keeping Company With The Canaanites (Part 2)

"..they put the Canaanites to tribute; but did not utterly drive them out." (Josh. 17:13)

Here's why they had a problem with their possession:

FIRST—They FAVORED some Canaanites. (v.13) says, *"they put the Canaanites to tribute..."* The word *"tribute"* refers to slave labor. The Israelites said, "Rather than driving them out, we'll make slaves out of them. We'll be better off with them in the land." So, those were the Canaanites they favored.

Do you have a Canaanite that you are showing favor to? Is there some sin or habit in your life that you think you're better off keeping around? Maybe there are some Canaanite friends that God has told you to get rid of, yet you are still hanging around them.

SECOND—They FEARED some Canaanites. In (v.16) they say, *"all the Canaanites that dwell in the land of the valley have chariots of iron..."* There were some Canaanites they didn't think they could drive out of the land because they had *"chariots of iron."*

The Israelites had a problem with their possession because some Canaanites they *favored*, and some Canaanites they *feared*. Some sins they felt they could handle, and other sins they thought that they could not overcome at all.

Is that the way you are? Are there certain things in your life that you say, "I can handle that," and so you don't get rid of them. But there are other things in your life that you say, "I can't handle that," and so you don't get rid of that either? Don't keep company with the Canaanites. Drive them out, today, and walk in victory!

A Sword By Your Side

"For the builders, every one had his sword girded by his side, and so builded." (Neh. 4:18)

It is interesting to note that as Nehemiah and the people were rebuilding the wall of Jerusalem, they kept a sword with them. In the Bible, a sword is a picture of the Word of God (Eph. 6:17). Notice some thoughts about a sword.

FIRST—The PLACE of the Sword. It says that every builder had his sword *"by his side."* If the Bible is the *"sword of the Spirit"* as Paul described it, then we need it readily available! The closest place to keep the Word of God is in your heart. David said, *"Thy word have I hid in mine heart, that I might not sin against thee"* (Ps. 119:11).

SECOND—The POWER in the Sword. The sword of the Spirit is very different than the sword on the battlefield. The sword on the battlefield is there to *take* a life. The sword of the Spirit *gives* life! But just as Nehemiah, and his builders, kept a sword nearby for protection against attacks from the enemy, God has given us His Word to defend ourselves from the attacks of Satan.

THIRD—The PRACTICE of the Sword. There is no use in having a weapon that you do not know how to use. In order for their sword to protect them, these builders had to be skilled in using their sword. The best way to be skilled with the Bible is to use it every day! Read, it; study it, memorize it. Then you will be ready when Satan attacks.

God has given us the perfect weapon against Satan…THE BIBLE! Don't neglect it. Hide it in your heart so that when Satan comes around you will have your sword by your side.

The High Cost Of True Love

"And the king David said unto Araunah, Nay; but I will surely buy it of thee at a price: neither will I offer burnt offerings unto the LORD my God of that which doth cost me nothing." (2 Sam. 24:24)

David had been offered a cheap and easy way to show his love and devotion to God, but he knew that the value of true love is shown by the price you are willing to pay for it.

1. The CLAIM That Love MAKES. David speaks about *"the LORD my God..."* There is something possessive and personal about love. David isn't just speaking about "a" God; he says this is *"my"* God.

2. The CONSTRAINT That Love KNOWS. A mother's love for her child will cause her to give of herself for that child without a moment's hesitation. That mother's life is given to meeting the needs of that young child all because of her love. Likewise, David is not thinking about what he can GET from God, but what he can GIVE to God because he loves Him.

3. The COST That Love DEMANDS. It was the cheapness of the offer that repulsed David. True love is not only willing to pay a price, but love insists that there should be a price to pay! David said, *"I will surely buy it of thee at a price."* A heart of true love and devotion to God will cost you something. And, when you truly love someone, you don't mind the cost!

4. The CHOICE That Love EXERCISES. It was David who spoke up, first. He could have had it easy and worshipped God at no cost to him, but it was his CHOICE not to do so. He knew that cheap worship isn't true worship. David had a choice to make, and so do you and I. Will we settle for a cheap, easy, type of worship, or say (like David), *"I will surely buy it of thee at a price..."*

First Things, First

It was the top of the ninth inning with two outs. The score was tied and the team's power hitter was at the plate. The ball was thrown, the batter swung and hit the ball deep into center field. The batter rounded the bases and crossed home plate for what seemed like a home run to win the ball game. But all the excitement turned to dismay when the umpire called him out for missing first base!

Sometimes, in all the excitement, we get ahead of ourselves and forget to put first things, first. Jesus, therefore, reminds us of what is to be our first priority in life when He said...

*"But seek ye **first** the kingdom of God, and his righteousness; and all these things shall be added unto you." (Matt. 6:33)*

FIRST—Notice the PRESENCE of the King. We are exhorted to seek a kingdom but you cannot have a kingdom without a king. The King of this kingdom is Jesus Christ and to seek His kingdom means two things: 1) It means that we accept Him as OUR King. 2) It means I am to submit to His authority as my King.

SECOND—Notice the PRIORITY of the King. There will be constant rivals in our lives trying to lure us away from Christ and His authority. Therefore, we must determine that nothing else will take *"first"* place because that is reserved for Jesus.

THIRD—Notice the PROMISE of the King. If we will seek God's kingdom first, God gives us a wonderful promise *"and all these things shall be added unto you."*

Is Jesus the King of your life? If not, seek Him, today. Trust Him, not only as your King, but as your Lord and Savior!

The Courage Of Conviction

"But Daniel purposed in his heart that he would not defile himself with the portion of the king's meat, nor with the wine which he drank:" (Dan. 1:8)

If you live for God, at some point, you will have to make a choice to go along with the world, or stand up for Christ. The key to taking a stand is having a conviction which means to be so thoroughly convinced something is true that you are willing to take a stand for it regardless of the consequences. Notice some things about Daniel's conviction:

FIRST—The SOURCE of His Conviction. Daniel's convictions came from the Word of God. The reason he refused to eat the king's meat and drink the king's wine was because it would have caused him to violate the Old Testament dietary laws. His love for God's Word gave him the conviction he needed to take a stand when necessary.

SECOND—The SPIRIT of His Conviction. Next, it says Daniel *"requested of the prince of the eunuchs that he might not defile himself."* He didn't blow up with a sanctimonious, super-spiritual attitude. He simply *"requested"* to *"not defile himself."* Sometimes our attitude can be the very thing that helps or hurts our stand for Christ.

THIRD—The SIGNIFICANCE of His Conviction. God blessed the stand Daniel took. (v.15) *"And at the end of ten days their countenances appeared fairer and fatter in flesh than all the children which did eat the portion of the king's meat."* Because Daniel took a stand for God, God took a stand for Daniel and everyone saw the results!

Ask the Lord, today, to help you develop some convictions in your life, and then give you the courage to take a stand.

Are You Going For The Jugular?

Matthew 18 tells of a servant who owed a great debt and was forgiven by his master, but then went right out and found a man who was indebted to him and (v.28-29) says:

"But the same servant went out, and found one of his fellowservants, which owed him an hundred pence: and he laid hands on him, and took him by the throat, saying, Pay me that thou owest. And his fellowservant fell down at his feet, and besought him, saying, Have patience with me, and I will pay thee all."
(Matt. 18:28-29)

Are we sometimes guilty of not showing mercy to others in areas in which God has shown mercy to us? Do we hold others to a standard that even God does not impose on them? Even this hard-hearted servant's master did not take him *"by the throat"* as he did to the man who was indebted to him.

I believe we should have some biblically guided standards that we live by. But if we are not careful, we can end up holding others to a higher standard than God, Himself, holds them to. Sometimes in our passion for serving God (which is a good thing), we put expectations on others who have not grown spiritually in the areas in which we have grown and then take them *"by the throat"* instead of having patience with them and lovingly teach them as they grow.

This man went for the jugular! Remember, the jugular veins are what bring blood from the head back to the heart. In his rage, this wicked servant was cutting off this man's blood supply to his heart! If we show no love or mercy to those who are weaker than we are spiritually, what will it do to their heart?

He Worketh The Work Of The Lord

"Now if Timotheus come, see that he may be with you without fear: for he worketh the work of the Lord, as I also do." (1 Cor. 16:10)

Paul said they were to RECEIVE Timothy and RESPECT Timothy as a man of God because *"he worketh the work of the Lord."* Your pastor might not be the most talented or gifted but he should be loved and respected because *"he worketh the work of the Lord."*

Timothy was young. He was certainly no Apostle Paul but that was not what was important. He was doing the same work as Paul and therefore he deserved the same respect. Paul said 'Timothy is doing the same work *"as I also do."'* In other words, "The way you treat him (Timothy) is the way you are treating me."

Be careful how you treat your pastor. If God has called a man and sent a man, then the way you treat HIM is the way you are treating GOD. Pray for your pastor. Love your pastor. Encourage your pastor. Your pastor has a huge target on his back. Satan is after him and would like to destroy his testimony and his effectiveness for Christ all because *"he worketh the work of the Lord."*

Practical Ways to Pray for Your Pastor:
- *Pray for God to protect his testimony.*
- *Pray for God to protect his marriage.*
- *Pray for God to protect his family.*
- *Pray for God to give him a fresh Word from God every time he preaches.*
- *Pray for God to give him a fresh anointing every time he preaches.*
- *Pray for God to give him wisdom and discernment as he leads the church.*

A Simple Way To Disprove Evolution

"So God created man in his own image, in the image of God created he him; male and female created he them."
(Gen. 1:27)

To disprove the Theory of Evolution, you do not need to know physics or be a scientist educated in Paleontology. All you really need to do is look at the blood in your own body. Did you realize that the way God designed your blood disproves evolution?

"Platelets" play an important role in preventing the loss of blood by beginning a chain reaction that results in blood clotting. As blood begins to flow from a cut, platelets respond to help the blood clot and to stop the bleeding after a short time.

Platelets promote the clotting process by clumping together and forming a plug at the site of a wound and then releasing proteins called "clotting factors." These proteins start a series of chemical reactions that are extremely complicated. Every step of the clotting must go smoothly if a clot is to form. READ THE LAST SENTENCE AGAIN!

If just ONE of the clotting factors is missing or defective, the clotting process does not work.

"So, what does this have to do with Evolution," you ask? Simply this: to form a blood clot there must be 12 specific individual chemical reactions in our blood. If evolution is true, and if this 12-step process didn't happen in the first generation NO creatures would have survived. They all would have bled to death! So that teaches us that man did not evolve over billions of years. Everything came about at the same time because it was created by God!

B.A.I.K.

"For where envying and strife is, there is confusion and every evil work." (James 3:16)

A boy showed up at school with the letters B.A.I.K. on his shirt. A friend asked him what the letters stood for and he said, "It stands for Boy, Am I Konfused." His friend said, "But you don't spell 'confused' with a K." The boy replied, "Well, evidently you don't know how confused I am!"

James said, *"where envying and strife is, there is confusion..."* James says there are two specific things to look out for when life seems to be confusing.

FIRST—Confusion comes from ENVY. When you become envious or jealous of another person, you have become more focused on what you *don't* have than on what God *has* given you. Envy and jealousy will bring confusion and instability into your life because it takes your focus off of God and puts it on someone else.

SECOND—Confusion comes from STRIFE. The word *"strife"* refers to a contentious spirit. When someone has a contentious spirit, it is evidence of pride in their heart because (Prov. 13:10) says, *"Only by pride cometh contention..."* Pride comes when we think only of ourselves.

God never intended for us to live a life of confusion. In fact, (1Cor. 14:33) says, *"For God is not the author of confusion, but of peace..."* If you allow envy and strife into your life it will mess you up; it will mess with your mind. You'll end up more confused than a Chameleon in a bag full of Skittles! So, keep your heart and mind right, and you'll be surprised how much stability you will have in the decisions you make.

Lesson Learned

"It is good for me that I have been afflicted; that I might learn thy statutes." (Ps. 119:71)

When I first started school as a child, I couldn't wait; it was going to be so much fun. And it was, until one day something very strange happened. The teacher said, "Today, we are going to have a test over all the material you have been taught. Wait...what? A test? You mean I was supposed to be remembering everything you've been teaching me? I think I am ready to go home now!

But, as I soon found out, tests were a normal part of school life. You can only go so long in school without having to take a test. And something else I found out was the higher up in school you get the tougher the tests are! It is one thing to have a test on your colors or on your ABC's, but when you throw Algebra, Trigonometry and Calculus into the mix...that launches you into a whole new universe!

As long as there are lessons to be learned, there will be tests. And tests are not just for school, they are also for life...especially the Christian life. Even the psalmist said he was thankful for the afflictions he had gone through because they taught him something. His afflictions had taught him to learn God's statutes.

Lessons and tests are no fun, but they do accomplish something. Just like troubles and trials in our lives, they teach us to depend more on God than on ourselves. We learn more about God through a storm than we sometimes do in a Sunday School Class.

So, if you are going through a trial, ask God to teach you the lesson He wants you to learn, so that you can pass the test with flying colors!

When You're Needing God's Leading

"I being in the way, the LORD led me..." (Gen. 24:27)

Abraham sent his servant to find his son a bride. Imagine being given the task of finding your employer's son a wife. What a responsibility! But in this story, we learn some truths about how to get guidance from God.

1. Let God CHOOSE the way. In (v.12), as the servant starts on his way, he prays, *"O LORD...send me good speed this day..."* The first thing in getting guidance from God is to let Him choose the way. Don't impose your will on God; surrender to His will for you.

2. Let God CONTROL the way. This servant had no control over the circumstances of his journey. He was sent out by his master, Abraham. The key to finding direction is this: don't surrender to a PLAN, surrender to a PERSON. God's will is not just a *roadmap*, it is a *relationship*. The more you develop your relationship with God, the more control God will have in your life, and the easier it will be for Him to lead and direct you.

3. Let God CONFIRM the way. There are several ways in which God confirms His direction in your life. *First*, He confirms it through His Word. He will never lead you contrary to His Word. *Second*, He also confirms it through prayer. *Thirdly*, He confirms it through godly counsel. You will never go wrong if all three of these are in agreement.

4. Let God CLEAR the way. Satan will put some obstacles in your path, hoping to trip you up. Sometimes it may be mountains in our way that make it seem impossible to move forward. God may remove those mountains, or it may be His will for you to climb them!

Mercy, Peace, And Love

"Mercy unto you, and peace, and love, be multiplied."
(Jude 1:2)

Jude gives us three special things that God wants to have present in the life of every believer: **mercy**, **peace** and **love**. In fact, not only does He want them present, He wants them to be multiplied. Let's look at what each of these bring to our lives.

FIRST—MERCY Looks UPWARD. Mercy looks upward to our relationship with God. Mercy and grace are flip sides of the same coin. MERCY is when God *does not* give us what we *do* deserve and GRACE is when God *does* give us what we *do not* deserve. God's mercy is what should drive us to the Throne of God.

*"Let us therefore come boldly unto the throne of grace, that we may obtain **mercy**, and find **grace** to help in time of need." (Heb. 4:16)*

SECOND—PEACE Looks INWARD. The word "peace" means to join together; to join that which was separated. That's what Jesus did on the cross—He made peace between us and the heavenly Father. If you do not know Jesus Christ as your Savior, you don't know real peace! Jude said, "May God's peace be multiplied in you."

THIRD—LOVE Looks OUTWARD. Love looks outward to our relationships with others. If you have the love of Jesus in your heart, it won't stay in, it will have to come out. In fact, Jesus said that love is one of the evidences by which the world will know we are His disciples. Are these three things being multiplied in your life? If not, ask Him to let His mercy, peace, and love shine through you into the life of someone else, today.

God's Waiting Room

"And therefore will the LORD wait, that he may be gracious unto you...blessed are all they that wait for him."
(Isa. 30:18)

One of my least favorite things to do at the doctor's office is to sit in the waiting room. But, sometimes God puts us in His "waiting" room. See, God is never in a hurry. He works at His own pace. God isn't as interested in TIME as He is in TIMING. In other words, God's timing is always perfect, so we much rest in the fact that God always knows what to do and, most importantly, when to do it.

Isaiah starts off this verse by saying, *"And therefore will the LORD wait."* Isaiah tells us that sometimes we are waiting on God because He is waiting on us! He is often holding back His answer to us because we may not be ready to receive it. Notice two reasons God's waiting room is so important.

FIRST—It's A Matter of GRACE for US. Isaiah says that the Lord sometimes waits *"that He may be gracious unto you..."* In other words, God is so sovereign that He knows that the *right answer* at the *wrong time* can hurt us more than help us. If you have not received your answer, just trust that God has your best interest in mind for not revealing it, yet. Trust that He is being gracious to you.

SECOND—It's A Matter of GLORY for HIM. Next, Isaiah says, *"and therefore will He be exalted."* The second reason God hasn't answered you, yet, is because He is waiting for the perfect moment which will bring Him maximum glory.

Wait on the Lord because when you do, you will be rewarded because the last part of the verse says, *"blessed are all they that wait for him."*

The Calmness Of Contentment

"Not that I speak in respect of want: for I have learned, in whatsoever state I am, therewith to be content."
(Phil. 4:11)

When things don't go according to our plans, the stress can produce anxiety in our spirit. But Paul had learned the secret to calming his spirit no matter what his circumstances were. How did he do it? He learned to be content.

FIRST—Paul Was TEACHABLE. He said, *"I have learned..."* Contentment doesn't just happen; it is something we must learn. It is a lesson God is constantly trying to teach us. Sometimes we look at the lives of others and we get discontent with where our life is, so God has to bring circumstances into our life in order to teach us a lesson about contentment.

A lady, whose child was born with a disability, began to get depressed because of what her child was going through. After staying with her child at the hospital for weeks, her spirit began to change. When asked what had made the difference, she said, "The more I walked the halls and met other parents whose children were far worse off than mine, I began to thank God. There were parents having to deal with children who were facing things I didn't have to deal with and it made me thankful."

SECOND—Paul Was FLEXIBLE. Next, he said, *"in whatsoever state I am..."* If Paul was up on the mountain-top with everything going great, he was content. But he had also learned to be content when the bottom fell out and he was getting beaten or had been thrown into prison.

When we are content with where God has us, it brings a calmness to our life that nothing else can because we realize that God is still in control!

146

When Evil Seems To Pay

"..fret not thyself because of him who prospereth in his way, because of the man who bringeth wicked devices to pass." (Ps. 37:7)

Sometimes it can get very frustrating when it seems that the ungodly are going unpunished; when it seems as if they are getting away with their wickedness.

But, in Psalm 37, David has been reminding God's people not to worry about what the ungodly are doing. In (v.1) he says, *"Fret not thyself because of evildoers..."* We can get our attention on them and become envious of the fact that they seem to be prospering, even when we are struggling.

There are two reasons why David says we should not focus, fret, or be frustrated over the apparent prosperity of the wicked:

FIRST—Because of the DEMISE of the UNGODLY. (v.2) says, *"For they shall soon be cut down like the grass, and wither as the green herb."* As Christians, we are not to look at the wicked as if they will get away with their wickedness. Not so. God is keeping an accurate record of their evil. They may stand up proudly and boast of their success in wickedness, right now, but make no mistake about it, there is coming a day when they *"shall soon be cut down..."*

SECOND—Because of the DESTINY of the GODLY. (v.9) says, *"but those that wait upon the LORD, they shall inherit the earth."* One day the tables with turn. Those who are prospering in their wickedness, today, will be cut off, tomorrow. But God's people who are suffering, today, will be exalted in the end.

Don't let Satan get your eyes on the wicked around you. Just remember, God has the accurate record.

God's Promise To The Elderly (Part 1)

"And even to your old age I am he; and even to hoar hairs will I carry you: I have made, and I will bear; even I will carry, and will deliver you." (Isa. 46:4)

I recently turned 51 years old. And as young as I still am....and, yes, I am STILL young...I am already noticing that it is no fun getting older. I am realizing that as you get older your body starts to change without your permission! Someone said you know you are getting old:

- *When everything hurts, and what doesn't hurt, doesn't work!*
- *When your knees buckle, but your belt won't!*
- *When you sit in a rocking chair and can't get it going!*
- *When you sink your teeth into a steak and they stay there!*
- *When every time you see a pretty woman, your pace-maker makes the garage door go up!*

Someone asked Robertson McQuilkin, "Why does God let us get old and weak? Why must I hurt so?" To which he replied. "I'm not sure, but I have a theory. I think God has planned strength and beauty of youth to be physical, but the strength and beauty of age is spiritual. We gradually lose the strength and beauty that is temporal, so we'll be sure to concentrate on the strength and beauty which is forever."

Old age may not be all that it is cracked up to be, but God has a promise just for the elderly.

In fact, tomorrow, I will give you *three* specific promises God gives to the elderly.

God's Promise To The Elderly (Part 2)

"And even to your old age I am he; and even to hoar hairs will I carry you: I have made, and I will bear; even I will carry, and will deliver you." (Isa. 46:4)

Notice three promises God gives to the elderly:

FIRST—He Will STRENGTHEN You. He said, *"even to hoar hairs will I carry you."* The word *"hoar hairs"* means gray hairs. One of the first things an elderly person begins to lose is their strength. They don't have the endurance they once had in their youth. The word *"carry"* means to carry a heavy burden. God promises to strengthen you and help you carry the heavy burden of old age.

SECOND—He Will SUSTAIN You. Next, He said, *"..I will bear."* The word *"bear"* means to lift up; to aid; to support. Aren't you glad that when the gray hairs come and your natural strength starts to leave, that God is still there to lift you up and sustain you? He is not promising to give you the physical strength you once had, but He can sustain you, spiritually, no matter how old you may be!

THIRD—He Will SAVE You. Lastly, He said, *"..and will deliver you."* One of the meanings of this word *"deliver"* is to preserve. What a comfort to know that when old age comes on and your memory isn't what it used to be, God will still preserve you. You may have forgotten many things you have done or things God has done, but your salvation and your fellowship with God aren't dependent upon what you can remember, but upon what God remembers!

It can be easy for the elderly to feel forgotten and all alone. But here is a great reminder from God that *"even to your old age"* and *"even to hoar hairs"* God is always there to strengthen, sustain, and preserve you!

Putting Up With The Atheist

"Love your enemies, bless them that curse you, do good to them that hate you, and pray for them which despitefully use you, and persecute you;" (Matt. 5:44)

Years ago there was a Christian who agreed to take in an elderly, weary traveler into his house for a night's rest. After they ate, the Christian asked the gentleman, "How old are you?"

"Almost a century old," the old man replied.

"Are you a religious man?" asked the Christian.

"No. I do not believe in God," the atheist answered.

The Christian was infuriated. He opened his door and said, "I cannot keep an atheist in my house overnight."

The old man hobbled out into the cold darkness. Later, the Lord spoke to that Christian man and said, "Why did you let him go?"

The man replied, "I turned him out because he was an atheist, and I could not endure him overnight."

The Lord replied, "Son, I have endured him for nearly one hundred years. Don't you think you could endure him for one night?"

It's easy to love those who love us. But it is when we are treated in an unkind, unfair, or even hateful manner that we have an opportunity to stand out as light in this dark world. In fact, the very reason we are to love our enemies is that we may show them we have a different Father than them. Jesus said in (v.45) *"That ye may be the children of your Father which is in heaven..."* This man in our story had an opportunity to show the love of Jesus to that elderly atheist, and he missed it.

So, when someone treats you ugly, you repay their ugliness with godliness. Because, in the process, you are leaving a testimony that cannot be denied.

Just One More Nibble

*"With my whole heart have I sought thee: O let me not
wander from thy commandments." (Ps. 119:10)*

If you have the privilege of living in a rural
community, like I do, you get to see things you will never
see in a big city. For instance, one morning while I was in
my office at the church, I happened to look out my window
and just a few feet away there stood a cow staring back at
me as if to say, "What are you looking at?" I couldn't help
but wonder how in the world a cow ended up outside my
office window. It turns out, of course, the cow had
wandered outside of its pasture. I guess you could say it left
the **pasture** to come see the **pastor**!

When asked how a cow gets itself lost, one farmer
said, "Well, the cow starts nibbling on a patch of green
grass, and when it finishes, it looks ahead to the next patch
of green grass and starts nibbling on that one. Eventually, it
ends up nibbling on grass that is next to a hole in the fence.
It then sees another patch of grass on the other side of the
fence that looks appealing, so it leaves the fenced area and
begins nibbling on that grass. The next thing you know, the
cow has nibbled itself into being lost."

I got to thinking…that is how it is with backsliders,
too. Most people who are away from God did not set out to
backslide. They just followed one desire after another, from
one patch of green grass to another, until they nibbled
themselves through God's fence and strayed away from
God. Even the psalmist said, *"O let me not wander from thy
commandments."* He didn't want to foolishly follow desires
that might lead him away from God's pasture.

So, keep your eyes on Jesus, today. Watch where you
are walking because just one more nibble and you might
find yourself in the wrong pasture!

Worship In A Box (Part 1)

*"..there came a woman having an alabaster box of
ointment of spikenard very precious; and she brake the box,
and poured it on his head." (Mark 14:3)*

Mark reveals to us what could be the greatest illustration of true worship in the Bible. Today, we have been conditioned to think of worship that only happens on Sundays, between the hours of eleven and twelve. Furthermore, we have been led to believe that worship can only happen when external circumstances are just right; we must have the lighting right and the mood just right or else we cannot really worship.

Let us notice some characteristics of true worship that came from a little Alabaster box.

FIRST—TALKING Wasn't Enough; She Had to GIVE. You've heard the saying, "Talk is cheap." That is so true. Anyone can talk about how much they love Jesus. It is easy to stand up in church and sing, "Oh, How I Love Jesus," but this woman didn't just talk about it. She evidenced her true devotion to Christ not by **talking** but by **giving**; not by what she **said** but by what she **shared**.

SECOND—CHEAP Wasn't Enough; She Gave Something COSTLY. The ointment she gave to Jesus wasn't cheap perfume she got on discount from the dollar store. No, the Bible says it was *"very precious."* They think that when they put that dollar bill in the offering plate, the angels in heaven must have folded their wings and stood in awe of their spirituality. But the truth is, what most of us want to offer God, today, is cheap worship. We don't want to be inconvenienced when it comes to our Christianity.

Don't let Satan rob you of true, genuine worship. Sure, it will cost you something, but it is so worth the cost!

Worship In A Box (Part 2)

"..there came a woman having an alabaster box of ointment of spikenard very precious; and she brake the box, and poured it on his head." (Mark 14:3)

Yesterday, we saw the first two characteristics of true worship that came from a little Alabaster box. Today, let's look at the last two.

THIRD—PART of it Wasn't Enough; She Gave it ALL. The Bible says that when this woman broke open her Alabaster box of precious ointment, she *"poured it on his head."* She didn't keep anything for herself; she gave it all to Jesus! That is a result of true, heart-felt worship. Too many Christians come to church to supposedly worship, yet they hold back on God. They live their Christian lives afraid to give it all to Jesus. They are afraid to let go and truly worship because of what someone else might say. This woman didn't really care what the others would say. Her focus wasn't on THEM, it was on JESUS!

FOURTH—UNBROKEN Wasn't Enough; It Had to be OUTPOURED. The special fragrance from this little box would never have been experienced by Jesus, and the rest of the house, unless the box had been broken. Often, people think that because they aren't the "perfect little Christian" the cannot truly worship God. They think that since they have a tainted past, and a broken life that somehow God doesn't want their worship.

Listen, my friend, it is just the opposite! It was BECAUSE this box was broken that Jesus was able to receive her worship. It is BECAUSE of your broken past that you have every right, and may I say responsibility, to worship God! Jesus is not looking for perfect people, He is looking for broken people who have given their brokenness to Him. THAT is the fragrance that blesses the Lord!

Mr. Glory-Face

"A merry heart maketh a cheerful countenance..."
(Prov. 15:13)

It is told that when the great Adoniram Judson went as a missionary to Burma, he had such a burning desire to preach the gospel before he had even learned the language that he walked up to a Burman and embraced him. The man went home and told his wife that he had just seen an angel! Because Christ was so radiant on Mr. Judson's countenance, the people began calling him, "Mr. Glory-Face." What would others call you because of your countenance?

We don't realize it, but sometimes the countenance on our face is not that good. I've seen people whose countenance looks like they are mad all the time. What kind of countenance do you display at home, at work, or at school? Your countenance says a lot about you to others.

A cheerful countenance begins on the inside. The Bible says that it is *"A merry heart"* that gives us *"a cheerful countenance."* In other words, the look on our face is affected by what is in our heart!

So, how can we maintain *"a cheerful countenance"*? We do this by maintaining *"A merry heart."* The word *"merry"* means to be glad; to rejoice; to be joyful. When we maintain a heart of thankfulness to God and rejoice in all He has and is doing in our lives, it will affect our affect our countenance!

Take some time, today, to rejoice and be glad for who God is and what He has done for you. Not only will it brighten your day, it will brighten your countenance, as well. Who knows, those around you might just start calling you, "Mr./Mrs. Glory-Face."

God Washed Her Brain

*"And be not conformed to this world: but be ye
transformed by the renewing of your mind..." (Rom. 12:2)*

There is a story of a missionary who was imprisoned
by the Japanese. At the concentration camp where she was
held as a prisoner, the penalty for having even a portion of
the Bible was death. However, she was able to smuggle in a
small Gospel of John in her winter coat. Every night she
would pull the covers over her head, and with a small light,
she would read a verse in John, then put herself to sleep
memorizing that verse.

After some time, she had memorized the entire Book
of John. When she would wash her hands, she would take
one of the pages and dissolve it with soap and water, then
flush it down the drain. "And that is the way," she said,
"that John and I parted company."

Later, just before her release, a newspaper reporter was
interviewing this missionary lady and heard her story of
memorizing God's Word. As the other prisoners were
released, the reporters noticed they walked out of the camp
shuffling their feet with their eyes to the ground, little more
than lifeless robots. But this missionary came out of the
camp as bright as a button. Someone was heard to ask, "I
wonder if they managed to brainwash her?" The Reporter
who had interviewed her replied, "No, because God washed
her brain."

As a Christian, you do not have to be conformed to this
world. In fact, the Bible says you can be transformed *"by
the renewing of your mind."* Don't let the world's
philosophy and false ideas control your mind. Get in God's
Word and let it cleanse you and renew you. Let God wash
your brain!

3 Reasons For Unanswered Prayer

"Ye lust, and have not: ye kill, and desire to have, and cannot obtain: ye fight and war, yet ye have not, because ye ask not." (James 4:2)

It is easy to become discouraged when it seems our prayers have not been answered. We pray and pray for something, yet the answer never seems to come. Why is that? May I suggest three reasons?

1. The PRACTICE of Prayer Has Been DISCONTINUED. Often, the reason for unanswered prayer is unoffered prayer. James says, *"ye have not because ye ask not..."* Jesus said to His disciples, *"..when thou **prayest**, enter into thy closet and when thou hast shut thy door, **pray** to thy Father..." (Matt. 6:6)*. There was an expectation that if the disciples wanted the Father to hear their prayer and reward them openly, they must first pray.

Sadly, not only has prayer been discontinued in the life of many Christians, it has also been discontinued in the life of many churches, too!

2. The PERSON Who Prays Has Been DISQUALIFIED. The second possible reason for unanswered prayer is that the person who is praying has been disqualified because of sin in their life. God will not listen to our prayer when unconfessed sin is in our life.

3. The PETITION in the Prayer Has Been DELAYED or DENIED. The third possible reason for what seems like an unanswered prayer is that sometimes God's answer is "Yes," sometimes it is, "No," and sometimes it is, "Not now." You see, even when the answer is, "No," or "Not now," that IS an answer.

God has a reason for not answering your prayer at this particular moment. But just hold on...the answer is on its way!

Thy Will Be Done

"Thy will be done in earth, as it is in heaven." (Matt. 6:10)

There is a struggle in the life of every believer between wanting to do OUR will and wanting to do GOD's will. Often, we get too impatient waiting on God's will so we run ahead of God and try to accomplish our will, instead.

FIRST—God's Will is a Matter of DISCERN-MENT. Before we can do God's will, we must discern what God's will is. Paul prayed that the Colossians *"might be filled with the knowledge of his will in all wisdom and spiritual understanding;"* The great thing about it is that God doesn't want it to be difficult for us to discern His will. That's why the best place to find God's will is in God's Word!

SECOND—God's Will is a Matter of COMMIT-MENT. It is not enough to KNOW God's will; we must be willing to DO God's will. Jesus didn't say, "Thy will be known." He said, *"Thy will be done."* There must be a commitment to obeying the will of God once God reveals it to you. Next, He said, *"Thy will be done in earth."* If God's will is to be done on earth, it is up to us as believers to do it. We must be committed to helping God fulfill His will on this earth.

THIRD—God's Will is a Matter of ENJOYMENT. The psalmist said in *(Ps. 16:11) "..in thy presence is fulness of joy; at thy right hand there are pleasures for evermore."* There is nothing more enjoyable than knowing God's will and doing God's will. It is enjoyable because there is joy in serving Jesus! Why? Because we realize we get to be a part of God's plan for this world. What an honor! What a privilege! Surrender yourself to obeying God's will and living for Him every day. It's the greatest life there is!

157

The Attraction Of Your Reaction
(Part 1)

"The LORD is gracious, and full of compassion; slow to anger, and of great mercy." (Ps. 145:8)

If there is one thing that will make us stand out from the world it is our reaction to how others treat us. The world says, "Do unto others BEFORE they do unto you!" But the Bible says God has a different reaction. Despite how the world treats the Lord, the Bible says He is still *"gracious, and full of compassion; slow to anger, and of great mercy."*

Over the next several days I want to give you eight tips that will help you react differently to others.

1. Don't Judge their PRESENT by their PAST. Everyone has a past. What if everyone judged you, today, based on a bad decision you made years ago. Not only have we all made bad choices, but people do grow and learn from their mistakes. Who they are today, may not reflect who they were when they made that bad choice. So, instead of judging their past, help them create a new future.

2. Put your EARS in GEAR, and your MOUTH in PARK. If there's one thing that is hard to find these days, it is a good listener. James said in (James 1:19) *"Wherefore, my beloved brethren, let every man be swift to hear, slow to speak..."* Often, we do not hear what the other person is saying to us because we are too busy trying to respond.

One of the best things you can do for someone is to hear them out. Listen to what they are saying, and you might even hear what they are NOT saying!

The Attraction Of Your Reaction
(Part 2)

"The LORD is gracious, and full of compassion; slow to anger, and of great mercy." (Ps. 145:8)

Yesterday, I gave you the first two tips to help you react differently to people.

3. Be kind, not because of WHO THEY ARE, but because of WHOSE YOU ARE. Some people can be plain rude! But that does not give us an excuse to be equally as rude. It is easy to treat those right who treat us right. But true Christianity shines when we love those who are hateful to us. In fact, that is what Jesus commanded of us when he said, *"Love your enemies" (Matt. 5:44).*

We don't treat others right because of who they are, but because of who WE are. We belong to Jesus! That is why Jesus said in the very next verse: *"That ye may be the children of your Father which is in heaven..." (Matt. 5:45)*

4. Don't try to make yourself look BIG by making others look SMALL. The moment you think you have the right to belittle someone because you think you are better than them is the moment you show everyone else how small you really are. James reminds us that the Christian life is not about showing partiality to others. James said, *"My brethren, have not the faith of our Lord Jesus Christ, the Lord of glory, with respect of persons" (James 2:1).*

When we react to others the way Jesus would react, *"gracious, and full of compassion; slow to anger, and of great mercy,"* there will be an attraction to our reaction. Tomorrow, I will give you the last four ways we should react to others.

159

The Attraction Of Your Reaction
(Part 3)

"The LORD is gracious, and full of compassion; slow to anger, and of great mercy." (Ps. 145:8)

5. Remember, everyone has a story. Their actions may stem from something they have gone through in the past, or something they are dealing with right now. The point is, everyone has a story. That rude waitress that messed up your order has a story. That problem student in your class has a story. Their story may not EXCUSE their actions, but it may help EXPLAIN their actions. So, remembering that they have a story will help in how you respond to them.

6. Instead of magnifying their FAILURE, help them SUCCEED. There is a saying, "Never look down on someone unless it is to help them up." Sure, that person might not be as successful as you are, but you have no idea how far they may have come from where they were to where they are right now.

7. APPRECIATE those who have supported you, FORGIVE those who have hurt you, and HELP those who need you. This pretty much says it all. There is no room in life for grudges and bitterness. Be thankful for those whom God has used to help you, but forgive those who have hurt you and tried to make you fail. Help those who need you because often it might even be the person who previously hurt you.

8. Your PLEASANTNESS leaves a door open for your WITNESS. When you respond to hatefulness with hatefulness, you are closing the door on any opportunity you may have in the future to share the gospel with them. Therefore, it is imperative that your reactions show them, not just WHAT, but WHO is in your heart...JESUS!

4 Miracles At Midnight

*"And at midnight Paul and Silas prayed, and sang praises
unto God: and the prisoners heard them."
(Acts 16:25)*

Paul and Silas had been beaten, bound, and were
barely making it. They were sitting in a cold, dark prison at
the midnight hour. But even though they could not get out,
God could get in! He came into that prison and performed
four miracles at midnight. Let's look at them.

Miracle #1—The SAINTS Were SINGING. The
Bible says they *"prayed, and sang praises unto God."*
They were singing after all they had been through? How
could they do that? There is only one way...GOD! Only
God can give you the grace and the strength to sing when
you feel like weeping.

Miracle #2—The STRONGHOLD Was SHAKEN.
(v.26) says, *"And suddenly there was a great earthquake,
so that the foundations of the prison were shaken:"* The
jailer needed to be saved, but he was no doubt a hardened
man. So God had to produce a **shake up** for the jailer to
wake up!

Miracle #3—The SUICIDE Was STOPPED. (v.27)
says the jailer *"drew out his sword, and would have killed
himself, supposing that the prisoners had been fled."* He
knew his life was at stake if the prisoners were gone. Paul
saw what he was about to do and *"cried with a loud voice,
saying, Do thyself no harm: for we are all here."*

Miracle #4—The SINNER Was SAVED. (v.30-31)
says the jailer *"brought them out, and said, Sirs, what must
I do to be saved? And they said, Believe on the Lord Jesus
Christ, and thou shalt be saved, and thy house."* Had Paul
and Silas not prayed and sang during their trial, this jailer
(and his family) never would have been saved.

161

Breaking Free From What Has You Bound

"And suddenly there was a great earthquake...and every one's bands were loosed." (Acts 16:26)

It is interesting that while Paul and Silas were praying and singing praises to God inside their prison cell at midnight, the Bible specifically says that *"there was a great earthquake"* and *"every one's bands were loosed."* Every cell door was opened and all of the shackles the prisoners were wearing were released!

Like prisoners in a prison cell, Satan also has people bound. Some are bound by lust and greed while others may be bound by bitterness, fear, or worry. When a prisoner is bound, it means they are not free to move around like they normally would. Those whom Satan has bound do not live in the freedom Jesus brings; they are restricted; they are bound by their sin.

It was God who brought the earthquake and it was God who loosened their bands, but what prompted God? What was it that got God's attention? I believe it was when Paul and Silas prayed and sang praises by faith. There is something about prayer and praise that gets God's attention!

Paul and Silas didn't have the strength to undo their shackles and open their prison door, but God did! You do not have the strength within yourself to loosen the grip of what has you bound...but God does!

Bring your shackles to Him. Pray and praise Him in spite of what has you bound. Let Him free you, today! Let Him loosen the bands that have you bound so that you can begin walking in victory!

Getting Past The Past

"..this one thing I do, forgetting those things which are behind..." (Phil. 3:13)

Two men were walking through the countryside toward another village. As they came near a river, they encountered a woman sitting there, upset because there was no bridge. The two men decided to help, so they joined hands and lifted the woman between them and carried her across.

Later on as they were walking, one of the men said, "Look how dirty my clothes got from helping that lady across the river." Another mile down the road and he complained again, "And my back is now hurting from lifting her up, too." A couple more miles went by and he said to his friend, "Why is it you are not complaining about it, too? Doesn't your back hurt, too?" His friend smiled and said, "No. Your back still hurts because you're still carrying the woman, but I sat her down five miles ago!"

That is how some people are today. They are still carrying the pain of the past. They are still bearing burdens of things done to them years ago.

The apostle Paul had many bad things in his past, but he determined to not think on them. He made a choice to forget *"those things which are behind."* He knew that you cannot move forward as long as you are holding on to the past.

Is something in your past hindering your progress forward for God? Let it go. Give it to Jesus and walk on in victory.

4 Lies About Temptation (Part 1)

"And when the woman saw that the tree was good for food, and that it was pleasant to the eyes, and a tree to be desired to make one wise, she took of the fruit thereof, and did eat, and gave also unto her husband with her; and he did eat."
(Gen. 3:6)

Temptation is certainly nothing new; it has been around since the beginning of creation. Ever since Lucifer fell from his exalted position, because of his pride, he has been trying to tempt man away from God. And because Satan is a liar, there are some lies he tells us about the temptations we face.

LIE #1—"I am being tempted because I did something wrong." Don't misunderstand; when you *fall* to temptation you *have* sinned. But just being tempted is not a sin, itself. Eve had done nothing wrong before her temptation. It was only when she gave in to the temptation that she sinned. The Bible says Jesus experienced temptation, yet we know He never sinned. You are not tempted because you did something wrong. You are being tempted in order to get you to do wrong.

LIE #2—"If I were more spiritual, I wouldn't be tempted with this." Different people are tempted by different things. What tempts me might not be a temptation for you. And what might be a temptation for you might not tempt someone else. No matter how spiritual a person is, temptation will come their way.

1Corinthians 10:13 says that temptation is *"common to man."* That doesn't mean it is common in the sense that every man is tempted by the same sin, but rather it is common in the sense that everyone is tempted by something. In other words, it happens to all of us!

164

4 Lies About Temptation (Part 2)

*"And when the woman saw that the tree was good for food,
and that it was pleasant to the eyes, and a tree to be desired
to make one wise, she took of the fruit thereof, and did eat,
and gave also unto her husband with her; and he did eat."*
(Gen. 3:6)

Today, let's look at the other two lies Satan tells us
about temptation.

LIE #3—"I am powerless against temptation."
Satan would have us believe we have no power to resist
temptation when it comes our way. Oscar Wilde said, "I
can resist everything but temptation." That may have been
true for Oscar, but that isn't true for a child of God.

In 1Corinthians 10:13, Paul says we do have a choice
when it comes to temptation. He said, *"There hath no
temptation taken you."* The word *"taken"* is referring to
being overtaken by temptation. In other words, when
temptation comes, it doesn't have the power to overtake us
unless we allow it to do so.

LIE #4—"It won't hurt to give in, just this once."
Clearly this is a lie because look at how Adam and Eve's
ONE time of giving in to temptation affected all of
mankind! This lie is so powerful because it says, "I can
stop at any time." It is like a chain smoker who says, "I can
quit smoking whenever I want" but they never seem to be
able to make that choice. Once you give in to temptation, it
makes it that much harder to resist the next time.

Many people have become life-long drug addicts all
because they decided to try drugs just "one" time. What
they didn't realize was that "one" time was all it would take.

Satan is a liar, and has been from the beginning. Don't
believe his lies regarding temptation. Tomorrow I will give
you some ways to overcome temptation.

8 Ways To Overcome Temptation
(Part 1)

"Thy word have I hid in mine heart, that I might not sin against thee." (Ps. 119:11)

Did you ever play with a couple of magnets when you were a child? If you did, you'll remember that the closer they got to each other, the harder it was to pull them apart. Temptation is like that. The more you dwell on it and the closer you let it get to you, the stronger its attraction will be. So, what are some ways in which we can overcome temptation?

1) Expect it. If Satan tried to tempt Jesus to sin, he will surely have a temptation just for you, as well.

2) Identify your weaknesses. (Hosea 4:6) says, *"My people are destroyed for lack of knowledge..."* Everyone has their own weaknesses. Identify what your weaknesses are so you can be prepared when temptation comes in that particular area.

3) Protect yourself ahead of time. Paul said in (Eph. 6:13) *"Wherefore take unto you the whole armour of God, that ye may be able to withstand in the evil day..."* The armor must be put on BEFORE the enemy attacks. A police officer doesn't wait until bullets are coming toward him to put on his protective vest. Likewise, you must put on God's armor daily so it will be in place when temptation comes.

4) Don't make provision for your flesh. (Rom. 13:14) says, *"make not provision for the flesh, to fulfil the lusts thereof."* Another way in which to protect yourself from temptation is by not putting yourself around the people, places, or things that stir up the temptation. Often, the reason we fall to temptation is because we have not protected ourselves ahead of time.

8 Ways To Overcome Temptation
(Part 2)

"Thy word have I hid in mine heart, that I might not sin against thee." (Ps. 119:11)

Today, let's see the last four ways to overcome temptation.

5) Ask God for the power to resist it. God promises us *"a way to escape" (1 Cor. 10:13).* James 4:7 says, *"Resist the devil, and he will flee from you."* He would not tell us to *"Resist the devil"* if it were not possible to do so. Through Christ, we have the power to resist his attacks.

6) Flee from it. Joseph was tempted with immorality by his employer's wife, but when she enticed him, he ran! (Gen 39:12) says, *"And she caught him by his garment, saying, Lie with me: and he left his garment in her hand, and fled, and got him out."* He did the right thing and ran away as quickly as he could. Usually, we fall to temptation when we think we are strong enough to stay around it.

7) Remind yourself of the consequences. In the moment of temptation, we rarely ever stop and think of the consequences of giving in to the temptation. God had told Adam and Eve that if they took of the tree of the knowledge of good and evil, they would die. Maybe if Eve had thought about the consequences, she would not have disobeyed. When you are tempted, stop and think, "How will this affect me? How will this affect those around me? What kind of embarrassment, shame, or guilt will this bring into my life?"

8) Learn from it. Identify what may have brought on the temptation. Where were you, who were you with, or what circumstances may have left you open to this temptation? Knowing this can help you avoid it the next time.

Needed: Men Full Of The Holy Ghost (Part 1)

"Wherefore, brethren, look ye out among you seven men of honest report, full of the Holy Ghost..." (Acts 6:3)

There is no greater blessing to a pastor, than godly deacons. Not only are they a blessing to their pastor, but they are also a blessing to their church. On the other hand, no one has done more damage to pastors and churches than carnal deacons.

Many people do not understand what a deacon is and what their purpose is. Notice the characteristics that the apostles said were necessary when choosing good, godly deacons.

FIRST—They were to be SAVED. (v.2) says these men were to be called out from among *"the multitude of the disciples"* which means they were to be a disciple, themselves.

SECOND—They were to be SERVANTS. The word deacon means "servant." The whole reason deacons were needed in the first place was because the widows were being neglected and the apostles said, *"It is not reason that we should leave the word of God, and serve tables."* The apostles' duties were to pray and study the Word of God in order to feed the people of God, spiritually. So, in order to free them up for that task, they needed other men who had a servant's heart who would come and take care of the business of meeting the widow's needs.

Contrast that with the idea in many churches that deacons are to sit on some "Board" and run the church and pastor, and in some cases tell the pastor what he can and cannot preach. Tomorrow, we will see the last two characteristics of godly deacons.

Needed: Men Full Of The Holy Ghost (Part 2)

"Wherefore, brethren, look ye out among you seven men of honest report, full of the Holy Ghost..." (Acts 6:3)

Yesterday, we saw that godly deacons are to be **saved**, and to be **servants**.

THIRD—They were to be SINCERE. Next, (v.3) says they were to look for *"men of honest report."* These were to be sincere men; men of honesty and integrity. Remember, they were going to be working closely with widows. Therefore, they were to be men of impeccable character and with a pure testimony lest rumors start of inappropriate behavior that could hurt them and the cause of Christ.

FOURTH—They were to be SPIRITUAL. (v.3) says they were also to be men *"full of the Holy Ghost and wisdom."* There would never be a deacon who was a problem to a pastor or church if they were truly *"full of the Holy Ghost."* Another reason deacons were needed was because (v.1) says there was beginning to be murmuring in the church. Deacons were called to help put down the murmuring.

This morning, pray for the deacons in your church. Call them by name. Thank God for them and encourage them as they encourage your pastor. Pray for God to help them be the serving, sincere, spiritual men God called them to be.

When You're In A Famine

"..there was a famine in the land. And a certain man of Bethlehemjudah went to sojourn in the country of Moab, he, and his wife, and his two sons." (Ruth 1:1)

The story of Ruth is a story of redemption. Redemption can only take place if something is lost. The book of Ruth begins with a family who is experiencing a great loss as a result of a famine. Let's look at this story and see how we should respond when we encounter a "spiritual" famine.

FIRST—The REASON for the FAMINE. When it seems you are experiencing a spiritual famine, before running away from it, stop and examine what may be causing it. (v.1) tells us this happened *"in the days when the judges ruled."* It also says, *"In those…every man did that which was right in his own eyes."* When a famine comes into your life, take some time to examine your life to see if there could be a reason why God would send it.

SECOND—The REACTION of the FATHER. (v.1) says it was *"a certain man"* who led *"his wife, and his two sons"* away from the land of promise. Fathers, it is up to us get our guidance from God, not impatiently move our families on a whim just because circumstances are not favorable.

THIRD—The RESULT for the FAMILY. Notice what happened next. (v.3) says that the father died and (v.5) says that both sons died, too! How sad to think that the very reason he moved his family there was in hopes of saving them during the famine. But, what a lesson we can learn from this! It is far better to remain in the land of promise where God has put us (even during a famine) than to try and make it by living among the ungodly.

My Bible Is Dry As Dust

"But his delight is in the law of the LORD; and in his law doth he meditate day and night." (Ps. 1:2)

One night, after a church service where R.A. Torrey was preaching, a man approached him and said, "I cannot get anything out of reading the Bible. My Bible is dry as dust! How can I make it come alive to me like it is to you?"

"Read it," replied Dr. Torrey.

"I have read it," the man said.

"Read it some more," was Torrey's reply.

"How?" said the man.

"Take a book of the Bible and read it twelve times a day for a month," Dr. Torrey answered.

"What book could I read that many times a day, working as many hours as I do?"

"Try Second Peter," replied Torrey.

The man began to read Second Peter three times in the morning, two or three times at noon, and three times in the evening. Soon, he was talking about Second Peter to everyone he met. The next time he saw Dr. Torrey he said, "Ever since I've started spending so much time reading the Bible it's as if the stars in heaven are singing the story of Second Peter. I read Second Peter on my knees, marking passages. Soon, my teardrops began to mix with the crayon colors I was marking it with and I said to my wife, 'I have ruined this part of my Bible.'" His wife said to him, "Yes, but as the pages have been getting black, your life has been getting white!"

The greatest way to fall in love with the Bible is to first fall in love with its Author! Fall in love with Jesus and you will find that the Bible is no longer as dry as dust.

The Delight Of Delighting

"Delight thyself also in the LORD; and he shall give thee the desires of thine heart." (Ps. 37:4)

I believe this may be one of the most misunderstood verses in the Bible. Some seem to think this verse is saying that if you are saved God should grant all your wishes as if He were a Genie in a bottle. We know this verse does not mean God will grant all of our desires, because not all of our desires are godly. We can have selfish desires, and fleshly desires, and lustful desires, and God cannot fulfill those in our lives because He is holy.

Likewise, the wicked will not see their true desire come to past. The ungodly are constantly searching for that which will satisfy them, only to be disappointed. (Ps. 112:10) says, *"..the desire of the wicked shall perish."* They are searching for something to bring them peace, but they can never seem to find it. Why? Because contentment and peace are only found in Jesus Christ. Therefore, *"..the desire of the wicked shall perish."*

But there is a delight to those who are delighting in the Lord. And that is that the godly WILL have their desires come to past. Because, when you delight in the Lord more than anything else, God will give you the right things to desire in your heart. And once you desire what God desires, He can then *"give thee the desires of thine heart."*

If all of your desires are fleshly desires, then God can't give those to you. So, make sure your desires are God's desires. The right desires are those which will make you more like Christ. And you can be sure that when you desire to be more like Jesus, that is a desire He will grant!

A Dead End Job

"Labour not for the meat which perisheth, but for that meat which endureth unto everlasting life..." (John 6:27)

Jesus was trying to teach the people that in life there are things which are temporary and things which are eternal, and one who is wise will labor for that which is eternal.

The truth Jesus is trying to teach us is that we should put more effort into our *spiritual* welfare than we do into our *physical* welfare. Let me give you an example: the average church member spends more time preparing themselves physically to come to church than they do preparing themselves spiritually to come to church. They may spend an hour or more showering, ironing their clothes, putting on makeup, preparing their hair, brushing their teeth, etc. Yet, they don't spend 15 minutes preparing their hearts to receive and obey the sermon they are about to hear!

Some will be the first in line to eat food at the church's cookout, where food for the **body** is given out. But they will come in late (if they come at all) to preaching time where food for their **soul** is being dispersed.

Laboring for that which is temporary, and will perish, is like working a dead end job! The wise man will lay up treasures in heaven. The wise man will labor for *"that meat which endureth unto everlasting life."*

Examine yourself, this morning. How many things are you involved in which have no eternal significance whatsoever. How much of your time is spent laboring on things which have no eternal impact for the kingdom of God? Something to think about.

173

The Key To Taking A Stand (Part 1)

"But Daniel purposed in his heart that he would not defile himself with the portion of the king's meat, nor with the wine which he drank: therefore he requested of the prince of the eunuchs that he might not defile himself." (Dan. 1:8)

While in captivity, Daniel was faced with a decision: eat and drink the king's food which had been likely offered to idols, or take a stand. He chose to take a stand. There will be times in life where, for the sake of your testimony as a Christian, you must take a stand. The key is knowing when and how to stand.

FIRST—He Knew WHEN to Take a Stand. There were some things the Babylonians tried to do to Daniel that he allowed and certain things he didn't allow. In other there words, he didn't take a stand on everything. Some Christians seem to take a stand on EVERYTHING! They fuss about everything little thing. Hey, not every hill is worth dying on!

Daniel didn't take a stand on everything. They deported him to a foreign nation....he didn't like it, but he let it go. They changed his name to one that would have been very offensive to him.....he didn't like it, but he let it go. They made him attend their schools....he didn't like it, but he let it go.

But then they offered him their food and he resisted it. Why? What was unique about the food that was not true of the other aspects of this trial? The food was a BIBLICAL ISSUE. Eating this food would have been a violation of Old Testament dietary laws, AND had probably been offered to their pagan gods.

So what determined when Daniel took a stand and when he didn't was whether or not he was in danger of violating the Word of God.

The Key To Taking A Stand (Part 2)

*"But Daniel purposed in his heart that he would not defile
himself with the portion of the king's meat, nor with the
wine which he drank: therefore he requested of the prince
of the eunuchs that he might not defile himself." (Dan. 1:8)*

SECOND—Daniel knew HOW to take a stand.
Notice that it says, *"therefore he **requested** of the prince of
the eunuchs that he might not defile himself."* He asked
permission to not have to eat the food. This is an important
component in taking a stand. He showed respect even while
taking a stand.

He didn't boycott the meat company. He didn't call the
ACLU and sue the King. He didn't accuse them of
violating his civil rights. He didn't play the "victim" card.

Taking a stand doesn't mean being rude, arrogant or
condescending; it doesn't mean beating someone over the
head with a Bible until they give in. Colossians 4:6 says,
"Let your speech be alway with grace..." We are to use
wisdom when we speak to others because the attitude with
which we speak, can affect the other person. Proverbs 15:1
says, *"A soft answer turneth away wrath: but grievous
words stir up anger."*

The better our attitude, the more effective our stand.
The problem with some Christians is that they have the
right message, but they have the wrong spirit. It's kind of
like my pastor used to say, "I like ice cream, but not in my
face." Some think the only way to present the message of
Christ is by getting in a person's face. That will not work,
my friend.

If we are going to be effective in taking a stand for
what is right, we need to know WHEN and HOW to take a
stand.

I Will Keep My Mouth

"I will take heed to my ways, that I sin not with my tongue:
I will keep my mouth with a bridle..." (Ps. 39:1)

Few things give us more trouble than our tongue. James said, *"the tongue is a fire, a world of iniquity..." (James 3:6).* How many times have you said something ugly or hateful, out of anger, only to regret it as soon as the words left your mouth? The trouble is we cannot take back hurtful words once they have been said. We can apologize for them, but it is too late...the damage has been done.

Someone can say something hurtful to you and then say they are sorry, yet you will still remember those words years later. Why? Because just saying the words, "I'm sorry" cannot erase the hurt that person caused with their tongue.

No wonder the psalmist said, *"I will take heed to my ways, that I sin not with my tongue..."* Sinning with our tongue is a very easy thing to do! So how can we keep from sinning with our tongues? The psalmist has the answer. He said, *"I will keep my mouth with a bridle..."*

A bridle is used around a horse's mouth. It includes a piece called a bit which lays on the horse's tongue. With a bridle on the horse's mouth, the rider can control that horse; he can direct that horse to go where he wants the horse to go. In other words, because of the bridle, the horse is under the control of its master!

As Christians, our tongue needs to be under the control of our Master, Jesus. Ask the Lord to help you guard your tongue and bridle your mouth, so that you will not say sinful things or say things in a sinful way, today.

Magnifying The Lord

"..let such as love thy salvation say continually, The LORD be magnified." (Ps. 40:16)

As a kid, I used to love playing with a magnifying glass because it could make even the tiniest of things look big. As I have gotten older, I have started using a magnifying lens on a regular basis; they are called "reading glasses!" For some reason, after I turned 40, everyone starting printing text much smaller than they did before. My reading glasses help make small text easier to read because it magnifies it; it makes it bigger.

The psalmist said, *"let such as love thy salvation say continually, The LORD be magnified."* Let's get one thing straight, right away...we cannot make God any bigger than He already is! Aren't you thankful that you serve a great big God? So, if we cannot make God bigger, what does the psalmist mean?

When we live after the flesh instead of walking in the Spirit, God becomes smaller in our lives. When we live in fear and anxiety and worry about the troubles we face, God seems smaller and smaller and our problems seem bigger and bigger.

But the more we stay in God's Word and walk by faith and not by sight, God becomes bigger to us. It's not that He GETS any bigger, it's that He gets magnified in our lives and we begin to see how big He really is!

Today, you will either make God appear small to those around you, or you will magnify Him in your life. Which will it be?

Follow Me

"Be ye followers of me, even as I also am of Christ."
(1Cor. 11:1)

Everyone has someone following them. Everyone has someone looking up to them. The singles look up to the young married couples and long for the day they too can be married like they are. Older teenagers look up to the single adults and long for the day when they will be out of school and have the "freedom" they see in the life of the singles. Thirteen and fourteen-year-old teens look up to the sixteen-year-olds who can drive a car. Younger children look up to the thirteen-year-olds and can't wait until they turn thirteen and can also be part of the teen youth group.

We all have someone looking up to us. Paul said, *"Be ye followers of me..."* Someone is following you but the question is where are you leading them? Paul was conscious of the fact that there were people following them so he wanted to be the right example by being a follower of Christ. If Paul followed Christ, then when others followed Him, THEY TOO would become a follower of Christ.

Mom and Dad, will your children become followers of Christ by following you? Hey, young married couples, single adults, and teenagers....will those who are looking up to you become followers of Christ by following you? Hey sir, or ma'am...will those whom you work with become a follower of Christ if they follow your example at work?

May our lives lead other lives to Christ when they follow our example in front of them.

Wait For It

"..tarry ye...until ye be endued with power from on high."
(Luke 24:49)

Jesus had just been crucified and buried. Now, as the disciples are assembled together, the resurrected Christ appears before them! Imagine how anxious they must have been to get busy serving the Lord and doing miraculous works, now that they know He had been raised from the dead. But, instead of telling them to hurry off and begin performing miracles, Jesus told His disciples that they were to wait in Jerusalem.

"What? Wait? But why?" they must have asked Him. So Jesus says to them, *"..behold, I send the promise of my Father upon you* **[the Holy Spirit]***: but tarry ye in the city of Jerusalem, until ye be endued with power* **[by the Holy Spirit]** *from on high."* In other words, Jesus was telling them not to try and do one single work for Him UNTIL the Holy Spirit was given to them.

What a lesson for us, today! We do not have to "wait" on the Holy Spirit like the disciples did because we are given the Holy Spirit the moment we are saved. BUT, though we do not have to wait on the PRESENCE of the Holy Spirit to do God's work, we must wait on the FILLING of the Holy Spirit to do God's work.

Trying to do God's work without the filling of the Holy Spirit simply means we are trying to do God's work through the power of the flesh. No, we must wait until we are sure that we are right with God and are being led by the Holy Spirit so that when we do **God's work**, it will be done **God's way**.

If you have sin in your life, then you are NOT filled with the Holy Spirit. Make things right, today, and be filled so you can get busy serving!

A Millionaire Unaware

"O the depth of the riches both of the wisdom and knowledge of God!" (Rom. 11:33)

There is a famous oil field in Texas called the "Yates Pool." During the depression, this field was owned by a sheep farmer named Yates. Mr. Yates struggled to make enough money with his ranch to even make the interest payment on his mortgage.

It wasn't until a seismographic crew from an oil company came and asked Mr. Yates if they could check for oil, that they discovered a vast oil reserve under his land. At 1,115 feet they struck oil, giving 80,000 barrels a day and Mr. Yates owned it all! He had been living in poverty for years never realizing the millions of dollars that was literally under his feet.

That is the way some Christians are living, today. They are living in spiritual poverty, barely making it, all because they don't realize how rich they are in Christ. God said, *"My people are destroyed for lack of knowledge: because thou hast rejected knowledge..."* (Hosea 4:6).

God's people are being destroyed, today, because of our lack of wisdom and knowledge of God. Paul said, "If you only realized *'the depth of the riches with of the wisdom and knowledge of God'* you would not be living in spiritual poverty."

Don't continue walking in spiritual ignorance. Get into God's Word and grow so that you will not become a millionaire unaware.

Full Of The Bible

"Jesus answered him, saying, It is written, That man shall not live by bread alone, but by every word of God."
(Luke 4:4)

When the Bible becomes a part of us, it renews our mind and as a result we begin to think like Jesus. And when we think like Jesus, it changes the way we respond to temptations.

A great example of this was a high school student whose school band was performing on a Caribbean cruise. One night his friends tried to entice him into the ship's bar, but Jeff (whose mother was an alcoholic) had memorized verses in Proverbs about the dangers of drinking alcohol. He refused his friends invitation to go have a drink and quoted to them *(Prov. 20:1)* *"Wine is a mocker, strong drink is raging: and whosoever is deceived thereby is not wise."*

They replied, *"Come on, Jeff. Just one beer won't hurt."* He replied by quoting (Prov. 23:32), *"At the last it biteth like a serpent, and stingeth like an adder."* They accused him of rejecting their company, to which he said, *"My son, if sinners entice thee, consent thou not" (Prov. 1:10).* After he quoted that last verse, one of the boys was heard to say, "Come on, let's go, guys. He's so full of the Bible we can't do anything with him!"

That is how Jesus defeated Satan when He was being tempted in the wilderness; He used the Word of God. Wouldn't it be great if the next time Satan tried to tempt you, he finally gave up and said, "I'm leaving. They are so full of the Bible that I can't do anything with them"

Read, study, and memorize God's Word. Not only will it fill you up, it will also defeat Satan, too!

Are You Causing Others To Stumble?

"It is good neither to eat flesh, nor to drink wine, nor any thing whereby thy brother stumbleth, or is offended, or is made weak." (Rom. 14:21)

A very important principle is given here to every believer. We are not to take part in anything which might cause another believer to stumble or be tempted to sin. Alcohol is specifically mentioned here. There are many believers who have fallen for the lie that "social drinking" is somehow okay. Often those who do so use the excuse that it's not hard liquor or real strong alcohol, therefore, it isn't that bad.

But the issue here isn't how strong the drink is because Paul even says here to avoid *"wine."* The issue at stake is your testimony. Paul specifically mentions drinking wine and eating meat (*"flesh"*), referring to eating the meat which had been sacrificed to idols in that day. But he didn't stop with that, he then says we are not to do *"any thing whereby thy brother stumbleth, or is offended, or is made weak."*

There many things which this world does, especially things which affect the body, that believers are to avoid. Just because it is popular or "cool" does not mean it is the best thing for your testimony. Younger believers, who are still growing in their faith, are watching you. And the liberty you are taking in the world, might cause them to stumble or be made weak in their faith.

The Bible says we are to *"Abstain from all appearance of evil" (1Thess. 5:22)*. Is there something you are involved in which might be causing others to stumble? Ask God to reveal it and then avoid it!

How To Pray For Our Nation

"If my people, which are called by my name, shall humble themselves, and pray, and seek my face, and turn from their wicked ways; then will I hear from heaven, and will forgive their sin, and will heal their land." (2Chron. 7:14)

In just a couple of days we will celebrate a very important day in the life of our country: Independence Day! Every year we set aside July 4 as a day to celebrate the freedom we have as a nation.

There are so many good things about America that we should thank God for; so many liberties we have, most of which no other country on earth enjoys.

But for all the good that is in America there is also much evil and wickedness. All it takes is a quick look at the rapid moral and spiritual decline to know that, more than anything, America needs revival!

But, according to the Bible, revival only comes through prayer. Therefore, for the next few days, I want to give you some specific ways in which you can pray for our nation and our leaders. Psalm 33:12 says, *"Blessed is the nation whose God is the LORD..."*

Today, I want to give you a specific prayer you can begin praying for our nation, using 2Chronicles 7:14.

"Father, I humble myself before You and seek Your face. I ask You to heal our land. I ask You to grant me a repentant spirit so I may be an instrument that ushers in Your blessing for this nation. Turn our hearts toward You and remind us that, as a nation, we have no hope apart from You and Your mercy. Forgive our sin and heal our land."

183

How To Pray For Our President & Vice President

*"Blessed be the name of God...he removeth kings, and
setteth up kings: he giveth wisdom unto the wise, and
knowledge to them that know understanding:"
(Daniel 2:20-21)*

Today, I want to focus on how to specifically pray for
our President and Vice President.

In our text verse, we see that God removes kings and
also sets them up. He gives them wisdom and knowledge.
If there is anyone who needs wisdom and knowledge it is
our President and Vice-President!

We have no idea the amount of opposition they face
every moment of every day. The pressure must be
incredible. There is pressure from liberals as well as
conservatives. There is pressure from the powerful, the
wealthy, and the wicked...all wanting them to make
decisions that will benefit them.

How will they be able to cut through the clutter and
make the right decisions for our country? They need
wisdom and knowledge that only God can give them. How
will they get it? Through prayer! Here is a prayer you can
begin praying for them right now.

*"Father, I thank you for America and the freedom You
have given to us. I thank You for our leaders. I ask that
You give them the courage to make decisions that honor
You despite the opposition. Give them Your wisdom,
knowledge, and discernment. I ask that You bless and
protect their marriage and children. Put a hedge of
protection around them physically and, most of all, may
they grow to love You more and more each day."*

How To Pray For Members Of Congress & The Supreme Court

"I exhort therefore, that, first of all, supplications, prayers, intercessions, and giving of thanks, be made for all men; For kings, and for all that are in authority; that we may lead a quiet and peaceable life in all godliness and honesty." (1Tim. 2:1-2)

Today, we will end this series of devotionals looking at how we can specifically pray for the members of Congress and the Supreme Court. They especially need our prayers because the Bible says in Ephesians 6:12 that Satan seeks to influence world leaders.

PRAYING FOR MEMBERS OF CONGRESS:

"Father, I pray that the members of Congress will seek Your wisdom and direction. I pray they will seek Your face and honor Your Word. A house divided against itself cannot stand, therefore, I pray for them to be unified in righteousness for the sake of the nation. I pray for those in Congress who are saved that they might stand boldly for right and I pray for those who are lost that You will turn their hearts to You and be saved."

PRAYING FOR MEMBERS OF THE SUPREME COURT:

"Father, I pray that each Justice will recognize their own inadequacy apart from You. I pray they will fear God and glorify Him through their actions. And I pray that the Supreme Court would honor biblical values in their rulings and decisions."

Are You Listening?

"He that hath an ear, let him hear what the Spirit saith unto the churches." (Rev. 3:22)

There have been times when I was watching something on TV and my wife started talking to me. After a few minutes of talking without hearing a response from me she would stop and say, "Are you listening to me?" I wonder if sometimes when the Holy Spirit is trying to speak to us, He doesn't ask the same question.

FIRST—Notice who is to HEAR. *"He that hath ears..."* Not everyone can hear. Unbelievers do not have spiritual ears to hear spiritual things. (1Cor. 2:14) says, *"But the natural man receiveth not the things of the Spirit of God: for they are foolishness unto him: neither can he know them, because they are spiritually discerned."* But equally as sad is the fact that even among Christians, not everyone who CAN listen to the Spirit, DOES listen to the Spirit.

SECOND—Notice who is to be HEARD. *"let him hear what the Spirit saith..."* The Holy Spirit is speaking and is to be heard. He should be heard because He is God! He is to be heard because He communicates the will of the Father and Son to us. He is to be heard because He convicts us of sin. He is to be heard because He is the one Who illuminates the Scriptures to us when we read them.

THIRD—Notice WHAT is to be heard. *"what the Spirit saith unto the churches."* It is important that you faithfully attend church. Why? So you can hear *"what the Spirit saith unto the churches."* The Holy Spirit will speak through your Sunday School teacher and pastor as they teach and preach the Word.

So, the question isn't "Is the Spirit speaking?" The question is "Are you listening?"

Better Than The Mighty

"He that is slow to anger is better than the mighty; and he that ruleth his spirit than he that taketh a city."
(Prov. 16:32)

There is nothing more powerful than our spirit, and few things can cause more harm than a bad spirit. A bad temper can ruin relationships. Wars have been fought between nations because the leaders could not control their tempers. Therefore, the Bible says that one who has control over his temper, by ruling his spirit, is *"better than the mighty."*

One meaning of the word *"mighty"* refers to a mighty hunter. *(Gen. 10:8-9)* *"Nimrod..began to be a mighty one in the earth. He was a <u>mighty</u> <u>hunter</u> before the LORD..."* A mighty hunter can conquer the wildest of beasts, yet, the person who *"ruleth his spirit"* is said to be able to conquer something even better than a hunter. Our text verse says you are *"better than the mighty"* if you can do two things:

FIRST—Be Slow to Get Angry. Some people have a very short fuse and live as if every little thing will set them off. Someone has said, "He who angers you controls you" and there is a lot of truth in that statement. *(James 1:19)* says, *"let every man be swift to hear, slow to speak, slow to wrath:"*

SECOND—Rule Your Spirit. *"and he that ruleth his spirit than he that taketh a city."* In other words, a person who can rule his own spirit is mightier than one who can conquer an entire city. Wow! That is mighty!

Today, Satan may use someone to try and anger you or make you lose your temper. Don't let them control your spirit. Ask God for the strength to not lose your temper and lose your testimony. Ask Him to help you be *"better than the mighty."*

Why Weepest Thou?

"And they say unto her, Woman, why weepest thou?"
(John 20:13)

It was the morning of the resurrection and Mary had rushed to the tomb, only to see two angels in white where her Lord's body had been. Just as Jesus had wept earlier, at the tomb of His friend Lazarus, Mary began to weep at the tomb of Jesus.

The angels spoke to her and said, *"Woman, why weepest thou?"* Usually, when angels appeared in the Bible, the first thing they said was, *"Fear not,"* because their very presence shocked and frightened people at first. But it's almost as if Mary isn't concerned at all about these strangers from another world because she is so grief-stricken.

When the angels asked, *"Why weepest thou?"* she said to them, *"Because they have taken away my Lord..."* If that were possible, that would be reason enough to weep, for sure. I believe the whole of creation, and the angels themselves, might weep if someone could take away our Lord!

But praise be to God, NO ONE can take away our Lord!!! *"Why weepest thou?"* the angels say. The reason He is not here at the tomb is because *"He is risen!"*

May I ask you the same question, this morning? *"Why weepest thou?"* Why are you downcast, discouraged, and depressed? No one can take away your Lord for He has promised He *"will never leave thee, nor forsake thee"* *(Heb. 13:5).*

Rejoice today! No matter what you may be going through; no matter what you may lose in this world, you can't lose Christ! The world may take away everything you own, but they cannot take away your Lord!

188

A God Of The Details

"But the very hairs of your head are all numbered."
(Mark 10:30)

Details matter. A wealthy woman who was traveling overseas saw a bracelet she thought was too irresistible not to buy. So she sent her husband this cable: "Have found wonderful bracelet. Price $75,000. May I buy it?" Her husband promptly wired back this response: "No, price too high." But the cable operator accidentally omitted the comma, so the woman received the message: "No price too high." She bought it. What a difference a small comma made!

The Bible says that God knows the number of *"the very hairs of your head."* Details matter to God. John R. Rice said, "God cares about the details. If you comb out some hairs in the morning, the record in Heaven in changed."

FIRST—God NOTICES the Little Things. When you look at creation you see that God took care of the tiniest little details. What an encouragement to know that no matter how "small" you think something is that you are doing for the Lord, He notices it! He sees it and will one day reward it.

SECOND—God CARES about the Little Things. God isn't just concerned with the "big picture," He is concerned with every aspect of your life. The verse before our text verse says God cares so much for His creation that He even notices every bird that falls from the sky! Wow!

Listen, friend, if God cares enough to see every bird that falls, how much more does He care about you? (v.31) says, *"Fear ye not therefore, ye are of more value than many sparrows."* Don't let Satan tell you that you are small in God's eyes. God sees what you are doing.

Heart Problems

"..he, being grieved for the hardness of their hearts..."
(Mark 3:5)

The American College of Cardiology reports that Cardiovascular disease accounts for approximately 800,000 deaths in the United States. You cannot continually have heart problems without it eventually taking your life. The Bible says there are "spiritual" heart problems that can also affect a person's life.

FIRST—A HARD Heart. There was a man whose hand was withered. The religious Pharisees watched whether Jesus would heal this man on the Sabbath just so they could accuse Him. It didn't matter that this man needed help, the heart of these Pharisees was so hardened that they didn't care about him. They only cared about themselves. Their heart had become hardened because of their stubbornness.

How many times have we, as Christians, hindered God from working a miracle in our lives because we had allowed our heart to become hard and stubborn?

SECOND—A BLIND Heart. Ephesians 4:18 speaks of unbelievers who have their *"understanding darkened, being alienated from the life of God through the ignorance that is in them, because of the blindness of their heart:"* Because their heart was blind, they were ignorant and alienated from *"the life of God."*

Maybe you have never trusted in Jesus as your personal Saviour. You are blinded to the love, joy, and peace that God can bring to your heart. Call on Him in faith and repentance, and receive His forgiveness today. Maybe you are a believer whose heart has become hard and stubborn because of sin. Confess it, today, before your heart problem kills you, spiritually!

Yesterday's Oil

"And it came to pass..that..the oil stayed." *(2 Kings 4:6)*

Here we see a widow. She was in debt and had no means by which to pay her bills. She came to the prophet Elijah and asked what she could do. After she gathered empty vessels, at the prophet's command, she began to pour out the little oil she had into these vessels. When she had no more vessels to pour into, *"the oil stayed."* She stopped receiving fresh oil because she stopped going to the cruse. In other words, she stopped **receiving** because she stopped **pouring**!

Thank God for the oil God gave you yesterday, but yesterday's oil is not good enough for today. You need fresh oil, today! This widow had to pour out yesterday's oil in order to receive today's oil. In other words, she had to be willing to **pour out** before God could **pour in**. She had to empty her cruse out before God could fill her cruse up!

God wants to give you fresh oil every day, but you must be willing to use the oil He gave you yesterday if you want Him to give you more oil, today. How many sermons has God allowed us to hear that was fresh oil from God, yet we never obeyed what we heard? We wasted the oil God gave us.

When she stopped pouring out into other vessels, the oil stayed. When she stopped going to the cruse, she stopped receiving fresh oil. As long as you keep going to the cruse, you will find the fresh oil you need; but when you stop going to the cruse the oil will stay in your life and you will have to live on yesterday's oil.

Are you living on yesterday's oil? Has the oil stayed in your life? Don't waste the oil God gave you, yesterday, so that He will give you fresh oil, today. Don't live on yesterday's oil.

The Harmfulness Of Idleness

"And he called his ten servants...and said unto them, Occupy till I come." (Luke 19:13)

The word *"occupy"* literally means "keep busy." In other words, this man was saying, "Keep busy till I come." There is little that will kill a person's spiritual life like idleness will. There is an old saying that says, "Idle hands are the Devils' workshop."

FIRST—Idleness results from having no goal or purpose. To be idle is to be lazy or to avoid work. Idleness is not the same as rest, which the Bible commends. Rather, idleness is doing **nothing** when you should be doing **something**. God wants us working with purpose, and that purpose is to glorify God with our lives.

SECOND—Idleness leads us into temptation. When we are idle, we are more prone to give in to temptation. Without focus, our minds more easily stray and we are more easily enticed by our sinful desires and the sinful pleasures of the world.

THIRD—Idleness often leads to other sins. A state of idleness is often accompanied by other sins, such as stealing and gossiping. 1Timothy 5:13 says, *"they learn to be idle, wandering about from house to house; and not only idle, but tattlers also and busybodies, speaking things which they ought not."*

It is not that Christians are to be workaholics or have no pleasures that they enjoy; rather we are to live our lives with purpose, doing all things—including rest and relaxation—for the glory of God.

Don't become idle. Make it your goal every day to live for God and bring glory to Him.

Bright Light Christians

"That ye may...shine as lights in the world;" (Phil. 2:15)

When writing to the Philippian believers, Paul encourages them to be *"blameless"* and *"without rebuke"* and to *"shine as lights in the world."* In other words, we are to be bright light Christians!

FIRST—Bright lights attract. Turn on a lightbulb outside at night and just watch how quickly it attracts a multitude of gnats and other flying insects. There is something about light that is attractive to these creatures. Likewise, since the Bible says that Jesus is the light of the world, the light of our lives should ***attract*** others to Jesus, not ***repel*** them.

SECOND—Bright lights guide the way. Imagine trying to drive your car at night without using the headlights. That would not only be crazy, it would be dangerous! Why, because the headlights light the path for us to travel. Our lives should shine brightly in this dark world so that others can plainly see the way to Jesus!

THIRD—Bright lights repel darkness. No amount of darkness can put out a light. You may be tempted to think that your little light in this vast world of darkness doesn't matter, but it does! One single star doesn't produce much light, but when combined with millions of others, they can light up the sky!

One final thought. Stars don't try to be stars. When you see them twinkling in the night sky, they are they just are being themselves. Don't try to be something you aren't. Walk with God and let Him shine through you as you go about your day, today.

Constructive Or Destructive?

"Death and life are in the power of the tongue: and they that love it shall eat the fruit thereof." (Prov. 18:21)

We grow up hearing the saying, "Sticks and stones may break my bones, but words will never hurt me." That saying is not true. Words CAN hurt us! To show how powerful our words are, the Bible says that both *"Death and life are in the power of the tongue."* See, it's not always about WHAT you say, but HOW you say it that also matters.

FIRST—Are your words DESTRUCTIVE? It first says our words can promote *"Death."* Destructive words tear down. Paul said in (Eph. 4:29), *"Let no corrupt communication proceed out of your mouth..."*

Destructive words are often said in anger. They seek to damage, discredit and destroy. We are NOT to use destructive words with others because that is *"corrupt communication."*

SECOND—Are your words CONSTRUCTIVE? Next, it says our words can promote *"life."* Constructive words seek to edify the other person. The next part of (Eph. 4:29) says we are to speak words which are *"..good to the use of edifying, that it may minister grace unto the hearers."* It can be difficult when someone comes at you with harsh, angry, destructive words. That is why the Bible says our response to them should be soft, because *"A soft answer turneth away wrath: but grievous words stir up anger"* (Prov. 15:1).

Today, think about the words you use, but especially HOW you respond to others. Seek to edify your spouse, your children, and your co-workers with words that *"minister grace unto the hearers."*

The Missing Piece

"From whom the whole body fitly joined together and compacted by that which every joint supplieth..."
(Eph. 4:16)

My wife loves to put together jigsaw puzzles. I admit that I don't have enough patience to sort through thousands of tiny pieces of a puzzle until it is completed, but my wife can. She could sit there for hours, perfectly content, to meticulously assemble one piece after another until the whole picture comes together.

As satisfying as it is to finally see the puzzle completed there is nothing more frustrating than to spend all of your time finding all the right pieces, only to get down to the end and be missing a key piece to the puzzle.

It doesn't matter if the missing piece is in the middle or on the edge. Every piece is an important piece because it is part of the puzzle.

Paul said that every member of the body of Christ is important because we are *"fitly joined together."* In other words, God made you, and gifted you as you are so that you can contribute something to the body of Christ.

Just as every piece of a 1000 piece puzzle is important, so is every member of the body of Christ. Often, Satan tells us we are worthless and unimportant in the body of Christ, but nothing could be further from the truth!

Don't sell yourself short. Jesus certainly hasn't! He said you are special, you are important, and you are needed! Don't be the missing piece.

An Anchor For Your Soul

"Which hope we have as an anchor of the soul, both sure and stedfast..." (Heb. 6:19)

I am not into boating, although I enjoy riding in a boat. And I certainly am not a sailor. But I do know enough about boats and ships to know that they each need an anchor. An anchor is there for one main purpose...to steady the boat and to keep it from drifting and getting off course.

God's Word says that in this dark day in which we live, *"we have...an anchor of the soul."* And, praise God, His anchor is *"sure and stedfast."*

What is this *"anchor of the soul"* that God has given to us? It is the promise of God's immutability. In (v.17) it says, *"Wherein God, willing more abundantly to shew unto the heirs of promise the **immutability** of his counsel, confirmed it by an oath:"* Then, in (v.18) it says, *"That by two **immutable** things, in which it was **impossible for God to lie**..."* The word *"immutable"* simply means God never changes! It means that when He promises us something, it will surely come to pass. Why? Because it is *"impossible for God to lie."*

When the storms are beating on your ship and you feel like you are about to go under, just remember that God has given you *"an anchor of the soul."* You have something in your soul that is *"sure and stedfast";* something that will keep you steady in the rough waters of life.

Take some time this morning to thank Him for never changing. Thank Him for the *"anchor of the soul"* He has given to you and that, in Him, you can weather any storm!

Does God Care About My Pain?

"Behold, I go forward, but he is not there; and backward, but I cannot perceive him:" (Job 23:8)

When suffering comes into our lives, we ask ourselves questions like: "Where is God in all of this?" "Why doesn't God do something about it?" "Does He really care?"

I am sure Job asked those questions, and more, when everything he had was taken away from him. Let's learn some lessons about God, from the suffering of Job.

FIRST—God's presence is not always evident. Job was discouraged because he could not perceive God's presence in his suffering. Job said in (v.3), *"Oh that I knew where I might find him."* He felt he was all alone in his suffering. He said in Job 30:20, *"I cry unto thee, and thou dost not hear me: I stand up, and thou regardest me not."* It can be discouraging when we feel we are suffering alone, and God seems nowhere to be found.

SECOND—God is keenly aware of your suffering. Even in the midst of it all Job recognized God was there all along. In (v.10) he said, *"But he knoweth the way that I take..."* Job said, "Even though I don't know where God is, He knows exactly where I am and that is what's important."

THIRD—God is actively working on your behalf. In (v.9) Job said God was working *"On the left hand"* and *"on the right hand."* Then, he said in (v.10) *"when he hath **tried** me, I shall come forth as gold."* He knew that his suffering was a trial sent by God. He did not understand everything God was doing, or even WHY God was doing it, but what helped him was to know God was doing SOMETHING!

God hasn't forgotten about you. He knows what you are going through and He's working in the midst of it. So, don't give up! God does care and is working for your good and for His glory if you will let Him.

Alone In The Desert

"And the child grew, and waxed strong in spirit, and was in the deserts..." (Luke 1:80)

One of the most rugged and dramatic figures we read about in the New Testament is John the Baptist. There was no one else like him then and no one else like him since. There are two things which made John stand out.

FIRST—His COMMUNION with GOD. It says he *"waxed strong in spirit..."* That does not surprise us because the more time you spend with God, the stronger your spirit will become. But he also spent most of his time alone; it says he *"was in the deserts..."* It seems that a time of isolation has been the lot of every great man. Even though Jesus loved people, He, too, found it necessary to be alone at times in order to commune with the Father. (Mark 1:35) says, *"And in the morning, rising up a great while before day, he went out, and departed into a solitary place, and there prayed."* What a reminder that to be great with God, we must spend time alone with Him.

SECOND—His CONTEMPT of the WORLD. John's *dress* was different than the world's dress; he wore camel's hair. His *diet* was different than the world's; he ate locust and wild honey. His *dwelling* was different; he lived in the deserts. Everything about him showed that he rejected the things this world seems to value most. He had a contempt for this world because it was at odds with what God says is most important.

We can be great for God, too, but to do so means we must have a regular communion with God and a contempt for the things of this world.

Don't Over-Think It

"Be not wise in thine own eyes: fear the LORD, and depart from evil." (Prov. 3:7)

Here's a riddle for you. A man is walking down the road. There are no lights, no moon, and he is dressed in all black. A car drives down the same road. The car has no lights on, yet the driver swerves and misses the man at the last second. How did the driver see him?

Don't overthink it. It's simple...it happened during daylight!

God never intended for the Christian life to be complicated, but man often tries to over-think the Christian life and make it more difficult than it should be.

In our verse this morning, God makes it really simple for us. He says that living the Christian life is as simple as this: *"Be not wise in thine own eyes."* In other words, don't be so full of pride that you think YOU have all the answers. The reason many are not reading and studying the Bible daily is because they don't feel they need God's wisdom. They are *"wise in* [their] *own eyes."*

"So how do we not become wise in our own eyes," you ask? He tells is in the rest of the verse.

FIRST—Fear the Lord. To fear the Lord means to serve Him with reverence and awe. Hebrews 12:28 says it this way, *"..let us...serve God acceptably with reverence and godly fear:"* The Psalmist put it this way in Psalm 33:8, *"Let all the earth fear the LORD: let all the inhabitants of the world stand in awe of him."*

SECOND—Depart from evil. Departing from evil means to run from sin as quickly as it appears. Don't over-think the Christian life, just live in awe of God and depart from evil and you will be a success!

A Double-Minded Man

"A double minded man is unstable in all his ways."
(James 1:8)

In the verses before this, James tells us to ask God for wisdom. "Why is that important," you ask? Because *"A double minded man is unstable in all his ways."* A double-minded person is one who says they want the wisdom of God, but then goes to this person or that person to get their opinion, too.

A double-minded person is one who lacks godly wisdom. Therefore, James said in (v.5), *"If any of you lack wisdom, let him ask of God, that giveth to all men liberally, and upbraideth not; and it shall be given him."* We need wisdom so that we will not become double-minded, trusting God one minute and doubting Him the next.

The danger in being *"double-minded"* is that you become *"unstable"* in all your ways. You will have no stability in your life. Why? Because you have no solid foundation; it's constantly changing as people's opinions change.

Wisdom is being able to correctly interpret our circumstances in light of what God is trying to accomplish in our lives. Therefore, James says we need wisdom in order to interpret our circumstances properly, or else we will stay frustrated and discouraged.

Determine to get your wisdom from God, not man, so that your life will be built upon God's Word which will never let you down!

The Greatest Title In The World!

"James, a servant of God and of the Lord Jesus Christ..."
(James 1:1)

In a day where many are concerned about titles and accolades, James reminds us that one of the most important titles we hold is simply *"a **servant** of God and of the Lord Jesus Christ."* Not only did the Apostle Paul also call himself *"a servant of Jesus Christ"* (Rom.1:1), but it is even said of Jesus that He *"made himself of no reputation, and took upon him the form of a **servant**..."* (Phil. 2:7)

James could have bragged that he was an Apostle, a leader of the Church at Jerusalem, and even the brother of Jesus, but he doesn't do that. He wasn't trying to lift himself up. He wanted to lift Christ up!

You may be the CEO, or have some high position at your place of employment but remember that, first and foremost, you are *"a servant of God and of the Lord Jesus Christ."* See, you are not a plumber, or mechanic, or nurse, or (whatever your job title is) that just happens to be a Christian. Rather, you are a Christian that just happens to be a plumber, mechanic, nurse, etc.

So, let's ask ourselves this question: "How can I best serve Jesus as I go about my day, today?" Or another way to ask it is "As I go about my day, how can I best live out my life as a servant of Jesus Christ?"

A Stinky Prayer

"Then Jonah prayed unto the LORD his God out of the fish's belly, And said, I cried by reason of mine affliction unto the LORD, and he heard me; out of the belly of hell cried I, and thou heardest my voice." (Jonah 2:1-2)

It is not unusual for a man to pray, but what IS unusual is WHERE Jonah is praying. He is praying *"out of the fish's belly."* Now, I have prayed in some strange places, but I have NEVER prayed from a fish's belly...and hope I never do!

My first thought here is that God sometimes has to allow us to get into "stinky" situations in order to get our attention. Fish smell...so I have to think that a fish's belly REALLY smells! But because Jonah was living in rebellion, running from God, God had to prepare a "stinky" circumstance to get his attention. And nothing will get a man's attention like being swallowed by a fish!

The second thing I notice is that when Jonah prayed, he said, *"thou heardest my voice."* There are no circumstances too bad but what God cannot hear you when you pray. Do you know how God was able to hear Jonah's prayer, even from the bottom of a fish's stinky belly? Because God was listening for his prayer!

God had not abandoned Jonah; God was preparing Jonah. And God has not abandoned you either. The circumstances you are facing may stink, but God may be using them to humble you and get your attention back on Him.

Jonah was in some stinky circumstances, but in the midst of those circumstances it says he *"prayed unto the LORD."* Don't let your circumstances silence your prayers. God is listening for you, call out to Him, today.

202

A Reason To Rejoice

*"Let the brother of low degree rejoice in that he is exalted:
But the rich, in that he is made low..." (James 1:9-10a)*

Two different types of people are mentioned in this verse: The Poor believer (*"the brother of low degree"*) and the Rich believer. What is interesting is that both are told to rejoice because of their circumstances. Let's look at them backwards.

SECOND—The RICH are to rejoice. It is easy to imagine a rich believer rejoicing; he has riches. Anyone could rejoice if they were rich. Ah, but he isn't telling the rich man to rejoice in his riches. He says the rich man is to rejoice *"in that he is made low."* What does that mean?

The biggest temptation for the rich man is to trust in his riches. Therefore, the rich believer should rejoice when God allows circumstances into his life which bring him low because it will keep him from trusting in those riches instead of trusting in God.

FIRST—The POOR are to rejoice. It says *"the brother of low degree"* is to rejoice. "Now, preacher, I can certainly understand how the rich believer can rejoice, because after all, he is rich! It's easy to rejoice when you have everything you need, but how can the poor believer be expected to rejoice," you ask?

The poor believer may not have much money, but he should rejoice because God has given him "true" riches which cannot be taken away. Riches often bring more heartache and trouble than you realize. Therefore, *"the brother of low degree"* is to be thankful for the things he has which money cannot buy!

So, no matter which place you find yourself, today (poor or rich), if you are a child of God, you have a reason to rejoice!

Look What's Below You!

"The eternal God is thy refuge, and underneath are the everlasting arms..." (Deut. 33:27)

I remember as a child, one time my dad, my brother, and some friends went camping together. Our camp site was next to a lake and one day we went into the lake to play in the water. At the time, I wasn't a good swimmer, so my dad held on to me and led me out into water that was over my head.

What my dad was doing was more than a swimming lesson, it was a lesson in trust. Though I was afraid of the deep waters, I knew my dad loved me and would not let anything happen to me, so I held on to him as tightly as I could.

Sometimes, our circumstances can make us feel we are in over our heads. God assured us in Isaiah 46:4, *"And even to your old age...I will carry, and will deliver you."*

Rest in His promise, this morning, that even though He may sometimes lead you into deep water, He is right there with you, upholding you.

Thank God we are always safe and secure, even in the worst of circumstances because underneath us are God's *"everlasting arms"*!

Well, Look Who's Here!

"The thief cometh not, but for to steal, and to kill, and to destroy: I am come that they might have life, and that they might have it more abundantly." (John 10:10)

It is easy to watch the news or see what is going on in the world around us and say, "What is this world coming to?" The first part of our verse reminds us that Satan (*"The thief"*) has come and his only mission in this world is *"to steal, and to kill, and to destroy."* But I am glad he is not the ONLY one who has come!

I like how one preacher put it. He said, "The early Christians did not say in **dismay**, 'Look what the world has come to' but they said in **delight** 'Look what has come to the world!'" Jesus said, *"I am come!"* Praise the Lord, things started looking up when Jesus came!

Oh, dear child of God, lift up your head this morning because Jesus has come.

See, God doesn't expect **us** to clean up this world. We do not have the power to clean it up. We cannot change a sinner's heart, but we can point the sinner to the One who *can* change his heart...JESUS!

When you begin to feel discouraged with the events that are happening all around you, just remember that Jesus has come to this world and, best of all, HE'S COMING AGAIN! And He will one day take us to a "better" world; one without sin, sorrow, sickness, or Satan! Praise the Lord!

Follow, First

*"And he saith unto them, Follow me, and I will make you
fishers of men." (Matt. 4:19)*

We often focus on the last part of this verse where
Jesus says, *"I will make you fishers of men."* But before
Jesus tells them what **HE** will do, He tells them what
THEY must do, *"Follow me."* In other words, before they
could be **FISHERS**, they had to be **FOLLOWERS**.

Sadly, we are living in a day of instant gratification,
instant communication, and instant Christianity. We think
we can be godly without first spending time with Jesus. But
before the disciples could ever be successful in fishing for
men, they had to spend time following Jesus. *"Follow me,"*
Jesus said, THEN *"I will make you fishers of men."*

That same principle is true in every other area of our
lives, as well. We will never be what we should be unless
we learn to follow Jesus, first. Before you can be the
husband, father, wife, or mother you should be...you must
follow, first.

Are you single, looking for a mate? Are you seeking
the one whom you are to marry? Here is some great advice.
Stop **LOOKING** and start **FOLLOWING**! Jesus said to
these fishermen, *"Follow me."* Why? Because Jesus knew
where the *real* fish were! And Jesus knows where your
future spouse is, too! So the best way to find them is by
following Jesus, first.

What is your goal in life? What is it you are trying to
achieve? Whatever it is, if God is not at the center of it, it is
doomed to fail. So the best way to guarantee your success
in whatever you are doing is to follow, first!

You've Got A Friend In Me

"A man that hath friends must shew himself friendly..."
(Prov. 18:24)

Jesus was a friendly person. In fact, He had such a loving disposition that even children felt comfortable coming up to Him. Here are four thoughts about how to make friends and build better relationships with others.

FIRST—Accept yourself. That doesn't mean you believe that you are all you want to be or should be. It simply means that you see yourself as a worthwhile person, created by God, redeemed by God, and precious to God.

The reason peer pressure has such a strong influence in some people's lives is because they feel that they are only worth something if that other friend likes them. When you see yourself valuable, because GOD says you are, then the threat of losing a friend won't bother you.

SECOND—See the value in everyone. One reason people were attracted to Jesus was that He valued them. He did not consider any person to be unimportant. He saw every person as a special creation of God and therefore precious to Him.

THIRD—Be friendly and show God's love to everyone. Love is the foundation upon which friendships are built. Since we know God loves everyone, we should too. Our **friendliness** opens the door for our **witness**.

FOURTH—Show an interest in others. You will make more friends just by showing a genuine interest in them than you will trying to get them interested in you. By the way, this is the secret to overcoming being an introvert! If you want to get people talking, just ask them about their family, their job, or their hobbies. And if you want to get a grandparent REALLY talking, just ask them about their grandchildren!

3 Ways To Combat Criticism

"But they held their peace, and answered him not a word: for the king's commandment was, saying, Answer him not."
(Isa. 36:21)

When the king of Assyria criticized Hezekiah and Israel's ability to defend themselves, Hezekiah told the people to *"answer him not."* He knew God would vindicate Israel in the end, so the criticism didn't matter.

Instead of answering your critic, here are three ways to combat the criticism:

FIRST—Don't Let Criticism Stop You From Doing Right. Your critic would love to know they stopped you from doing right by making you stop to give them an answer. When someone criticizes you, the best answer is no answer at all! Just keep on doing right because time will vindicate you in the end.

SECOND—Take Your Criticism to the Lord. Instead of answering the king of Assyria, (Isa. 37:1) says Hezekiah *"went into the house of the LORD."* Your critic wants nothing more than to draw you into an argument or fight. Don't do it. As soon as you fight back, they win. Instead, take it to the Lord.

THIRD—Pray for Your Critic. Praying for your critic allows God to begin working in their heart. But it does more than that; it allows God to work in YOUR heart, as well. Praying for your critic is important because it will prevent bitterness from growing in your heart toward them.

Let's face it...everyone will face criticism at some point. But don't let it stop you from doing right. Take it to the Lord and let Him deal with it for you so you can keep on serving Him with a clean heart.

Timely Help For Troubled Hearts

"Let not your heart be troubled: ye believe in God, believe also in me." (John 14:1)

Just before Jesus spoke these words, the disciples had become troubled. Jesus and the disciples were sitting in the Upper Room and Jesus drops a bombshell! He tells them that one of them is a devil! Then He says that Peter would deny Him before the cock crows. And if that were not enough, Jesus then says that He is leaving them soon. So, they were full of anxiety and fear because of a **devil**, a **denier**, and now the possibility of being **deserted**! No wonder Jesus begins chapter 14 by saying to them, *"Let not your heart be troubled..."*

"How can you expect us to not be troubled," the disciples must have wondered. Sensing their struggle, Jesus says to them, *"ye believe in God."* Notice there isn't a question mark at the end of that phrase because this is not a question; it is a statement. Jesus said, "I know ye believe in God." In other words, Jesus was saying to them, "Why should your heart be troubled if you believe in God."

Jesus is asking us the same question, today. If we believe in God; if we believe there is a God Who created this whole world of ours and that same God knows and loves us; if we believe that we are His child....then what in the world should cause our hearts to be troubled?

If *"ye believe in God"* then that is enough to put your fears to rest. If *"ye believe in God"* that is enough to calm our greatest anxiety.

So, the question is: Do you believe in God? Do you trust that He knows what is best for you? If so, rest in that fact. Let the fact that God is still in control calm your weary spirit this morning. Walk in victory, today. Why? Because *"ye believe in God."*

God Has A Bush For You

"And the angel of the LORD appeared unto him in a flame of fire out of the midst of a bush...and the bush was not consumed. And Moses said, I will now turn aside, and see...why the bush is not burnt." (Exod. 3:2-3)

One of the most interesting and compelling stories in all the Old Testament is the story of Moses and the burning bush. This burning bush experience transformed Moses forever. Up until then, Moses was just a shepherd, keeping his father-in-law's flock on the backside of a desert. But, like everyone, when you encounter the presence of God your life will be forever changed!

Long before Moses **encountered** the bush, God had **planted** that bush. God wanted to meet with Moses because He had a huge plan for Moses to one day lead the Children of Israel out of bondage. But He needed to prepare Moses for such an undertaking.

God had this bush waiting for Moses but He needed to get Moses to that bush. God has a plan and purpose for you, too, but He needs to prepare you for your purpose. Before Moses could lead people, he had to learn how to lead sheep.

Before God ever put Moses in the spotlight, He prepared him alone in a desert. The desert experience was necessary in order to prepare Moses for something greater.

Think about this: God brought Moses to the desert, because that was where God was going to meet with Him! Moses saw more of God in that bush, and in that desert, than he ever saw back in the palace of Pharaoh!

If you are in your wilderness experience right now, the best way to find your purpose is to let God prepare you in your wilderness time. Stay faithful. God has a bush for you, too!

The Hardest Thing In The Christian Life

"Wait on the LORD: be of good courage, and he shall strengthen thine heart: wait, I say, on the LORD."
(Ps. 27:14)

Back when I was in school, I still remember one of my teachers saying, "Patience is a virtue that carries a lot of WAIT." That really didn't mean much when I was younger but, oh, how I understand that now as an adult! Because we live in such an "instant gratification" type of world where we expect everything immediately, it can be difficult to have patience.

One of the hardest things in the Christian life can be learning how to wait. Twice, in this short verse, the psalmist reminds us that we are to *"Wait on the Lord."* Now, I believe that carries with it two implications.

FIRST—It Means Waiting FOR the Lord. Often, we find ourselves waiting ON someone. All it takes is a trip to the doctor and you will find yourself being put into a "waiting room." Why, because you must wait ON the doctor. Sometimes God doesn't move as quickly as we think He should, but He is teaching us to wait ON Him.

SECOND—It Means Waiting UPON the Lord. When you go to a nice restaurant, you will likely be served by someone called a "waiter" or "waitress." They are there to serve you; to make sure you have what you need when you need it. Their service is not about them, it is about you. As Christians, we are to wait UPON the Lord. We are there to serve Him, making sure HIS will is done, not ours.

Changed!

"But we all, with open face beholding as in a glass the glory of the Lord, are changed into the same image from glory to glory, even as by the Spirit of the Lord."
(2 Cor. 3:18)

In this chapter, Paul reminds us that unbelievers have a *"veil"* upon their heart Verse 14 says that their minds are *"blinded."* Until they are saved, they cannot truly behold *"the glory of the Lord." "BUT,"* Paul says, *"we all"* (those of us who have been saved and have had the veil removed) CAN behold *"the glory of the Lord."*

Praise God, we can get a glimpse of His glory! How? By looking into the mirror of God's Word! Friend, if you are not in His Word, you will not behold His glory.

And notice Paul says that the purpose of *"beholding...the glory of the Lord"* is so that we might be *"changed into the same image."* Friend, the reason we read God's Word and the reason we go to church to hear God's Word taught and preached, is so that it will get inside of us and change us from the inside out! If you are not being changed by what you are reading or hearing preached, something is not right.

Every day, we are to be in the Word of God, beholding God's glory so that later the world might get a glimpse of God's glory IN US! Are you being changed into the image of Christ? You may be the only image of Christ your co-workers, or friends see.

Let them see something real!

Fake New; Fake Christians

*"Ye hypocrites, well did Esaias prophesy of you, saying,
This people draweth nigh unto me with their mouth, and
honoureth me with their lips; but their heart is far from
me." (Matt. 15:7-8)*

We hear a lot about "Fake News" today, and have all
seen the many sensational storylines which turned out to be
false. We must also constantly be on guard against email or
phone scams which are fake.

The sad fact is, we also see a lot of "Fake News" in the
church, as well. I am talking about the many hypocrites
who call themselves "Christians" yet do not live the
Christian life apart from church. They act like the most
spiritual person you ever met, while at church. But, come
Monday morning, they are as carnal as the worldly crowd
they associate with. Jesus said, *"This people draweth nigh
unto me with their mouth, and honoureth me with their lips;
but their heart is far from me."*

So, how can we tell who a REAL Christian is? It's
really pretty simple. John tells us that those who are true
blue Christians will have an "outward evidence" of their
belief. Their walk will match their talk!

*"If we say that we have fellowship with him, and walk
in darkness, we lie, and do not the truth:" (1John 1:6)*

What about you? Do you call yourself a Christian?
How would someone know that beyond hearing you talking
about it? Could a complete stranger observe you for a day
and know, based on your life, that you are a Christian?

Turn Your Frown Upside Down

"Thou hast made known to me the ways of life; thou shalt make me full of joy with thy countenance." (Acts 2:28)

The Bible has a lot to say about our countenance. The word "countenance" in the Bible refers to the expression on your face that others see when they look at you. The Bible says there is a direct link between our heart and our face. In others words, the attitude of our heart will affect the expression on our face!

We can have a **PRIDEFUL** countenance. (Ps. 10:4) *"The wicked, through **the pride of his countenance**, will not seek after God: God is not in all his thoughts."*

We can have a **SAD** countenance. (Matt. 6:16) *"Moreover when ye fast, be not, as the hypocrites, of a **sad countenance**..."*

We can have an **ANGRY** countenance. (Gen. 4:5) *"And Cain was very **wroth**, and **his countenance fell**."*

We can have a **TROUBLED** countenance. (Dan. 5:6) *"Then the king's **countenance** was changed, and **his thoughts troubled him**..."*

But we can also have a **CHEERFUL** countenance. (Prov. 15:13) *"A merry heart maketh a **cheerful countenance**..."*

The Bible also indicates that our countenance can be changed by others. We can actually sharpen the countenance of a friend. (Prov. 27:17) *"Iron sharpeneth iron; so a man **sharpeneth the countenance** of his friend."*

I believe as Christians, we should watch our countenance. Our faces should exhibit the happy, joyful heart within us. The best way to have the right countenance, is to let Jesus change it! (Psa 4:6) *"LORD, lift thou up the light of thy countenance upon us."*

Above The Clouds

"Is not God in the height of heaven? and behold the height of the stars, how high they are!" (Job 22:12)

Years ago we boarded an airplane, flying to visit a mission field. It was a dark, dreary day. As the airplane taxied down the runway, all you could see were dark clouds and rain coming down. The airplane took off and began to climb in altitude. We climbed higher and higher, then all of the sudden something surprising happened.

As I was looking out the window, I could see as we broke through the dark clouds. Almost instantly, all we saw was the sun shining above those clouds. There was no more darkness; there was no more rain. It all looked so cheery and calm. We were above it all.

I thought to myself, we are seeing our dreary day from God's viewpoint! Above the clouds everything was good. Above the clouds there was no rain. The same day that was dark and dreary to us was bright and sunny to God.

Job said, *"Is not God in the height of heaven?"* In other words, as long as God is still on His throne, everything is going to be ok! It may seem like your life is one big dark cloud. It may seem as if the sun will never shine again, but God sees a different picture. It is never dark where God is!

Just stay faithful and keep on praying. Soon, you will break through the dark clouds of your circumstances and you will see a brighter day!

You Had It Coming

*"For what glory is it, if, when ye be buffeted for your
faults, ye shall take it patiently? but if, when ye do well,
and suffer for it, ye take it patiently, this is acceptable with
God." (1Pet. 2:20)*

Someone said, "Don't tell everyone your troubles
because half the people you tell them to don't want to hear
it and the other half probably feel you had it coming!"

We know we deserve it when we receive retribution
for something bad we did. But the sad truth is, sometimes
you will forgive others, serve others, love unconditionally,
and STILL you will be done wrong! In other words,
sometimes it just doesn't seem fair.

So Peter wants to set the record straight. He says that if
a person does wrong and then suffers the consequences,
even though he or she patiently endures the punishment,
nobody applauds. But—AND DON'T MISS THIS—when
you do what is **right** and suffer for it with grace and
patience, GOD applauds! God takes notice of your patient
suffering and will reward you for enduring it when you
suffer wrongfully.

Therefore, live so that when you stand before God at
the Judgment and He rewards you for your faithfulness, He
will say, "Congratulations! You had it coming!"

What Are You Doing Here?

"And he came thither unto a cave, and lodged there; and, behold, the word of the LORD came to him, and he said unto him, What doest thou here, Elijah?" (1Kings 19:9)

One of the things I love about the Bible is that it gives us the good, the bad, and the ugly. It doesn't sugarcoat things. God shows us the best and worst of even His greatest servants. And that is important because sometimes we forget that the greatest men in all the Bible were still just men. They had faults and failures just like us,

Case in point, Elijah. God had just given Elijah one of the greatest victories ever seen up on Mount Carmel. He had just seen the miraculous happen when God sent fire down from heaven to consume his sacrifice, proving to 850 false prophets that Jehovah is the one, true, God.

Yet, as soon as Queen Jezebel heard of the demise of her false prophets, she was so angry that she sent word that she would kill Elijah. In fear, Elijah is on the run, hiding from this angry Queen. He goes into a cave to hide out. He thinks he is all alone in that cave, but he is not. God is there, too!

And God says to Elijah, *"What doest thou here, Elijah?"* In other words, God said, "What are you doing hiding out in this cave, Elijah? I didn't tell you to come here. I am Jehovah God. I am the one who called you. I am the one who just proved myself by sending fire down from the sky. Why are you hiding out in a cave from an angry Queen?"

Maybe God is asking you the same question, today. *"What doest thou, here?"* Why are you letting fear, anxiety, and worry, determine your course of action? Maybe you are even running from God (like that's even possible). *"What doest thou, here?"*

Sweet Meditation

"My meditation of him shall be sweet..." (Ps. 104:34)

In this busy, non-stop, hectic culture in which we live, Bible meditation has become a lost art. The average Christian, if they read the Bible at all, doesn't take the time to digest what they have read. Yet, they wonder why they are not strong, spiritually.

The Psalmist said, *"O how love I thy law! it is my **meditation** all the day" (Ps. 119:97).*

It is not in the honey bee's touching of the flowers that produces the honey, but in its abiding for a time on the flowers and drawing out their sweetness that is vital. Likewise, in order to digest the real sweetness of God's Word often requires meditating upon it.

Someone said, "If I had only three minutes for a devotional time, I would spend one minute reading the Bible and two minutes meditating on what I had read."

Today, more people are struggling depression, anxiety and thoughts of suicide in record numbers. It is evident that what we think about and meditate on affects our mental health and stability. God knew this when He told us to meditate on His Word.

If Bible meditation is new to you, I wrote a book called *The Power of Meditating On Scripture* that will help you get started. It will teach you, step-by-step how to meditate on Scripture. You can get it on Amazon.com.

When Chickens Come Home To Roost

"Whoso diggeth a pit shall fall therein: and he that rolleth a stone, it will return upon him." (Prov. 26:27)

Solomon gives us a principle here that is reiterated throughout the Bible and that principle is you will reap what you sow. King David said it this way in Psalm 7:16, *"His mischief shall return upon his own head, and his violent dealing shall come down upon his own pate."* But this principle is most clearly given by Paul in Galatians 6:7 where he wrote, *"Be not deceived; God is not mocked: for whatsoever a man soweth, that shall he also reap."*

You are either in the **sowing** stage or the **reaping** stage. Therefore, think about what kind of harvest you want to reap and sow to that end. If you want to reap the right kind of harvest, you must sow the right kind of seed.

Think about what kind of **ADULT** you want your child to become and begin sowing those character traits in them while they are still young. What kind of Christian will your child be based on what you are sowing in their lives today?

Think about what kind of **MARRIAGE** you want to have and begin sowing to that end, right now. Don't wait until your marriage is in trouble to seek help. Sow the right kind of marriage so you will reap the right kind of marriage.

Think about what kind of **REWARDS** you want to receive at the Judgment, and sow to that end. As long as you have breath, you can still sow more for Jesus Christ.

Your chickens will eventually come home to roost. Make sure you are sowing the right things, today, so that you will reap the right harvest in the end.

Who's In The Cockpit?

"The steps of a good man are ordered by the LORD: and he delighteth in his way. Though he fall, he shall not be utterly cast down: for the LORD upholdeth him with his hand." (Ps. 37:23-24)

Have you ever experienced turbulence while flying on an airplane? Turbulence is basically instability in the air around a plane caused by winds and air pressure. It can make any passenger feel nervous when the airplane hits turbulence.

Years ago my wife and I were flying back from a conference in Texas. We were on a smaller plane when, all of the sudden, we hit turbulence. That little plane vibrated as if it was hitting speed bumps in the air. It is enough to make your heart skip a beat.

It wasn't until later I learned that it is an extremely rare thing for an airplane to crash as a result of turbulence. In fact, I learned that airplanes are designed to withstand most any turbulence they encounter. The flight crew knows this, too. That is why, even when turbulence seems bad to us, the flight crew continues to serve food as if nothing is wrong. They are used to it.

The pilot isn't worried over turbulence, either. He has the knowledge and wisdom to guide the plane safely to its destination. One reason the flight crew doesn't get nervous during turbulence is because they trust the pilot.

What a spiritual lesson for us as well. At some point or another, we will hit turbulence in our lives. Circumstances will shake our world up! But in the midst of it all we can have peace in our soul when we know Jesus is our pilot and He is always in control. If Jesus is in the cockpit, there's no need to fear. Turbulence is nothing to Him. After all, the winds obey His will!

You're Not Thinking Right

"The thoughts of the righteous are right: but the counsels of the wicked are deceit." (Prov. 12:5)

The Bible has a lot to say about your mind and what you think. What you think about will eventually control you. That is why Satan battles for control of our minds constantly. He knows that if he can defeat us mentally, he has us!

Our mind is where we struggle with fear, anxiety, worry, lust, anger, and bitterness. That is why Paul gives us a whole list of things to think about that will prevent Satan from getting a foothold in our mind (Phil. 4:8).

Out text verse says, *"The thoughts of the righteous are right."* To have the right thought life, you must first be righteous. In other words, it means living right. If you are not living right, if you have sin in your life, your thought life will be all messed up. Your thought life will never be right when it is guided by your flesh instead of by the Holy Spirit.

If you think you are a worthless person with no value to God....you're not thinking right.

If you think your sin is too bad to ever be forgiven...you're not thinking right.

If you think that God cannot use you because of past mistakes...you're not thinking right.

If you think that it is too late to start over with God...you're not thinking right.

Satan wants to fill your mind with all kinds of thoughts of fear and doubt about God. But God loves you. He has always loved you and He will never *stop* loving you! So, stop giving Satan rental space in your head. Evict him, today!

Now (Part 1)

"..behold, now is the accepted time; behold, now is the day of salvation." (2Cor. 6:2)

It may be hard to believe, but in that little word "now" lies one of the deepest secrets of the Christian life. We know that sinners are encouraged to come to Jesus for salvation, "now." Don't delay another moment.

But I believe there is another great truth hidden in this word "now." This morning, we will look at the first truth.

FIRST—"now" means that the abundant Christian life is not lived in the PAST. Many believers cannot move forward, spiritually, because they cannot get past their past. They can't seem to break free from past sins they have committed, even though those sins have been forgiven.

Just as we cannot allow past sins (which have been forgiven) to hold us back, we cannot live on past victories, either. The exhortation is not "THEN WAS the day of salvation," but rather "NOW is the day of salvation." The victorious Christian life is to be lived, not in the past, but right now!

If Satan can get you constantly focused on your past, it will defeat you "now." So, whatever sin or failure may be in your past, leave it there...in the past. Ask the Lord for grace to live for Him, right "now," moment by moment.

Now (Part 2)

"..behold, now is the accepted time; behold, now is the day of salvation." (2Cor. 6:2)

Yesterday, we saw that one meaning of *"now"* means that the abundant, Christian life is not lived in the PAST.

SECOND—*"now"* means that we do not live in the FUTURE. Yes, we will be in our glorified bodies one day. Yes, we will have a mansion in Heaven one day. While we do not know all God has waiting for us one day, but we do know something right *"now"*... 1John 3:2 says, *"Beloved, now are we the sons of God..."* That is who we are right *"now,"* praise the Lord!

THIRDLY—*"now"* means we are to live the abundant Christian life in this very moment! We can get so fixated on the past or on the future that we forget to abide in Christ right *"now."* Paul said, *"Behold, now is the day of salvation."*

Yes, Jesus saved me when I trusted in Him as my Lord and Savior, but Jesus also saves me right *"now"*! In other words, Jesus is to me, right *"now,"* at this very moment, all that the Father gave Him to be!

Aren't you thankful you don't have to wait until you get to Heaven to have the peace, and grace, and mercy Jesus has for you. No, my friend, if you will walk with Him and abide in Him you can have it right *"now."*

From Your Heart To Your Lips

"Brethren, my heart's desire and prayer to God for Israel is, that they might be saved." (Rom. 10:1)

Paul said that his *"heart's desire"* was that Israel *"might be saved."* That is what burdened him. That was what weighed heavily on him. What do you do when you find yourself burdened down with a heavy burden on your heart? We know what Paul did...he prayed!

He said, *"my heart's desire and **prayer to God**..."* Paul turned his desire into a prayer, He turned his burden into a prayer. He took the very thing which was overwhelming him and turned it into a prayer to God. Paul could not save Israel, but he knew God could!

We will all face difficulties and trials in our lives. But God wants us to take our desires, our burdens, and our anxieties, and turn them into prayers. Paul decided the best way to handle the burden he was bearing was to get it from his heart to his lips.

The best Christians are not those who have no burdens, but rather those who have learned how to turn their burdens into prayers. Paul turned his *"heart's desire"* into a *"prayer to God."* What about Jesus? When He was in the Garden of Gethsemane and was facing His crucifixion, the toughest part of His earthly life, what did He do? He prayed! If Jesus, who was God in the flesh, felt the need to pray, how about us? How much more should WE see the importance of taking our burdens to the Lord in prayer?

How often are we guilty of taking our burdens to everyone else except the Lord? I saw a quote on Facebook that said, "Have you prayed about it as much as you have talked about it?" What a convicting thought.

Whatever your burden is, turn that *"heart's desire"* into a *"prayer to God."*

God Wants Your Weakness

"And he said unto me...my strength is made perfect in weakness. Most gladly therefore will I rather glory in my infirmities..." (2Corinthians 12:9)

Too often, we make the excuse that we aren't strong enough to do what God has asked us to do. I have seen men, whom God was calling to preach, run from that call because they didn't feel they could be a good enough speaker.

Maybe God has asked you to do something for Him and you are using the same excuse. If that is the excuse you are making, think about this...what if God is asking you to serve Him out of your WEAKNESS, not out of your STRENGTH?

God can use your strengths, to be sure, but more often than not, God seems to choose to use our weaknesses rather than our strengths.

*"But God hath chosen the **foolish** things of the world to confound the wise; and God hath chosen the **weak** things of the world to confound the things which are mighty;" (1Cor. 1:27)*

When was the last time you realized that God has a plan for your weaknesses? That can be an uncomfortable thought, can't it? We would rather build God's kingdom through our gifts, not our gaffs. We'd prefer to serve our Savior from our savvy, not our shortcomings.

Yet, it is through our weaknesses that we are reminded how much we must depend upon Him. It is also while serving though our weaknesses that God's grace is ever more real to us.

What Are You Leaving Behind?

"A good man leaveth an inheritance to his children's children..." (Prov. 13:22)

Often, when we think of the word *"inheritance"* we think of money. So, when we think of leaving an inheritance to our children and grandchildren, we think of leaving them money. But an inheritance can mean much more than money.

My grandparents and my parents have given to me something money cannot buy...a godly heritage! One set of grandparents lived in the city and owned businesses, while my other grandparents lived and worked on a farm. Both sets of my grandparents were very different in the way they lived but they had one thing in common...they both loved and served the Lord.

As parents, we naturally want what is best for our children. We work and work and work, hoping to provide for them financially, and that is good. But too many parents end up providing **material** things but not **spiritual** things for them. We teach our children how to be good ball players, or successful business men and women, but we fail to give them the thing they need most...a godly heritage. As a result, they may end up becoming a **good** man or woman, but not a **godly** man or woman.

When you are dead and gone, what will your children and grandchildren remember about you? Will they remember all the things you missed because you were always working to make an extra dollar? Or will they remember family altars and serving the Lord together at church?

Every day, you and I are building our children's inheritance by the way we live. So, what are YOU leaving behind?

Out Of Order

"Let all things be done decently and in order."
(1Cor. 14:40)

When writing to the church at Corinth, Paul told them that everything in the church ought be done *"decently and in order."* Why? Because *"God is not the author of confusion..."* (1Cor. 14:33). So, we know that the church should have an order to it. But what about our personal lives?

If the church should be a place of order, because God is in control there, shouldn't our personal lives also reflect order since God is supposed to be in control of us?

Now, I understand that some people can become OCD about things and some things can be taken too far, but the average Christian isn't usually guilty of having their lives TOO orderly, but rather not orderly enough. And I am not just talking spiritually, either.

You would be surprised how many people struggle week after week with just getting to church on time. Now, I know that emergencies can happen in anyone's life. Anything from unexpected traffic, to the baby getting sick at the last minute can make even the most organized person late. But I am not talking about rare emergencies. I am talking about those whose daily life seems to be so unorganized that they are always late and unprepared for things.

In one church I pastored, we had a young couple with only one child who could never seem to get to church on time. Yet, we also had another couple with four children who usually got there early!

Just like God's church, our lives should also reflect order. If this devotion hits home with you, tomorrow I will give you some practical tips that will help you.

4 Tips To Organizing Your Life

"Let all things be done decently and in order."
(1Cor. 14:40)

Yesterday, we saw that, because God is a God of order, our lives should reflect order, too. Here are some tips that can help you stay organized and reduce stress.

TIP #1: Assess how long it takes you to drive to church (or wherever you are going). If I am going somewhere I don't *normally* go, I will look it up on my GPS the night before so I have an idea of what time I will need to leave in order to be there on time.

TIP #2: Realistically assess how long it takes to get yourself ready. Most unorganized people underestimate the time it takes to do things, therefore they are always late. If you are constantly 15 minutes late, begin getting ready 15 minutes earlier than normal, the next time.

TIP #3: Save yourself time and stress in the morning by preparing everything the night before. Preparing your family's Sunday clothes on Saturday night will help ensure you don't waste time on Sunday morning trying to decide what to wear and getting it ready.

TIP #4: Invest time in training your children to help with cleaning chores. Most moms stay tired and stressed out because they can never keep their house clean. If you have children, teach THEM to pick up after themselves. One mom said her philosophy was:

- *If you can take it out, you can put it away.*
- *If you can open it, you can close it.*
- *If you can turn it on, you can turn it off.*

Even a toddler can be trained to put toys away. A great way to teach them is by making it a fun game that you play along with them until they can do it by themselves. The time you invest at first, will pay off great dividends later.

228

Forget The Fancy Words

"But when ye pray, use not vain repetitions, as the heathen do: for they think that they shall be heard for their much speaking." (Matt. 6:7)

Do you know someone that when they are called on in church to pray, they can pray the most beautiful prayers? It seems there are some who always seem to have the right words when it comes to public prayers. Then, there are others who are terrified to pray in public because they do not feel they say all the right words.

There have been times when I was in such a deep, dark, place that I wasn't even sure HOW to pray. If you had been listening to my words, you would have probably not even heard a coherent thought coming out of my mouth because my heart was so broken.

If you are one of those people who feel you don't pray beautifully-worded prayers, then let me say this to you...forget the fancy words! You can't impress God with fancy words, anyway.

Think about it. When your child, or grandchild, comes to you asking you for something, you aren't critiquing the words they use. You are interested in THEM, not how eloquently they are communicating with you.

God loves YOU, not the fancy words you use when praying. Stop trying to impress God, or others, when you pray and simply talk to Him from your heart. It is your heart, not your fancy words that gets God's attention.

Come Apart Before You Come Apart

"And he said unto them, Come ye yourselves apart into a desert place, and rest a while: for there were many coming and going, and they had no leisure so much as to eat."
(Mark 6:31)

I have heard preachers who bragged about the fact that they never took a vacation, as if it was a sin for them to take some time apart from the ministry to rest. Compound that with the 24/7 fast-past world we live in where, if you do rest, you feel as if the world passes you by.

So, true rest has become a lost art in our culture. If anyone knew what it was like to be busy, it was Jesus. But it was also Jesus who said to His disciples, *"Come ye yourselves apart into a desert place, and rest a while..."*

Some REST When They Should Be WORKING. We see it in every church. 80% of the work is done by only 20% of the members. You visit the average church and you will find that the majority of work is done by the same, dedicated, faithful few. 20% of the people are *working* while the other 80% are *watching*.

Some WORK When They Should Be RESTING. There is nothing spiritual about never taking a rest. In fact, I believe the opposite is true. The longer you work without a physical and spiritual rest, the more you open yourself up to temptation by Satan. Remember, it was after Jesus had fasted 40 days, and was weak, physically, that Satan came to tempt Him.

Don't rest when you should be working, but also learn that there needs to be times of rest. You must learn to rest so that you will be more effective for Christ when you ARE working.

So, take some time to come apart before you come apart!

How Effective Is Your Word?

"By faith Noah, being warned of God of things not seen as yet, moved with fear, prepared an ark to the saving of his house..." (Heb. 11:7)

Both Noah and Lot lived just before a terrible judgment fell from God. Noah was preparing for a flood and Lot was preparing for God's judgment to fall on Sodom and Gomorrah, where he and his family lived. Two different men facing two different judgments with two different outcomes.

When NOAH spoke, his family MOVED. Noah's family was saved from the flood because they heeded their father's word. Noah was warning them about something they had never even heard of before...water falling from the sky. Yet, Noah's word carried weight with them. Why? The Bible says Noah *"moved with fear."* Because his family saw HIM obeying God's Word, THEY obeyed Noah's word.

When LOT spoke, his family LAUGHED. What a different reaction Lot received than Noah did. But Lot set himself up for failure from the beginning. The Bible says that Lot *"lifted up his eyes, and beheld all the plain of Jordan, that it was well watered every where, before the LORD destroyed Sodom and Gomorrah...Then Lot chose him all the plain of Jordan..."* (Gen. 13:10-11).

Lot lived by gratifying his fleshy desires. Therefore, his family learned to do the same thing. Therefore, Lot's word of warning meant nothing to them.

What kind of an impact are *you* having on *your* family? How effective is *your* word as a parent? Our children and grandchildren are watching us. May we be the example before them we need to be. May they see US obeying God's Word so that THEY will obey it, too!

Just Enough To Get By

*"And whatsoever ye do, do it heartily, as to the Lord, and
not unto men;" (Col. 3:23)*

I was in a church, once, and they were having some
serious issues with the sound system. Some days it would
work fine, then all of the sudden in the middle of a service
it would just go haywire. We began to investigate, and to
our surprise, we found that it looked as if a 5-year-old had
wired it together! There were wires going everywhere and
many were only loosely connected. It was evident that
whoever installed that sound system did just enough to get
by.

How many of us do the same thing in our spiritual
lives—cutting corners because no one is watching? We
think we can cut corners in our daily walk with God. We
think we can cut corners in our church attendance.
Basically, we think it is okay to do just enough to get by.
What we forget is that even when others aren't watching,
the Lord is.

Too many Christians, today, do just enough to get by.
That is why our churches are filled with mediocre
Christians. The Bible says that whatever we do, we should
do it *"heartily, as to the Lord."*

When you have your daily devotional time, is your
heart in it? When you go to church, is your heart in it?
When you teach Sunday School, sing in the choir, clean the
church, keep the nursery, is your heart in it? Or are you
doing just enough to get by?

Something to think about.

A Walking Advertisement

"Ye adulterers and adulteresses, know ye not that the friendship of the world is enmity with God? whosoever therefore will be a friend of the world is the enemy of God." (James 4:4)

Years ago, in a church I attended, there was a blind man who had been a member there before I came. They said that even though he was blind he carried his Bible with him everywhere he went. Finally, out of sheer curiosity, someone asked him, "If you cannot see, then why do you carry your Bible around with you?" With a smile on his face, he replied, "Because it's good advertisement. It lets people know whose side I'm on!"

Did you know that every day, everywhere you go, you are a walking advertisement? That's right! You are either an advertisement for the world, or for God.

By the way you live each day, would others say you look and act like a friend of the world, or do you look and act more like a friend of God? There is an unseen battle raging, and we must choose a side. Remaining neutral is not an option in this war.

As followers of Christ, it should be evident in our daily choices whose side we are on. Are you a walking advertisement for God at work? Do those you work with know, without any doubt, whose side you are on? Are you a walking advertisement for God at your school? What about around your closest friends?

You are an advertisement one way or another. By your life you either represent the Lord or your own fleshly desires. So, the question today is who are you a walking advertisement for?

Drifting Away

"Therefore we ought to give the more earnest heed to the things which we have heard, lest at any time we should let them slip." (Heb. 2:1)

The story is told of the English explorer, Edward Parry and his crew, who were exploring the Arctic Ocean. They needed to travel north to continue their exploration, so they determined their location by the stars and began their dangerous journey.

After many hours of walking, they stopped, exhausted. While they were resting, they decided to get their bearing to determine how far they had traveled. When they did, they made a horrifying discovery. They found that they were now further south than when they first started! "How could that have happened? How is that even possible?" they asked themselves. What they discovered was they had been walking on an ice floe (a sheet of floating ice) that was traveling faster south than they were walking north.

No wonder the writer of Hebrews gives us the warning to *"give the more earnest heed to the things which we have heard, lest at any time we should let them slip."* See, we can read the Bible, pray, and even attend church faithfully, and still let our lives slip, spiritually. How? By not taking *"heed to the things which we have heard."*

Just SEEING a Stop sign doesn't prevent a car crash. It is only when you HEED the Stop sign that you prevent crashing into another car coming the opposite direction.

Likewise, in order to keep our lives from slipping, spiritually, we must not only READ but HEED what God's Word tells us. Otherwise, we will find that our lives drifted further than we ever expected.

Where's The Fruit?

*"He that abideth in me, and I in him, the same bringeth
forth much fruit:" (John 15:5)*

Clara Peller was a manicurist who, at the age of 81,
was hired to be in a commercial and ended up having her
short, three-word speaking part become one of the most
iconic phrases of all time! It was a 1984 commercial
launched by the fast-food chain Wendy's.

The commercial portrayed a fictional fast-food
competitor called "Big Bun," where three elderly ladies are
served an enormous hamburger bun containing a tiny little
hamburger patty. While two of the women are commenting
on the size of the bun, they are interrupted by 81 year
Peller, who looks down at the tiny burger and yells out,
"Where's the beef?"

The phrase became a part of American pop culture.
After that commercial aired, people everywhere were
saying, "Where's the beef?" When something didn't seem
to live up to the hype, or when a person didn't get what
they were expecting, they would say, "Where's the beef?"

I wonder if many times God doesn't look down at our
lives and say, "Where's the fruit?" Where is the evidence
of a Spirit-filled, daily walk with God? We say we have
been saved. We say that the Holy Spirit lives within us, but
where's the fruit?

So, what's the answer? Jesus said, *"He that abideth in
me, and I in him, the same bringeth forth much fruit:"* The
secret to bearing fruit is to abide in Christ.

Where's the beef? I don't know. But I know where the
fruit is; it is in the life of a believer who is walking in
fellowship with Jesus!

Afraid Of God

"For I know the thoughts that I think toward you, saith the LORD, thoughts of peace, and not of evil, to give you an expected end." (Jer. 29:11)

Do you know what is keeping many people from completely surrendering to God? FEAR! But it's not just fear of man; they are afraid of GOD! Satan has caused them to view God as a threat to their plans, rather than the fulfiller of their dreams. They have their life all planned out and they are afraid God is going to mess things up.

Well, let's get one thing clear right up front. If our future plans do not include serving the Lord, and living in a way the glorifies Him, then our plans SHOULD be messed up! Why should God bless anyone's plans that would ultimately lead them away from Him?

But there is no reason to fear God. The Bible teaches that God only wants the best for us, if we will trust Him.

FIRST—God said, *"For I know the thoughts that I think toward you..."* What a blessing to know He is thinking of us! And God's thoughts of us are *"thoughts of peace, and not of evil."* When you begin thinking God is out to get you, that thought is from Satan, not God.

SECOND—God said, *"..I know the thoughts that I think toward you...to give you an expected end."* When we live in trust and obedience to the Lord, we can be confident of an *"expected end."* We can expect to be blessed because that is what God has promised to those who live for Him.

Fear does not come from God, it comes from Satan. Don't fear God. Rest assured that if God were to change your plans, HIS PLANS would be far better than yours could have ever been, anyway!

Weighed In An Even Balance

"Let me be weighed in an even balance, that God may know mine integrity." (Job 31:6)

In the Bible, a balance refers to a pair of scales used for weighing commodities or goods. It was a system of measurement. Often, dishonest business men would use a "false" balance in order to charge their customer a higher price without them knowing it. Therefore, the Bible condemns a false balance.

"A false balance is abomination to the LORD: but a just weight is his delight." (Prov. 11:1)

Job was an honest man, and to prove his integrity he said to God, *"Let me be weighed in an even balance."* He wasn't afraid for God to judge him. He said, "I am being falsely accused by man, so God, I want YOU to judge my heart because I know you judge righteously. You know my integrity."

We sometimes forget that God already knows everything about us. He does judge us rightly because things we may hide from others are clearly seen by Him!

If you are living in sin, it should frighten you to know that God sees everything. But if you are living right, it should comfort you to know He sees it all. Others may falsely accuse your motives, but God sees your heart. He knows your integrity.

Just keep on doing right, knowing you are being weighed in an even balance!

A 100 Million Dollar Water Bill!

"Who gave himself for us, that he might redeem us from all iniquity..." (Titus 2:14)

It is not unusual to open your utility bill, only to find it higher than you expected it to be. But *The News & Observer* reported that Kieran Healy, of Hillsborough, North Carolina, received a water bill that would give a person a heart attack! The statement said that he owed 100 million dollars! Yes, you read that right. It seems there was a mistake made from an outside company which sends out payment reminder emails. Jokingly, Mr. Healy asked if he could make installment payments.

Could you imagine receiving such a bill, only to find out you really did owe that much? There would be no possible way to pay back that large of a bill.

Well, the Bible says that man owes an even LARGER debt...the debt of SIN! And no amount of money or good works will ever pay it off. Thankfully Jesus came and bore our sin on the cross and, as a result, He paid our sin debt in full! The Bible says He *"gave himself for us, that he might redeem us from **all** iniquity..."*

There will not be one person in heaven who can brag that they got there on their own. No one will boast of paying for their own sins. But for all eternity, the saints of every age will worship and glorify Jesus Christ alone for His death, burial, and resurrection which secured our eternal life!

Don't wait until you get to heaven. Take some time this morning to thank Him and praise Him for paying your sin debt in full.

Your Church Needs You

"..thou art Peter, and upon this rock I will build my church..." (Matt. 16:18)

Throughout the New Testament, the Bible emphasizes the importance of the local church. The church was started by Jesus and He is the builder of it. He said, *"I will build my church."* Now, He wasn't speaking of building a church out of wood or mortar. The building materials God uses to build His church are people...those who have been saved!

Satan constantly tries to diminish the importance of the church, but God thinks it is important. In fact, He said that it was so important to Him that He died for the church (Eph. 5:25)!

So if the church is important, AND the materials God uses to build His church are His children...that means YOU are important to the church. Your church needs you.

Your Church Needs You PHYSICALLY. A home without people living in it is not really a home; it is only a house. Likewise, a church without people is only a building. It is not the building that is the church. The PEOPLE are the church. The people can meet outside the building and still be the church. You can have church without a building, a piano, a sound system, pews, or even electricity. But you CANNOT have a church without people! So, your church needs you every time the doors are open.

Your Church Needs You SPIRITUALLY. There are churches that are alive, and churches that are dead. Since the church is made up of people, the atmosphere of a church is also determined by the people. Your church needs you to be spiritually alive when you go to church. It is up to YOU to help set the spiritual temperature in your church.

A Chorus From A Cave

"My heart is fixed, O God, my heart is fixed: I will sing and give praise." (Ps. 57:7)

When David penned this verse, it was during a very dark time in his life. He had already been anointed by God as the future king of Israel. He had been faithfully serving King Saul, but for his obedience, David had only received persecution and death threats from the king. David was on the run for his life and was hiding out in a cave.

Not only was David having to hide out from the king, but this anointed (but not-yet-appointed) king was leading a very discouraging group of men. 1 Samuel 22 describes them as being in *distress*, in *debt*, and very *discontented*. Not exactly the victorious, encouraging kind of people you hope to have with you during one of the darkest times of your life.

David was in a dilemma, and maybe you have been there, too. God's promises and David's circumstances were at odds. What God had promised and what David was facing were two completely different perspectives. Yet even when things didn't seem to be turning out the way God had promised, David found a way to *"sing and give praise."*

David was able to sing a chorus from a cave by allowing what he KNEW to be true about God steady him when he didn't SEE what God was doing. God had promised him a throne but all he saw was a cold cave. Yet he said, *"My heart is fixed."* In other words, he refused to let his circumstances direct his heart.

We have the same choice to make. Will we see this dark time as the birth of something new or the death of what we thought should be? Fix your heart upon God and then you can sing a chorus from your cave!

Blue Angels

"Then said Jesus unto his disciples, If any man will come after me, let him deny himself, and take up his cross, and follow me." (Matt. 16:24)

When I pastored in Florida, we took our boys one day to see *The Blue Angels*, the United States Navy's flight demonstration squadron. Watching their fighter jets screaming through the sky—flying in formation so close together they appear to be one, is impressive to say the least. As we watched the jets flying their tight formations, I thought to myself: How can they fly so close together and not lose control?

The answer is: they all follow the leader. All of the wing pilots must trust that the lead pilot is traveling at precisely the correct speed and trajectory. The wing pilots must surrender their will to lead and go their own way. If they are going to be successful, they must follow the leader.

The same is true, spiritually. Just as Christ is our leader, He has given us other spiritual leaders in our lives we are to follow. He has given children parents whom they are to follow as their spiritual leaders. He has given a husband as the spiritual leader the wife and children are to follow. He has given the church a pastor as the spiritual leader they are to follow.

Just like *The Blue Angels*, when we follow the spiritual leaders God has put in our lives (as they follow Christ), our lives will appear with Christ as one. Then others won't see us, they'll see Him!

Living Above It All

"If ye then be risen with Christ, seek those things which are above...Set your affection on things above, not on things on the earth." (Col. 3:1-2)

God never intended for us to live a life with our affections on this earth. He wants us to live a life that is above this old world. Paul says four things about our lives:

First—The TRANSFORMATION of our life. (v.1a) *"If ye then be risen with Christ."* You will never live the life God intended for you until you have first been saved *("risen with Christ.")*. Salvation is the first step.

Second—The DIRECTION of our life. (v.1b) *"seek those things which are above..."* The difference between a believer and an unbeliever is a believer seeks *"things which are above."* So, which direction is YOUR life headed? Are you living for the things of this world or are you seeking *"those things which are above..."*?

Third—The AFFECTION of our life. (v.2) *"Set your affection on things above..."* The word *"Set"* means it is an action on our part. It is our responsibility. What captivates YOUR affection more, earthly or heavenly things? It is only when believers focus on the realities of heaven that they can then truly enjoy the world their heavenly Father has created.

Fourth—The PROTECTION of our life. (v.3) *"For ye are dead, and your life is hid with Christ in God."* Notice it says, *"ye are dead."* We are to be dead to the direction and affection of this world. Why? Because our life is to be *"hid with Christ in God."* When we are *"hid with Christ in God"* that is where our focus will be; that is where our affection will be; that is where our attention will be.

242

When Something Bad Becomes Something Good

"It is good for me that I have been afflicted; that I might learn thy statutes." (Ps. 119:71)

It is hard to believe, but sometimes something bad can become something good in our lives. When David sinned against God, God brought affliction into his life... something bad. But David, realizing that his affliction was God's way of getting his attention, said, *"It is **good** for me that I have been afflicted;"* In fact, just a few verses earlier, David said, *"Before I was afflicted I went astray: but now have I kept thy word."*

No one likes affliction, but God often uses it to bring us back to where we should be. Often, it is only after trouble has come into our lives that God gets the most glory. As Spurgeon once said, *"We should never know the music of the harp if the strings were left untouched; nor enjoy the juice of the grape if it were not trodden in the winepress."*

Any painter will tell you that there must be shadows in a picture in order to bring out the light. Likewise, it is often the dark times and difficult trials that highlight the good grace and mercy of our Lord. Maybe you are experiencing a dark time in your life right now. Here are two things you can do:

FIRST—Make sure the affliction is not God's way of dealing with sin in your life. If there is sin in your life, confess it and repent.

SECOND—If there is no unconfessed sin in your life, ask God to help you trust Him in this trial so that He will be glorified. When God gets the glory from our trials, then something bad has become something good!

Pushing Your Panic Button

"And he was in the hinder part of the ship, asleep on a pillow: and they awake him, and say unto him, Master, carest thou not that we perish?" (Mark 4:38)

Have you ever encountered a situation that sent you into pure panic mode? Years ago, when our boys were little, we took them to an Atlanta Braves game. As we were making our way through the turnstile, we noticed that our oldest son had gotten separated from us. He had not come through with us and, because of the large crowd, we could not even see him!

My heart sank! I could only imagine that someone had taken him. I immediately jumped back over the turnstile and fought my way through the thick crowd of people, yelling his name. After a moment, I saw him. He was scared and crying, thinking we had left him. When I realized my son wasn't with us, my heart went into panic overdrive!

I can imagine that was what happened when these disciples were caught in the middle of a storm. There was thunder and lightning and the waves were crashing in on them filling the boat up with water. And to make matters worse, they looked back and Jesus was asleep. Time to hit the panic button!

Jesus was in the same circumstances they were in. The verse before this says the boat was about full of water which means Jesus was also surrounded by the water in the boat. Yet, He slept. How? Because God is never in a panic.

You and I do not have control over our circumstances, but God does! When Jesus spoke, the wind and waves ceased. What we need in our storm isn't a panic button. What we need is a word from the Lord. Before you panic, go to God and let His Word bring you peace.

244

A $10,000 Sinner

"Jesus saith unto them, Verily I say unto you, That the publicans and the harlots go into the kingdom of God before you." (Matt. 21:31)

The Bible says that when Jesus sat down to eat in the home of a Pharisee named Simon, a woman who was a harlot came in with an alabaster box filled with fragrant oil. She stood at the feet of Jesus weeping and began washing His feet with her tears and anointing them with her oil. This "woman of the night" had obviously repented of her sin because she sought Jesus out. It is very possible that the oil she was anointing His feet with were oils she may have used in her "former" sinful life. She would have no more need for these oils because she had given that life up.

Nearby sat Simon the Pharisee. In his heart he judges this woman's motives, knowing the life she had lived. So Jesus spoke up and told the story of two debtors. One debtor owed 500 denari and one owed 50. Neither could pay their creditor, yet he forgave them both.

Jesus was saying, "Simon, these two debtors are you and this woman. You see her as a $100,000 sinner, but you only see yourself as a $10,000 sinner. Her sin may be an outward sin of **passion**, but yours is an inward sin of **pride**, and neither of you can pay the debt you owe to God."

The lesson for us is this: Whether you see yourself as a $100,000 sinner or only a $10,000 sinner, all of us have a debt we cannot pay. But the good news is that Jesus died to pay for ALL of our sin debt, no matter how big it is! All that is required is recognizing, as this woman did, that you ARE a sinner and are in need of forgiveness.

Call out to God in prayer. Repent of your sin and walk in His forgiveness.

Coming Down From The Mountain

"..they came down from the mountain..." (Matt. 17:9)

The disciples has just been invited to witness one of the most spectacular sights recorded in all the Bible! They personally witnessed the transfiguration of Jesus Christ. Not only that, but they also witnessed the appearance of Moses and Elijah who stood with Jesus and spoke to him.

This scene had to have been the most exciting thing they had ever witnessed. No doubt it was easy for the disciples to shout while they were up on the mount of transfiguration. But then (v.9) says *"they came down from the mountain"* and almost immediately they encountered the devil at work.

I don't know about you but I love mountain-top experiences. I love it when God leads us up high in a church service and we experience His presence in a real way. And part of me wishes I could live up on the mountain and bask in that spiritual high every day. But that is not God's way. We cannot always live on an emotional high.

The danger in constantly seeking an emotional high is that you will go from place to place, following after this preacher or that preacher, never really being satisfied.

You see, God doesn't give us mountain-top experiences to LIVE ON, but to LEARN FROM. The disciples were to take their VISION from the mountain back down into the VALLEY.

We all love the mountain-top, but reality is...at some point (just like the disciples), we have to come *"down from the mountain."* Thank God he gives us times up on the mountain, but the test of true Christianity is not how long we SHOUT up on the mountain, but how much we SHINE down in the valley!

3 Ways To Handle Your Troubles

"For the enemy hath persecuted my soul; he hath smitten my life down to the ground; he hath made me to dwell in darkness, as those that have been long dead. Therefore is my spirit overwhelmed within me; my heart within me is desolate." (Ps. 143:3-4)

Let's face it, we all face times of trouble and temptation. What can we do when it comes?

First—FLEE It. The first thing we should do when trouble comes is to get away from it if possible. Even David said, *"O LORD...I flee unto thee to hide me" (v.9).* Paul told Timothy to *"Flee also youthful lusts" (2 Tim. 2:11).* If you know an area of weakness in your life, then flee that area. Paul said, *"But put ye on the Lord Jesus Christ, and make not provision for the flesh, to fulfil the lusts thereof" (Rom. 13:14).* But what if you can't flee it? Then...

Second—FACE It. David said the LORD is our *"strength in the time of trouble" (Ps. 37:39).* He gives us the strength to face the trouble from which we cannot flee. But He does expect us to do **our** part first. He didn't kill Goliath for David. He expected David to show up and do his part first. David had to **show** up, then **load** up (with 5 smooth stones). If we will do what we **can** do, God will then do what we **cannot** do.

Third—FAITH It. When you have faced it and it seems like it is too overwhelming to deal with, you will then have to "faith it." David showed up to fight Goliath but Goliath will still bigger and stronger than David was. That is when he had to "faith it" and trust God to do what only God could do.

Are you facing troubles? Ask God for the strength to Trust God then leave the results to Him by faith.

When Jesus Sat Down

"..when he had by himself purged our sins, sat down on the right hand of the Majesty on high;" (Heb. 1:3)

In the Old Testament, the priests would make continual sacrifices for sin. One sacrifice alone was never enough. But, when speaking of Jesus' sacrifice for our sins, the Bible says, He *"needeth not daily, as those high priests, to offer up sacrifice, first for his own sins, and then for the people's: for this he did **once**, when he offered up himself"* *(Heb. 7:27).* Why only once? Because He was the perfect sacrifice! No other sacrifice was needed.

It is interesting to note that the Old Testament priests never sat down—there were no seats in the sanctuary because they offered sacrifices day in and day out. Yet the writer of Hebrews says that Jesus *"**sat down** on the right hand of the Majesty on high;"*

Because the Old Testament sacrifices were temporary, more had to be offered constantly. But when Jesus, the PERFECT sacrifice, offered Himself, the Bible says He went back to the Father and *"sat down."* Wow! What a picture! In other words, what the Old Testament sacrifices could not do, Jesus did once and for all!

But Jesus is not done working. He is now our Advocate with the Father, interceding on our behalf. Romans 8:34 says, *"Who is he that condemneth? It is Christ that died, yea rather, that is risen again, who is even at the right hand of God, who also maketh intercession for us."*

Stop trusting in other things which aren't perfect. Put your trust in the One Who is the perfect, complete sacrifice for your sin...JESUS CHRIST!

When Prayer Becomes A Struggle

"And being in an agony he prayed more earnestly: and his sweat was as it were great drops of blood falling down to the ground." (Luke 22:44)

In a previous devotion I talked about turning your problem into a prayer. But what do you do when it is hard to pray? What do you do when praying becomes a struggle.

Well, first of all, prayer **can** become a real struggle. Don't feel you aren't spiritual just because your prayer time has become difficult. It will! When you pray, you are engaged in spiritual warfare. Satan fights our prayer time because it is the greatest weapon God has given us to defeat him with.

But the real question is what do you do when it becomes a struggle? What do you do when it seems your prayers are not rising past the ceiling?

Well, the Bible tells us that Jesus even struggled when He was praying in the Garden of Gethsemane before His crucifixion. In fact, it says He was literally *"in an agony"* while He was praying. So much so that *"his sweat was as it were great drops of blood falling down to the ground."* Now THAT is struggling in prayer!

So, what did He do? It says, *"And being in an agony he prayed more earnestly..."* He didn't stop praying when it became difficult. Rather, as His agony intensified, so did His praying! Someone said it this way, "When it seems hardest to pray, we need to pray the hardest." In fact, I believe that when it is hardest to pray, God blesses our prayers that much more.

Satan fights hardest when he is about to lose the battle. So, don't be surprised when it becomes difficult to pray. It may just mean you are closer to a victory than you realize!

Two Mormons In A Thrift Store

Recently, my wife and I were browsing through a thrift store. I love to look at the book section because I can usually find some really good Bible study books for under a dollar. This day was no exception. While my wife was looking around the rest of the store, I was loading up on books.

As I was perusing their religious book section, I noticed two Mormon "elders" come up beside me to look at books. While they were standing there, I began thinking to myself, "What can I say to them if we get into a conversation?" My mind was racing, searching for thoughts and scriptures I could give them.

Just then, one of them looked over at me and, seeing the stack of books I already had in my hand, said, "That's a lot of books!" Just then, my wife stepped up and said, "That's a lot of books" (For the record, it was only nine books). When she said that, the Mormons walked away.

But it did get me to thinking how that we should be ready to share the gospel with others whenever and wherever God opens up the opportunity. Peter said it this way: *"But sanctify the Lord God in your hearts: and be ready always to give an answer to every man that asketh you a reason of the hope that is in you..." (1Pet. 3:15)*

Don't let that verse scare you, It doesn't say you should have an answer to every question a person asks you. It simply says that you should be ready to share with anyone *"a reason of the **hope** that is in you."* If you have a hope of eternal life. Are you able to share with someone why you have that hope? Could you tell them how THEY can also have that hope? Think about how you would share the gospel with someone. That way you will be better prepared should you ever encounter two Mormons in a thrift store.

When You Can't See God

"Behold, I go forward, but he is not there; and backward, but I cannot perceive him: On the left hand, where he doth work, but I cannot behold him: he hideth himself on the right hand, that I cannot see him:" (Job 23:8-9)

Have you ever been in such dark circumstances that it seemed you could not find God? Have you ever prayed and it seemed as if your prayer never went past your ceiling? If any of these scenarios sound familiar, Job knew exactly what that felt like. He said he felt as if God had left him all alone. But in (v.10) we see three things that kept Job going during his trials.

FIRST—Job said, "He KNOWS me." (v.10a) *"But he knoweth the way that I take:"* Job said, "I may not know what God is doing, but I believe He knows exactly what I am going through. He knows the way I take."

SECOND—Job said, "He TRIES me." (v.10b) *"when he hath tried me..."* Job realized that this trial he was going through was just that...a trial; a testing from God. God may be allowing your trial to show you what is really in your heart.

THIRD—Job said, "He will REWARD me." (v.10c) *"I shall come forth as gold."* I love the optimistic faith Job had in the outcome of his trial. He didn't say, "I **hope** I pass this test" or "I **might** pass this test." No. He said, "Not only will I pass this test, but I will win the gold!"

Job said what we need to say during our trials. He said, "I cannot control my circumstances, but I can control my FAITH in the midst of my circumstances."

What a lesson for us during those times when we can't see God.

A Daily Choice

"..choose you this day whom ye will serve...but as for me and my house, we will serve the LORD." (Josh. 24:15)

Every day we get up, we have many choices to make like "What will I wear?" or "What will I eat?" But we also have another choice...will we serve the LORD?

FIRST—we must choose to serve the SAVIOUR. Joshua said, *"we will serve the LORD."* Without realizing it, we can actually become a slave to other things in life. Some are a slave to money. Others are a slave to their calendar, feeling they must do everything that comes their way. Sometimes it can be hard to know what to choose but Joshua said, "The choice is easy. My house will serve the LORD and no one else."

SECOND—we must choose to serve Him SINCERELY. In (v.14), Joshua said, *"Now therefore fear the LORD, and serve him in sincerity and in truth..."* In other words, we must serve Him from our heart, sincerely, not just with our lips. Anyone can "say" they are serving the LORD, but He wants us to serve Him *"in sincerity and truth."*

THIRD—We must choose to serve Him SOLELY. Next, in (v.14) he said, *"and put away the gods which your fathers served on the other side of the flood, and in Egypt; and serve ye the LORD."* God won't share the spotlight with anyone! We cannot serve many gods. We are to put away all other things in our life which compete for our worship and service. God wants us to worship and serve Him solely.

So today, and every day, we have a choice to make. Will we serve the gods of this world, or serve the one, true, LORD?

The Secret To Overcoming Your Circumstances

"We are troubled on every side, yet not distressed; we are perplexed, but not in despair;" (2Cor. 4:8)

Despite facing troubles on every side, Paul said he was *"not distressed"* about it. He admitted that there were times when he was *"perplexed"* about his circumstances, but he was never *"in despair."* So how did he do it? Here's his secret.

First—Paul KEPT the right PERSPECTIVE. Often, we don't see things as they are, but as we perceive them to be. Staying in the Word of God will help you keep the right perspective of your circumstances. It gives us the balance we need in life to see things from God's viewpoint, not ours. Because he kept the right perspective, Paul didn't look at the temporal; he looked at the eternal. He says in (v.18), *" ..we look not at the things which are seen, but at the things which are not seen: for the things which are seen are temporal; but the things which are not seen are eternal."*

Second—Paul CHOSE a right SPIRIT. Despite the fact that he never seemed to go a day without facing some kind of adverse circumstance, he didn't let it get him angry or bitter. You will never overcome your circumstances with a bad attitude. In fact, a bad attitude will only make your circumstances worse!

Third—Paul MAINTAINED a strong FAITH. He had faith in the future because He knew God was in control of his future. He had faith that no matter how bad today's circumstances are, there's a better day coming.

I Can Get It Clean

"But we are all as an unclean thing..." (Isa. 64:6)

One day, as a man was walking down the street, he noticed a store owner was washing the large plate-glass window of his store. The entire window was clean except for one soiled spot which the owner could not seem to remove no matter how much soap, water, or scrubbing he used.

Finally, after a while of working hard at it, one of his employees walked up to him and said, "You'll never get that spot clean, sir."

"Listen, young man," said the store owner, "I am the boss. I know more than you do about cleaning windows."

"Yes sir," said the boy, "But you will not get that spot clean."

Out of frustration, the man replied, "And what makes you think that?"

The boy said, "Because that soiled spot is on the inside!"

Man, in his attempt to earn his way to Heaven, tries to clean his soul from the stain of sin. He tries washing it with tears of sorrow. He tries scrubbing it with the soap of good works. He tries cleaning himself up through the efforts of religion. But all of this is to no avail. Why? Because the stain of sin is on the inside!

How many are in Hell, today, because they thought they could wash away their own sin through their good deeds? John makes it very clear that it is only *"the blood of Jesus Christ"* which *"cleanseth us from all sin."* (1John 1:7)

If you are not saved, trust in Jesus Christ as your Savior, today, and let Him wash away your sin once and for all!

Milk Your Own Cow

*"As newborn babes, desire the sincere milk of the word,
that ye may grow thereby:" (1Pet. 2:2)*

Years ago there was a Catholic man who got saved. Immediately he developed a love for the Word of God and began reading it every day. It wasn't long before the priest came by to check on him because he had not been back to the Catholic church.

When the priest arrived, he found this man sitting on the front porch with his Bible open, intently reading it. The priest said to him, "Don't you know it is dangerous for you to read the Bible without a Priest to explain it to you?"

The man replied, "But I just read where Peter said, *'As newborn babes, desire the sincere milk of the word,'* and I am a newborn babe, so I am hungry for the Word.'"

"Yes," said the priest, "But the priests are God's appointed milkmen. Only we can tell you what the Bible says."

The man thought for a moment and said, "I have a cow in my barn and recently I was sick and had to hire a man to milk my cow for me. I found out that he was stealing half of my milk and filling up the rest of the bucket with water. It sure was awful milk I was drinking. But now, I'm milking my own cow and it's cream I'm getting, not water!"

Sadly, even many preachers today are *watering down* the Word of God when they preach. When you pray this morning, thank God that you can read God's Word for yourself. What a privilege! What an honor! You don't have to depend on someone else. You can milk your own cow!

5 Lessons Your Child Learns From Hearing You Pray

"..one of his disciples said unto him, Lord, teach us to pray." (Luke 11:1)

There are five lessons your child will learn from hearing you pray.

FIRST—Your child will learn that there is a God. Your child is growing up in a world that is hostile toward God and toward Christianity. They will most likely encounter a teacher or friends who mock the fact that there is a God. So, hearing you pray reminds them that there really is a God in heaven.

SECOND—Your child will learn that you have a relationship with God. It is one thing to believe IN a God. It is another thing to KNOW that God in a personal way. When your child hears you pray, you are showing them that you have a personal relationship with God, and that they can have a relationship with Him, too.

THIRD—Your child will learn that God hears and answers prayer. As they witness answers to prayers they've heard you pray, it teaches them that God really does hear us when we pray.

FOURTH—Your child will learn that they are accountable to God. As they hear mom and dad submit themselves to God in prayer, they learn that not only mom and dad, but they, too, are accountable to God.

FIFTH—Your child will learn how to pray! Parents teach their children how to do just about everything, but few teach their children how to pray. The best way for them to learn to pray is by listening to you pray.

I Got Some Money!

"The heavens are thine, the earth also is thine: as for the world and the fulness thereof, thou hast founded them."
(Ps. 89:11)

One night, while on a trip, my wife and I stopped at a fast-food restaurant for a bite to eat. As I was waiting for my food to be prepared, I saw a mother come in with a little child. What really got my attention was the fact that this little boy had a handful of dollar bills in his hand and was waving them at everyone he saw.

When they got up to the counter to order their meal, the little boy waved the money at the cashier and said, "I got some money!" The cashier smiled and said, "Can I have some of that?" The boy turned and ran away saying, "No! It's all mine!"

Obviously that money had been given to that little boy by his mother. Yet, he acted as if HE was the one who had worked and earned it all by himself.

It got me to thinking how often we say that about the things which God has given to us. The Bible says, *"The heavens are thine, the earth also is thine:"* In other words, God owns the heavens and the earth. Yet, we act as though WE own everything we have.

Listen, you and I do not have one thing that God hasn't given to us. Every blessing we enjoy is from the good grace of a loving God.

The money in your wallet...*His.*

The health you enjoy...*His.*

The material possessions you have...*all His!*

James said that *"Every good gift and every perfect gift is from above, and cometh down from the Father of lights..." (James 1:17).* Thank Him for everything He has blessed you with this morning.

A Wild Ride At Walmart

"Wine is a mocker, strong drink is raging: and whosoever is deceived thereby is not wise." (Prov. 20:1)

Just when they thought they had seen it all, police officers in Wichita Falls, Texas, responded to a call from Walmart employees saying there was a woman driving around the parking lot on a cart while drinking wine from a Pringles can! Yes, you read that right.

Now, I can't even begin to imagine what that woman was thinking. I don't have a clue what thoughts were running through her head at the time. But I do know that she was proving the Bible to be true by her very actions because the Bible clearly says that *"Wine is a mocker..."*

Maybe that woman was under a lot of stress at work or at home. Maybe she just thought that she would drink a little to calm her nerves. Whatever the reason behind her decision to drink, I'm sure she never thought she would end up doing donuts in the Walmart parking lot while drinking from a Pringles can! Can you imagine the look on her face when she saw her picture on TV the next morning, after she had sobered up?

But that is how Satan works. He tells people that what they need is some substance in their system in order to deal with the pressures of life. When what they *really* need is not some SUBSTANCE, but the SAVIOUR!

Only Jesus can give us the peace and strength to face the daily challenges of life. We do not need a substance to be able to cope because, as Christians, we have something better...the Holy Spirit!

Don't run to a substance, turn to Jesus. He can give you what no substance can!

Preparing Others For Jesus

"In those days came John the Baptist...The voice of one crying in the wilderness, Prepare ye the way of the Lord, make his paths straight." (Matt. 3:1, 3)

When our President pays a special visit to a foreign nation, a large scale preparation is made before his actual arrival. An enormous amount of time is put into planning everything from security that must be in place, to the food they will take on Air Force One. It may take weeks, or even months, to plan one trip.

So, if that much time and effort go into planning for the arrival of an earthly leader, it should be no surprise that someone was sent ahead to prepare the way when the "King of kings" and the "Lord of lords" came into the world.

John the Baptist was the fulfillment of the prophecy in Malachi 3:1, *"Behold, I will send my messenger, and he shall prepare the way before me..."* The main message and ministry of John the Baptist was simply to *"Prepare...the way of the Lord."*

Did you know that we have the same mission? Our job in this world is to help *"Prepare...the way of the Lord."* By the way we walk, talk, dress, act, and react, we are either **helping** people see Jesus or **hindering** people from seeing Jesus.

Years ago I was knocking on doors and a man answered the door. When I invited him to the church I was attending at the time, he said, "Does (and he named a man in our church) go to your church?" I said, "As a matter of fact, he does." He then said, "Then I will never go there. I know how he lives." Oh my! Does your life prepare others to receive Jesus? Will they want to know Jesus based on what they see in your life?

259

4 Characteristics Of A Person God Uses

"Behold, I have seen a son of Jesse the Bethlehemite, that is cunning in playing, and a mighty valiant man, and a man of war, and prudent in matters, and a comely person, and the LORD is with him." (1Sam. 16:18)

If there is one thing that today's generation is lacking, it is character. David was greatly used of God because he had four characteristics that God could use.

FIRST—He was a hard worker. The reason David wasn't at home when Samuel came to anoint one of the sons of Jesse to be king was because he was in the field working. God will not use a lazy individual; He is looking for hard workers.

SECOND—He did right when no one was watching. His father did not have to be out in the field supervising him, making sure he did his job. He had the character to do his job even when no one was watching him.

THIRD—He prepared himself. The Bible says David was *"cunning in playing"* the harp. He was a skilled musician. It took a lot of practice and discipline to be a skilled harp player, but David prepared himself. It also says he was *"a mighty valiant man, and a man of war."* He was able to defeat Goliath because he had prepared himself for battle.

FOURTH—He was submissive to his God-given authorities. David was loyal to his leader before he ever became a leader himself. You are not qualified to be a leader until you are willing to follow leadership, yourself.

Do you want God to use you? Make sure you have these four characteristics in your life.

A Spiritual Sleeping Pill

"I will both lay me down in peace, and sleep: for thou, LORD, only makest me dwell in safety." (Ps. 4:8)

There is nothing more frustrating than not getting a good night's sleep. Tossing and turning all night long is no fun at all. While there are many reasons a person may not be able to sleep, many sleepless nights are simply the result of a failure to trust our burdens to our Heavenly Father's care.

Those nights of tossing and turning in the bed can often be attributed to more than a bad mattress or the wrong pillow. They are often the result of not casting all our cares upon the Lord. With the Lord's promise to never leave nor forsake us, along with His promise to lead, guide, and protect us, it should not be difficult for us to say with the Psalmist, *"I will both lay me down in peace, and sleep..."*

During one of the world wars, a little old lady in England had stood the nerve-shattering bombings with amazing peacefulness. When someone asked how she was able to be so calm and get a good night's rest each night, she said, "Well, every night I say my prayers and then I remember how the Bible says that God never slumbers nor sleeps. So I just pull my covers up and go on to sleep. After all, there's no need in both of us staying awake all night."

If stress and worry are keeping you up at night, cast your cares upon the Lord. Give them to Jesus. He never intended for you to stay awake all night worrying about them because the Bible says, *"..he giveth his beloved sleep" (Ps. 127:2).*

Trust Him with your cares. It is the best spiritual sleeping pill you will ever find!

When Happiness Leaves Your Happy Place (Part 1)

"Happy art thou, O Israel: who is like unto thee, O people saved by the LORD, the shield of thy help, and who is the sword of thy excellency! and thine enemies shall be found liars unto thee; and thou shalt tread upon their high places." (Deut. 33:29)

Moses was giving Israel one last challenge. He was reminding them that one of the things which should characterize them as God's chosen people was that they should be happy. Sure, they were about to go possess the land God had promised them, but they were to remember that their happiness wasn't in a PLACE. Their happiness was in the Lord!

What a lesson for us, today. Often you see people who are constantly moving. They can never seem to get settled because they think happiness is found in a place. As soon as they get bored where they are, they are off, seeking happiness somewhere else. Or you see a person who goes from one relationship to another because they think happiness is found in a person. Therefore, when their current relationship isn't as exciting anymore, they are off for a new adventure with another person, seeking that ever-elusive happy feeling again.

Don't fall for that trap. Seeking happiness in a place or a person will always leave you unhappy and discontent. Better than trying to find your "happy place," find your happiness in Jesus, who is EVERY place.

Tomorrow, I will give you three truths to remember that will keep Satan from stealing the happiness from your happy place.

When Happiness Leaves Your Happy Place (Part 2)

"Happy art thou, O Israel: who is like unto thee, O people saved by the LORD, the shield of thy help, and who is the sword of thy excellency!" (Deut. 33:29)

Yesterday we saw that Moses was giving Israel one last challenge. He was reminding them that, although they were about to possess the land God had promised them, their happiness wasn't in a PLACE or a PERSON, but in the Lord. Here are three truths to remember that will help you stay "happy" in the Lord.

FIRST—You were specially made by God. Moses said to Israel, *"O Israel: who is like unto thee..."* Just as Israel was a one-of-a-kind nation made by God, you are a one-of-a-kind person made by God. People lose their happiness in life because they are trying to be like everyone else. Be who God made YOU to be.

SECOND—You are saved. Next, Moses said, *"O people saved by the LORD..."* If for no other reason, you should be happy because you are saved! You have eternal life and a home in Heaven! What a reason to be happy.

THIRD—You are protected. Moses said, the Lord is *"the shield of thy help..."* Rejoice in the fact that God is not only your Father, but also your protector. And not only your protector, but He is *"the sword of thy excellency."* He can fight your battles for you. In fact, Moses tells them that God would take care of their enemies, as well. He said, *"thine enemies shall be found liars unto thee; and thou shalt tread upon their high places."*

If you are a child of God, remember that your happiness is not found in a PLACE or another PERSON; it is found in Jesus Christ, Who never fails!

Letting The Blind See Jesus

"The LORD openeth the eyes of the blind..." (Ps. 146:8)

As a result of an accident, a three-year-old boy named Louis became blind. For most people this would have been a crippling problem. But little Louis, who was born in 1809, was determined not to be limited by this blindness. Eventually, he was able to attend the National Institute for Blind Children in Paris and later even became a teacher there. He also became an accomplished musician.

In 1821, he met a soldier named Charles Barbier who explained a code system he had invented called "night writing." This allowed soldiers to communicate using combinations of 12 raised dots. Louis was intrigued by this idea.

Realizing its potential, Louis developed an even simpler system using only six dots. This system eventually became known as "braille," after his last name, Louis Braille. In 1827, he even published a book using this new technique which revolutionized life for the blind.

Sadly, blindness remains a serious problem to this day. But, thankfully, even those who are completely blind are still able to read, thanks to Braille's innovations.

As difficult a problem as physical blindness is, there is an even greater blindness people suffer from: spiritual blindness. Paul said their understanding is darkened *"because of the blindness of their heart" (Eph. 4:18)*. They are blinded to the gospel by the god of this world, Satan (2Cor. 4:4).

As you go about your day, think about the many around you who may be blinded to the gospel of Jesus. Be ready, because God may give you a divine appointment to share the gospel so that Jesus can open their blinded eyes!

Bob The Builder

"Therefore whosoever heareth these sayings of mine, and doeth them, I will liken him unto a wise man, which built his house upon a rock:" (Matt. 7:24)

My wife and I are in the midst of building a house. Let me rephrase that...my wife and I are in the process of having *someone else* build our house for us. I am no builder! I could probably build a birdhouse...maybe...after watching a YouTube video about it. But I do not have the knowledge, the tools, nor the expertise it takes to take on such a huge project like building a house.

I never knew so much went into building a house. And while I haven't done any of the building, myself, I have learned through this process a lot of what you SHOULD do and what you SHOULD NOT do to build the right kind of house. I do know the most important part of a house is the foundation. If the foundation is not solid, then it will affect the rest of the house.

In our text, Jesus is giving an illustration about two men who built themselves a house. One man was a wise builder and the other man was a foolish builder. One built his house upon a rock and the other foolishly built his house on the sinking sand.

Now, on the outside, both houses probably looked equally good. They both may have been painted nicely and beautifully decorated. But it wasn't until *"the rain descended, and the floods came, and the winds blew, and beat upon that house"* that you saw which house was strong enough to withstand the storm and which one crumbled.

Build your home on the right foundation, and I not talking about concrete and cinder block. I am talking about building your home on the solid rock, Jesus Christ!

The Truth About Your Troubles

"Wherein ye greatly rejoice, though now for a season, if need be, ye are in heaviness through manifold temptations:" (1Pet. 1:6)

God made every person unique. There are no two identical human beings. Even identical twins are not truly "identical." They are not exact replicas of one another. We are all unique, but there is one thing we ALL have in common...we ALL face troubles and trials. Peter gives us four truths about our troubles.

Our troubles are PRESENT. Peter said, *"ye are in heaviness..."* Troubles are a fact of life. In fact, Peter was writing to a lot of Christians who were currently facing persecution. They were literally *"in heaviness."* The truth is, as long as we are in this world, troubles will be a present reality for us. But just as our trials are ever present, our GOD is also ever present!

Our troubles are PLENTIFUL. *"through manifold temptations:"* It would be nice if we only faced a few trials in our lives. But the truth is, we will encounter *"manifold (many) temptations."* Sometimes we face them daily. If you overcome one temptation don't get too cocky because there is another one coming just around the corner!

Our troubles are PROBLEMATIC. They are *"manifold temptations."* Temptations can be quite problematic for us. They tempt us to sin against God and leave His plan for our lives.

Our troubles are not PERMANENT. *"though now for a season..."* Though we cannot escape our troubles, I am thankful that God says they will only last for *"a season."* It may seem like that trial you are facing will last forever, but hold on dear child of God, there will be an end to it.

A Forgery

"Every good gift and every perfect gift is from above, and cometh down from the Father of lights..." (James 1:17)

In the early 1960s, some unusual paintings featuring a person or animal with huge, sad eyes became popular. Some considered the work tacky, but others delighted in it. As the artist's husband began to promote his wife's creations, the couple grew quite prosperous. But the artist's signature—Margaret Keane—didn't appear on her work. Instead, Margaret's husband presented his wife's work as his own. Margaret fearfully remained silent about the fraud for twenty years until the couple's marriage ended. It took a courtroom "paint-off" between them to prove the true artist's identity.

As crazy as it was for the husband to take credit for his wife's paintings, it is no crazier than when we try to take credit for the blessings God has given to us. How often do we live our lives as if it belongs to us and not God?

When we make decisions for our lives without any thought about what God wants, then we are in effect committing a spiritual forgery. We want God's blessings, but we want to do things our way, not His.

So don't forget that *"Every good gift and every perfect gift is from above."* Everything you have, every blessing you have received (including life itself) was given to you by God. He is the owner, you are simply the manager of it.

He is the artist who is painting the portrait of your life. Therefore, ask God to help you live your life in such a way that the lost world around you will see His name on your canvas.

A Spiritual Workout

".. work out your own salvation with fear and trembling."
(Phil. 2:12)

Working out and becoming fit has become a multi-billion dollar industry. You can find virtually every type of workout program imaginable…and even some you *can't* imagine. There are aerobics classes, spin classes, yoga classes, and even a karaoke spin class where you sing while cycling! There are workouts with dogs, and even workouts with goats called "Goat Yoga." Whew! Just trying to list them all was a workout!

But there was one workout missing…a spiritual workout. The Bible says you are to *"work out your own salvation."* Notice it doesn't say to work FOR, but work OUT your salvation. The Bible clearly says that we cannot work FOR our salvation because it is *"Not by works of righteousness which we have done, but according to his mercy he saved us…"* (Titus 3:5).

You see, as God works our salvation IN us, we are to work it OUT. He does the internal part, but we do the external part. As He works in our hearts, then we let what He did in us come out of us for the world to see. So, every day we should be working out our own salvation.

We should work it out at HOME. A Christianity that doesn't work at home will not work anywhere. We are to be Christians at home before we are Christians anywhere else. If anyone should see Christ at work in our lives, it should be our family.

We should work it out at WORK or SCHOOL. It should start in the home, but it should spread to every other area of our lives. Others should see Christ in our lives by the way we walk, and talk, and relate to others. This morning, don't forget your spiritual workout!

Love Is A Six-Letter Word

"Husbands, love your wives," (Eph. 5:25)

Love is a misunderstood word, today. Sadly, it has been redefined by Hollywood and red-carpet celebrities to simply mean something we experience; something we "feel" when we find that "perfect" someone to share our lives with. They portray love as the feeling you should expect to have while you walk off into the sunset, as the credits begin to roll. But is that what love really is? No!

Love is a six-letter word: **C-H-O-I-C-E**.

Love is not passion, lust, or even romance. Love is more than a nice Instagram photo or the perfect Facebook post. Love is not something you fall into or fall out of; it is a *choice* you make even when your "feelings" tell you otherwise.

Love is choosing to love one moment at a time; one day at a time. Relationships do not fall apart overnight. They disintegrate in the same way they are built...one choice at a time.

The Bible says that *"God is love"* (1John 4:8). Therefore, let's see how GOD defines love.

FIRST—Love is choosing to GIVE. (John 3:16) says, *"For God so loved the world, that he gave..."* True love is not selfish, it is selfless. Because God loves us, He gave us the best He had to give, His *"only begotten Son."*

SECOND—Love is choosing to FORGIVE. True love not only **gives**, it **forgives**. Relationships fall apart because one or both people refuse to forgive. They cannot let go of an offense or past hurt. But true love forgives.

Today, remember that true love is more than a feeling; it is more than a dozen roses and a box of chocolates. Love is a six-letter word: C-H-O-I-C-E!

Death By Hoarding

"To every thing there is a season, and a time to every purpose under the heaven..." (Ecc. 3:1, 6)

74-year-old, Gordon Stewart, an eccentric hermit, hoarded so much junk and trash he had to burrow through it to get around his home. Then in January 2009 he evidently got lost in the maze of tunnels and died of thirst. He had filled the rooms of his house clear up to the ceiling with years' worth of old newspapers, garbage, and clutter, making it impossible to walk around. Neighbors said Mr. Stewart's home had been accumulating junk for at least 10 years. Towers of plastic bags could be seen piled up against his front window, while broken furniture, computer parts, and even an old TV spilled over onto his front lawn. A car dating back to the 1950's stood in the garage, untouched for years as garbage accumulated around it.

Neighbors finally called authorities after failing to see him leave his house for several days. When police arrived, the stench from the garbage was so foul they brought in a police scuba diving team with breathing apparatus to search the house. They crawled around through mountains of junk and garbage, searching the elaborate network of tunnels until they located Stewart's body. The compulsive hoarder is believed to have become disorientated inside the walls of rotting trash and unable to find a way out until he collapsed from dehydration.

We might shake our heads in disbelief that someone would want to hoard so much junk in his home, but many Christians are guilty of collecting the filth of this world and hoarding it in their hearts. How many Christians cannot find God's will because of the worldly "junk" that has filled their lives? How much of the world have you been hoarding?

How To Handle Rejection

*"He is despised and rejected of men; a man of sorrows,
and acquainted with grief..." (Isa. 53:3)*

Whether it is children on a playground, a boy asking a girl out on a date, or an employee asking for a raise, no one likes rejection. But Jesus knows exactly what it feels like to be rejected. Isaiah says that he was *"despised and rejected of men."*

Here are four truths to remember if you have experienced rejection.

FIRST—Rejection can be a sign you are doing right. Sometimes it boils down to choosing between the acceptance of others and the acceptance of God. Paul said in *(2Cor. 5:9) "Wherefore we labour, that, whether present or absent, we may be accepted of him."* When you choose to live for Christ, sometimes people will reject you.

SECOND—It is better to be rejected than to lower your standards. Sometimes a man or a woman is tempted to lower their standards in order to find someone, or to have certain friends. You are better off without those friends if you must lower your standards to get them.

THIRD—Focus on others who may need to be accepted. Instead of focusing on YOUR rejection, look for others who may also need a friend. Maybe God wants you to use your rejection to help someone else who may have also felt rejected by others.

FOURTH—God will NEVER reject you! No matter what others do, God said, *"I will never leave thee, nor forsake thee"* (Heb. 13:5). Take heart. You may have been rejected by others, but you are never alone!

God's Workmanship

"For we are his workmanship, created in Christ Jesus unto good works..." (Eph. 2:10)

Henry Steinway built his first piano in 1836 in the kitchen of his home in Germany–the same piano now displayed at the Metropolitan Museum of Art in New York City. Born in 1797, he would build 482 pianos over the next decade. Eventually, he and his family emigrated to the United States, establishing Steinway & Sons with the goal of manufacturing pianos.

It must have sounded like an unlikely business, but within three years, they were manufacturing more than 200 pianos a year. Because of the quality of their craftsmanship, Steinway developed a reputation for excellence. As a result, their pianos were sold the world over.

Today, the company so dominates the piano business that an estimated 97% of concert soloists choose to play on a Steinway.

Just as a Steinway piano is a reflection of its creator's workmanship, we (as Christians) are also a reflection of our Creator's workmanship. No matter where we go, everything we say and do reflects what others will think of Jesus.

Just as Steinway & Sons puts a lot of time and effort into crafting the finest piano they can, God has put a lot of time and effort into making us what He would have us be. Steinway's goal is to make the best piano possible. God's goal is to make us into the image of Jesus Christ.

Ask God to help you be the best representative of His workmanship in your life, today. Let others see the work God has, and is doing in you on a daily basis.

How To Get A Word From God

"And the LORD said unto Moses, Write thou these words: for after the tenor of these words I have made a covenant with thee and with Israel." (Ex. 34:27)

Moses was invited by God up on Mt. Sinai for a one-on-one, face-to-face meeting with God! Wow! Can you imagine having that privilege? The end result of that meeting was that Moses got a word from God. He got direction from God.

So, what steps did Moses take in order to get that word? What can we do to get a word from God, too?

FIRST—You must spend time with God. (v.28) says Moses was in God's presence for forty days and forty nights! This was no 5-minute meeting. I am not saying you must spend that much time with God before He will speak to you. But the lesson is, we cannot rush our time in God's presence and expect to get a word from Him.

SECOND—Get into a spirit of worship. After spending that much time in God's presence, (v.8) says Moses *"bowed his head...and worshipped."* Getting into God's presence will lead you into a spirit of worship which will prepare your heart to receive His word.

THIRD—Repent of known sin. Finally, in (v.9) Moses repented of the sins of Israel. He said, *"pardon our iniquity and our sin."* In order to receive a word from God, there must be a repentance of any known sin in our lives. Sin prevents God from hearing our prayers which will prevent us from hearing from God.

Every day we need a fresh word from God. Take time to get into His presence this morning and get the word you need!

273

Where Do We Go From Here?

"I will instruct thee and teach thee in the way which thou shalt go: I will guide thee with mine eye." (Ps. 32:8)

When Alexander the Great was leading his victorious armies down through Asia Minor, the great leader came to the foothills of the mighty Himalayas, beyond which lay the Khyber Pass and India. As far as Alexander was concerned, he was standing at the end of the world. You see, up until that time no maps had been made of the vast territory before him. As far as he knew he was marching his soldiers off the map of the world!

Often when ancient mapmakers reached the edge of what had been charted, they drew a line and depicted dragons and monsters beyond. You can understand why this practice didn't exactly encourage exploration. One Roman commander in the first century had led his troops beyond the line on the map into "dragon territory." He sent a courier back to Rome with an urgent message: "We have just marched off the map. Please send new orders."

Sometimes it seems as if such unforeseen circumstances of life come your way that you are left wondering, "Where do I go from here?" It seems as if your life has run out of map. Your life's GPS has gone blank and it is not rerouting you!

It can be difficult to keep moving forward when you aren't sure where forward even is! It can often strike fear in our hearts when we feel life has left us to walk on in unchartered territory.

Well, I have good news for you. God has already been where you are headed. You can rest assured that there is no uncharted territory with God because He created the territory!

Caught In Quicksand!

"Save me, O God...I sink in deep mire, where there is no standing..." (Ps. 69:1-2)

An Arizona man is lucky to be alive after he got trapped in quicksand in Utah's Zion National Park for several hours in freezing conditions.

Ryan Osmun was hiking with his girlfriend when they said she tripped in a shallow creek that turned out to be quicksand. Osmun said he went to help pull her out, but in the process, his entire right leg became swallowed by the sand.

"There was no chance of moving it at all. The sand had surrounded the whole leg and I couldn't move it," Osmun told CBS News. "The best way to describe it would be... standing in a huge puddle of concrete that basically dries instantly." Making matters worse, the area they were in had no cellphone reception.

Osmium's girlfriend tried to free him, unsuccessfully, before finally leaving to find help. "I thought for sure when she left that I would lose my leg," Osmun said.

Once rescuers found Osmun, they were surprised that he was even still alive. It took them over two hours to finally free his leg from the quicksand.

David knew what it felt like to sink in spiritual quicksand. He said, *"I sink in deep mire, where there is no standing..."* Sometimes we face circumstances in life which make us feel as if we are being swallowed up and cannot keep our heads above water. We feel as if we are doing all we can just to make it from day to day.

What did David do when he felt that way? He cried out to God. He prayed, *"Save me, O God!"* Don't underestimate the power of prayer. God is above any circumstances that may be swallowing you up.

Going In His Power

"And Jesus came and spake unto them, saying, All power is given unto me in heaven and in earth. Go ye therefore..."
(Matt. 28:18-19)

Before Jesus ascended back into Heaven, He gave His disciples clear directions about their mission. He reminded them that He has *"All power...in heaven and earth."* Not only did HE have power, but He was sending THEM in that power, as well!

In other words, Jesus was saying to them, "Since I have all power, YOU will also have access to that power when you go in my name." So Jesus said to them, *"All power is given unto me...God ye therefore..."*

There was a lot that He needed the disciples to accomplish. There was work to be done. There were souls to be saved. There were lives that needed to be changed...all through the power of Jesus.

Here's the great thing...just as God called and empowered His disciples in that day, He has called and empowered you, today! As a child of God, He has given you access to the same power He gave to His disciples because there is still a great work that needs to be done.

There are still souls that need to be saved. There are still lives that need to be changed. There are still people who need hope that only Jesus can give. But here's the key....you cannot accomplish this great task in your own power. That is why Jesus said in John 20:21, *"..as my Father hath sent me, even so send I you."*

You are not in this thing alone. You have a Heavenly Father above you and His Holy Spirit within you to empower you to share the gospel of Jesus with everyone you meet. The question is will you complete the mission you've been given? Can Jesus count on you?

Driving Down A Dead-End Street

"Yea, though I walk through the valley of the shadow of death, I will fear no evil: for thou art with me..." (Ps. 23:4)

It is said that, in South Africa, when a tribesman is about to take his last breath, a witch doctor will place in the man's hand a dead bone as sort of a "passport" into the world beyond. When I read that, I thought...what a sad attempt that is at human comfort when eternity is so close.

I am thankful I have a Savior who has taken the sting out of death. There is nothing to fear in death because when Jesus is present, nothing but the *"shadow"* of death remains. And just as the shadow of a knife cannot stab, and the shadow of a dog cannot bite, neither can the *"shadow of death"* harm the child of God!

I also read of an old Indian Chief who was told of Jesus Christ, but didn't feel he needed him. He said, "The Jesus road is good, but I have followed the old Indian road all of my life, and I will follow it to the end." A year later, as he lay dying, he searched in vain for comfort of his soul and some pathway through the darkness. Finally, he turned in desperation to the missionary who had been called to his bedside and whispered weakly. "Can I turn to the Jesus road now? My road stops here. There is no path through the valley."

How about you? Which road are YOU on? There is only ONE road that leads to Heaven. There is only one path that leads *"through the valley of the shadow of death."* Jesus said, *"I am the way, the truth, and the life: no man cometh unto the Father, but by me" (John 14:6).*

Come to Jesus. If you are on any other road, you are driving down a dead-end street.

5 Ways To S.E.R.V.E. Your Spouse

"..by love serve one another." (Gal. 5:13)

The world we live in mocks the idea of serving others. No one wants to serve; everyone wants to *be* served. But as Christians, we are called to serve one another. If we are to have a servant's hearts toward others, I believe that also includes our spouse. Here are five ways to S.E.R.V.E. your spouse.

S—STOP keeping score. Keeping score only produces selfishness. Jesus said, *"Thou shalt love thy neighbour as thyself..." (Mark 12:31).* You have no closer neighbor than your spouse. A great marriage is NOT 50/50. A great marriage is 100/100!

E—ESTABLISH good communication. A marriage is only as good as the communication between spouses. There is a difference between TALKING TO your spouse and COMMUNICATING WITH your spouse. *Talking* is just saying words. *Communication* means the other person understands what you are meaning by your words.

R—REMEMBER, you are serving God by serving your spouse. The Bible says, *"And whatsoever ye do, do it heartily, as to the Lord, and not unto men;" (Col. 3:23).* Therefore, how you serve your spouse is a reflection of how you are serving God.

V—VIGILANTLY protect the priority of your marriage. You need a strong marriage. Your children need you to have a strong marriage. Make your spouse and your marriage a priority. Remember...by your example you are teaching your children what kind of marriage THEY should have one day.

E—EDIFY your spouse daily. Look for ways every day to encourage and build your spouse up. Praise them every chance you get.

Ear Ticklers

"Prophesy not unto us right things, speak unto us smooth things..." (Isa. 30:10)

Isaiah was a preacher of righteousness. He uncompromisingly declared God's holiness and His judgment on Israel's sinfulness. As a result, he was not only hated and persecuted, but eventually martyred for his stand!

The people did not want him preaching against their sin. Instead, they said, *"Prophesy not unto us right things, speak unto us smooth things..."* In other words, they said, "Don't tell us what we NEED to hear; tell us what we WANT to hear."

The apostle Paul said that we will face the same kind of attitude in our day, as well. In 2Timothy 4:3 Paul said, *"For the time will come when they will not endure sound doctrine; but after their own lusts shall they heap to themselves teachers, having itching ears;"*

We are living in that day, today. People are not only living in sin but are flaunting it down main street for the world to see! Not only are they not ashamed of their sin, but they expect you to keep quiet about it. If you speak out against it, you will be in big trouble! And worst of all, this is even happening in the church!

But God did not call us to stay quiet. He called us to be salt and light in this evil world. He calls Christians to STAND UP and He calls preachers to SPEAK OUT!

If you have a pastor who preaches the Word without compromise, you ought to thank God for him. If you have a pastor who preaches against the sins of the day, you better lift him up in prayer because Satan will come after him with all he's got! What we need are not more "ear ticklers." It is not our EARS but our HEARTS that need to be touched.

Growing Down

"But speaking the truth in love, may grow up into him in all things..." (Eph. 4:15)

There was a woman who lived in Virginia years ago. Her unique story was told in the *Virginia Medical Monthly*. She had grown normally, married, and had three children. Life was good until the husband and father died when the children were in high school.

The mother became intensely devoted to her children. So much so that she changed her clothes to those of a girl of twenty, and joined in her children's parties and fun.

In a few years, the children noticed that as they grew older their mother was growing younger. Psychiatrists call it "personality regression," which means "a person going backward." Usually such people stop going backward at a certain age. But not this woman. She slipped backward at the rate of one year for every three or four months of time that went forward. Although she was 61 years old she acted and talked like a 6-year-old. She was sent to a sanitarium, where she insisted on wearing short dresses, playing with toys, and babbling like a child.

Then she became like a three-year-old; she spilled her food, crawled on the floor, and cried "Mama." Backward still further to the age of one, she drank milk and curled up like a tiny baby. Finally, she went back over the line and died!

Even worse than **physical** regression is **spiritual** regression. Peter says we are to *"grow in grace, and in the knowledge of our Lord and Saviour Jesus Christ"* (2Peter 3:18). The church isn't one giant nursery meant to pass out baby bottles and pacifiers to everyone who walks through its doors. It is a training ground for "growing up" into mature Christians.

How Do You Do That?

"And when they had set them in the midst, they asked, By what power, or by what name, have ye done this?"
(Acts 4:7)

Peter and John were being used by God in a mighty way. Not only had God given them boldness in their preaching, He was also performing miracles through them. One forty-year-old man, who had been lame from birth, was healed and went into the temple with Peter and John *"walking, and leaping, and praising God" (Acts 3:8)*.

The next day, the rulers, the elders, and the scribes met together and asked Peter and John, *"By what power, or by what name, have ye done this?"* They knew that having a lame man healed was not something you see every day. They knew there was something different about Peter and John and they wanted to know what it was.

I wonder, do sinners who are around you know there is something different about you? Do they see a difference in the way you walk, the way you talk, and the way you live for God? You and I may not be able to speak to a lame man and heal him like Peter and John, but by the way we live our lives the world should see the miracle God has worked in us!

Today, ask God to give you the courage and boldness to take a stand for Him. Determine to live so differently in front of those around you that they will want to ask you, "How do you do that?"

A Dead Man Saved Their Lives!

"In every thing give thanks: for this is the will of God in Christ Jesus concerning you." (1Thess. 5:18)

One stormy night in 1910, a group of traveling musicians arrived at the city of Riga, on the Baltic Sea, to fulfill a concert engagement. The weather was so bad, however, that the conductor of the orchestra tried to persuade the manager of the hall to cancel the concert. He felt sure that no one would venture out on such a rainy night.

The manager refused to cancel, but he did agree that if not even one listener turned up, the orchestra could leave early in order to catch the night boat bound for Helsinki, Finland.

When the musicians arrived at the concert hall they found only one person sitting in the audience—a stout old man who seemed to smile at everyone. Because of this one old man, the musicians were forced to play the entire concert and were unable to leave early to catch the boat. After the concert was over the old man continued sitting in his seat.

Thinking he was asleep, an usher nudged his shoulder. Only then was it discovered that the old man was dead. The musicians had played the entire concert for a dead man. But, ironically, playing for this dead man had actually saved their own lives because the boat they would have taken to Finland sank that very night with no survivors!

Sometimes we get irritated when circumstances don't go our way, but God's Word tells us that *"In every thing"* we should *"give thanks"* because we do not know how God might be using those bad circumstances for good in our lives.

Happily Ever After?

*"With all lowliness and meekness, with longsuffering,
forbearing one another in love;" (Eph. 4:2-3)*

"And they lived happily ever after." That is the usual ending of the typical fairy tale story. It doesn't matter what happens during the story, you know that everything will turn out ok. Everyone will end up living "happily ever after."

Sadly, in many marriages today, people think that living "happily ever after" is just that....a fairy tale! They think that there is no such thing as a happy, fulfilling marriage beyond the honeymoon. While it is possible, there are some obstacles to a "happily ever after" marriage.

PRIDE is an obstacle to a happy marriage. Our text verse says we are to live *"With all lowliness..."* Pride is the opposite of lowliness. Pride is lifting yourself up, not humbling yourself.

ANGER is an obstacle to a happy marriage. Next, it says, *"...and meekness."* Meekness means gentleness. Anger is the opposite of being gentle and kind. Nothing will destroy a "happily ever after" marriage quicker than an angry spirit directed toward your spouse.

QUITTING is an obstacle to a happy marriage. Lastly, it says, *"..with longsuffering, forbearing one another in love;"* That refers to the perseverance it takes to support your spouse and fight for your marriage even when it would be easy to walk away and quit.

So, how can you get the "happily" back into your "ever after"? Verse 3 says you do that by *"Endeavouring to keep the unity of the Spirit in the bond of peace."* Prayer is the difference between the best YOU can do and the best GOD can do!

Need I Say More?

""Wherefore, my beloved brethren, let every man be swift to hear, slow to speak..." (James 1:19)

Someone said, "Many things in life have been opened by mistake, but nothing more often than the mouth!" The truth is…we just talk too much sometimes. When all is said and done—there's usually more said than done!

FIRST—James says, "let every man be swift to hear..." That simply means you should be a ready listener before becoming a ready speaker. God gave us two ears and only one mouth for a reason!

SECONDLY—James says, "be…slow to speak." Why? Because sin is not too far behind! Prov. 10:19 says, *"In the multitude of words there wanteth not sin: but he that refraineth his lips is wise."*

In other words, the more we speak, the more likely we are to say something we shouldn't say. And Jesus said we are going to give account of EVERYTHING we say (Matt. 12:36-37). So, given that fact, James says, *"be…slow to speak."* Most of the trouble we get into, is because of our mouth. Someone said: "It would be better to keep your mouth shut and be thought a fool; than to open it and remove all doubt."

It takes as much wisdom to know when NOT to speak, as it does to know WHEN to speak. We need to be like the man about whom it was said he was so wise he could be silent in 7 different languages!

Proverbs 21:23 says, *"Whoso keepeth his mouth and his tongue keepeth his soul from troubles."* So, a great lesson for us to learn is this: not everything that pops into our MIND should proceed out of our MOUTH! Today, consciously think before you speak. And when you do speak, think to yourself, "Need I say more?"

A Spy In The Sky

"For the ways of man are before the eyes of the LORD, and he pondereth all his goings." (Prov. 5:21)

We live in the day where Big Brother is always watching you. There are cameras on just about every street corner. There are even certain apps on our cell phones which track our every move. On top of that, if you have a smartphone, it is probably listening to everything you say! It is enough to make a person paranoid.

One Sunday I was teaching my Sunday School Class and I said the word "Seriously" and all of the sudden my iPhone come alive and Siri said, "I will look that up for you!" #Creepy

What we forget is that long before there were satellites in the sky and GPS's on our phones, there was a God in Heaven who heard and saw everything we did. In fact, if you decided tomorrow that you would live off the grid, so that no one could track you, you still could not get away from God.

The writer of Hebrews put it this way: *"Neither is there any creature that is not manifest in his sight: but all things are naked and opened unto the eyes of him with whom we have to do" (Heb. 4:13).* In other words, you may be able to hide your actions from your spouse, your parents, or your pastor, but you cannot hide them from God. He sees it all! What a sobering thought.

God heard the gossip you spread on the telephone. He saw that website you viewed on the internet. He witnessed that picture you sent on Snapchat. He read that tweet and Facebook post you wrote. So, today, think about how your words and action reflect Jesus Christ. Because, even though others may not see, God does.

Missing The Main Attraction

"The eyes of your understanding being enlightened; that ye may know what is the hope of his calling, and what the riches of the glory of his inheritance in the saints,
(Eph. 1:18)

One year, my wife and I decided to take a two week vacation out west, which included Arizona and Nevada. While there, we took both of our boys with us and we took a trip to see the Grand Canyon. The day before we went to the Grand Canyon, a local told us a secret way to go that not many people know about and he said it would be less crowded than going in through the main entrance. He also told us that the way he suggested us go would also provide one of the best "first views" of the canyon.

We took his advice, and sure enough, there was little traffic that way and it was indeed a breath-taking first view of the canyon. I had seen pictures of it before, but none of them did it justice. As we made our way back around the canyon, we came to the Gift Shop, where everyone was trying to purchase souvenirs.

Could you imagine someone taking the time to drive all the way to the Grand Canyon, only to spend all of their time in the Gift Shop, never actually seeing the slender of the canyon, itself? That would be crazy! They would be missing the main attraction.

But, isn't that the way many people treat Jesus? He has so many spiritual riches to offer us, when we come to Him, yet we spend all of our time enamored with the "gift shops" of this world, missing out on the *true riches* that are in Christ.

Don't get so busy doing *good* things that it takes your attention away from the *main* thing...JESUS!

4 Ways To Keep The F.I.R.E. Of God Burning In Your Heart

"And they said one to another, Did not our heart burn within us, while he talked with us by the way, and while he opened to us the scriptures?" (Luke 24:32)

When we first got saved, our heart was on fire for God. But over time it is easy to let that fire die down, and even go out, if we are not careful. Here are four ways to keep the F.I.R.E. of God burning in your heart.

F—FORGET past failures. The quickest way to put out the fire of God in your heart is by focusing on all the past failures in your life. Rather, focus on present successes. Part of Paul's success was, *"forgetting those things which are behind" (Phil. 3:13).*

I—INTENSIFY your walk with God. Complacency is an enemy of a growing Christian. You cannot remain neutral and still grow. Strive to grow closer and be more faithful to God each day.

R—REPENT of sin immediately. Nothing will quench God's fire in a person's heart any faster than sin will! You cannot be on fire for God AND harbor sin in your heart at the same time. It is impossible. So, in order to keep God's fire burning in your heart, you must forsake sin immediately.

E—EMPHASIZE God's Word in your life. As Jesus was walking along with these two, discouraged believers, verse 27 says that Jesus *"expounded unto them in all the scriptures the things concerning himself."* After they heard the Word of God, they said, *"Did not our heart burn within us?"* God wants our hearts to stay on fire for Him. If you will do these four simple things, it will help keep the F.I.R.E. of God burning in your heart!

Falling Without A Parachute!

"Though he fall, he shall not be utterly cast down: for the LORD upholdeth him with his hand." (Ps. 37:24)

The record for surviving the highest fall without a parachute is held by a Serbian woman, Vesna Vulovic. On January 26, 1972, she was flying over the Czech Republic. Croat terrorists had placed a bomb onboard JAT Yugoslav Flight 364, on which Vulovic was a flight attendant. The 22-year-old wasn't even supposed to be on that flight; her schedule had been mixed up with another flight attendant.

The explosion tore the DC-9 to pieces, but Vulovic survived. She remained strapped into her seat in the middle section of the plane that was right above the wings. The assembly spiraled down 33,000 feet then struck the snow-covered flank of a mountain. Her injuries included a fractured skull, two broken legs, and three broken vertebrae, one of which left her temporarily paralyzed from the waist down. She was also in a coma for 27 days. She regained the use of her legs after several months of surgeries.

Can you imagine what that must have been like? Maybe not, but we know what it is like to fall, spiritually. I am so thankful that when a child of God does fall, the Bible says, *"Though he fall, he shall not be utterly cast down."*

If you have fallen into sin there is help, and there is hope! You can survive the fall! Jude 1:24 says that God is, *"..able to keep you from falling, and to present you faultless before the presence of his glory with exceeding joy."* What a blessing! What an encouragement!

If you have fallen, don't give up. Come to Jesus for forgiveness and cleansing.

She Prayed With Her Hands

"I thank my God, making mention of thee always in my prayers," (Philemon 1:4)

I once read a story of a nurse who had learned the importance of intercessory prayer. Since she used her hands as instruments of mercy and healing with those she was in charge of caring for, she also felt it was a natural thing to use them in her prayers for them as well.

When someone asked her how she prayed with her hands, she described it this way. Each finger represented someone she wanted to pray for.

- Her **thumb** was nearest to her and reminded her to pray for those who were closest and dearest.
- The **index finger** was used for pointing, so it stood for her instructors.
- The **third finger** was the tallest and stood for those in leadership.
- The **fourth finger** was the weakest, representing those in distress and pain.
- The **little finger**, which was the smallest and least important, reminded the nurse to pray for her own needs.

Maybe she learned to have a desire to pray for others by following Paul's example. He said in Philippians 1:4, *"Always in every prayer of mine for you all making request with joy."* Notice Paul said that he prayed for others *"Always"* and in *"every prayer"* of his. Wow! THAT is true intercessory prayer!

We need more intercessory prayer warriors, today. You don't have to use your hands, like this nurse. But however you pray, just pray!

Love In A Letter

"Ye see how large a letter I have written unto you with mine own hand." (Gal. 6:11)

Little Ruby was like most four-year-olds; she loved to run, sing, and play. But one day she started complaining about a pain she was having in her knees. Ruby's parents took her in for tests but were not prepared for the shocking results. It was determined that little Ruby had cancer—stage 4 cancer to be exact. Ruby was in serious trouble and was quickly admitted to the hospital.

Due to the seriousness of her condition, Ruby's hospital stay went longer and longer. She ended up staying over into the Christmas season which, for a little child, was very difficult.

One of Ruby's nurses came up with the idea to place a mailbox outside her room so family could send letters full of prayers and encouragement to her. They even posted on Facebook about Ruby's condition and that's when the volume of mail coming in from friends and complete strangers surprised everyone, most of all Ruby. With each letter received (more than 100,000 total), Ruby grew a little more encouraged, and she finally got to go home.

The apostle Paul knew that there is something about the power of encouragement. In his letters to the churches, he is always writing to encourage and edify other believers.

If we are not careful, we can get so busy living our own lives and dealing with our own problems that we fail to encourage others. Few people still write hand-written letters, but you can still make a phone call or send an encouraging text to someone that would lift their spirits.

Ask the Lord who it is that YOU could encourage today because one day it will be YOU who needs the encouragement.

Keeping Your Salvation Fresh

"And Moses said unto the people, Remember this day, in which ye came out from Egypt, out of the house of bondage; for by strength of hand the LORD brought you out from this place..." (Ex. 13:3)

The greatest day of anyone's life is the day they were born again. Once you get saved, one of the greatest tasks you will have is to keep it fresh each day. Let me show you ways you can keep your salvation fresh.

First—remember the day you got saved. In the verse above it says, *"Remember this day..."* Do you remember the day you got saved? You should regularly think back to the time when you accepted Christ as your Saviour and your life was changed.

Second—remember where you came from. You were delivered from the bondage of sin. If you are going to keep your salvation fresh, you need to remember what it was like before you got saved.

Third—Remember the blessings that salvation brought. Israel received many blessings by being delivered, and you received many blessings by being born again. Remember everything God has done for you since you've been saved!

Fourth—talk about your salvation to others. In (v.8), God told Israel to tell their children about their deliverance. If you want to keep your salvation fresh, then tell others about your salvation experience.

Fifth—sing about salvation. In (Ex. 15:1), Moses sang a song of deliverance. It is important that you listen to the right music, because whatever music you listen to is the same music you will sing. Friend, salvation is the greatest thing that will happen to your life. Don't let your salvation get stale; keep it fresh!

An Imaginary Crisis

"Take therefore no thought for the morrow: for the morrow shall take thought for the things of itself. Sufficient unto the day is the evil thereof." (Matt. 6:34)

Are you a "Worry Wart?" Do you worry over things that haven't even happened, yet? Maybe you are one of those who worries about the plane going down that you are flying on. Or maybe you worry about how you would pay the bills if you lost your job. Or maybe you are the type of parent who, if your child doesn't text you right back, fears the worst. You immediately imagine that they are lying in a ditch somewhere hurt and need help.

I have found that there are some people who, even if they don't have any legitimate things to worry about, will FIND something to worry about! There are even some who have a home-made survival pack all ready to go in case World War 3 breaks out or our power grid goes down!

As humans, we are often prone to worry. We fret and become anxious over circumstances that we aren't even facing, yet. That is why Jesus' reaction here, in Mathew 6, is almost humorous. It is as if Jesus is saying to these "Worry Warts," "Really? You don't have *enough* to worry about in your life? You don't already have *enough* challenges to face that you have to waste your energy mulling over imaginary ones?"

If that is you, His advice to you is stop worrying because *"the morrow shall take thought for the things of itself."* In other words, cross that bridge when you get there. Don't bring tomorrow's worries into today.

There is no reason to worry because the God of today's circumstances is also the God of tomorrow's circumstances.

Cast Clouts And Rotten Rags

"So Ebedmelech took the men with him, and went into the house of the king under the treasury, and took thence old cast clouts and old rotten rags, and let them down by cords into the dungeon to Jeremiah." (Jer. 38:11)

The message that Jeremiah was told to preach to the people of Israel was not a popular one. The princes of the kingdom had him placed into a horrible pit of mire where he was likely to die of hunger. Here are some lessons we learn from Jeremiah's pit experience.

FIRST—God can use anyone. Ebedmelech is not of the household of King David; he is not even an Israelite. He is a eunuch of Ethiopia. And yet, it is Ebedmelech that God uses to bring deliverance to the prophet Jeremiah.

SECOND—God can use anyone at any time. It seemed that the fate of Jeremiah was sealed. He was in a dungeon that he could not get out of on his own, so God sent the right man at the right time!

THIRD—God can use anyone at any time, in any place. Praise God for those whom He uses to encourage us when we are in the pit of circumstances.

FOURTH—God can use any thing. When Ebedmelech comes to the innermost prison, there are no cords to be found to let down to Jeremiah for his deliverance. Some old cast clouts and old rotten rags are found. They are tied together to make a rope. Jeremiah is told to place this homemade rope around his armpits and he is pulled to freedom.

You might feel like God could never use you. Be encouraged! If God can use old rotten rags for His glory, He can certainly use you!

293

From East To West

"As far as the east is from the west, so far hath he removed our transgressions from us." (Ps. 103:12)

When it comes to the sin we confess to God, the Bible says that God removes them *"As far as the east is from the west."* Now, if it had said He removes them "As far as the north is from the south" that is still quite a distance. If you were to begin at the South Pole and travel north, you would have to travel approximately 12,430 miles until you eventually reach the North Pole, the furthest a person can travel north.

Now that would be an amazing distance, to know that is how far away from us God has removed our sins. But it doesn't say that. It says God removes our sins, *"As far as the east is from the west."* Once you reach the North Pole, you immediately begin traveling south again.

But it is different when you travel east to west. When you start moving from the east to the west, there is no end! When you go west, you never stop going west. There is no point at which you have reached the end of west and begin going east again.

Praise God, that is how far away the Bible says our sin has been removed from us! That is how far God has removed our transgressions from us! God has removed them so far away that we will NEVER encounter them again!

5 Ways To Strengthen Your Marriage

"For this cause shall a man leave his father and mother, and shall be joined unto his wife, and they two shall be one flesh." (Eph. 5:31)

If you want to strengthen your marriage, here are five tried and true things you can begin doing today!

FIRST—Connect Spiritually. Marriage is a divine institution. Therefore, it is a spiritual union at its very core. You must have God, and His Word, as your foundation if you expect to have a successful marriage God can bless.

SECOND—Communicate Daily. Communication isn't simply talking TO someone, but talking WITH someone. Communication is making sure your spouse doesn't just hear, but understands what you are trying to say to them.

THIRD—Contact them Physically. Intimacy is a very important way to invest in your marriage. A couple who does not value or practice intimacy leaves themselves open to temptation. Many divorces have occurred because one or both spouses sought affection and intimacy outside of the marriage.

FOURTH—Compliment them Regularly. Learn to leave little notes for your spouse. Nothing will brighten their day like finding an unexpected note that reminds them how much you love them. Love notes are not just for when you are dating, they are important AFTER marriage, too!

FIFTH—Confess and forgive Instantly. Even the best of marriages have arguments and disagreements. But successful marriages learn how to deal with them when they come. When you are hurt, be willing to forgive immediately.

Stick On Jesus!

"Now there was leaning on Jesus' bosom one of his disciples, whom Jesus loved." (John 13:23)

Last Summer, my wife and I decided to spend our vacation in Washington, D.C. It was a great trip. We got to see so many wonderful sites which had tremendous historical significance. I wasn't brave enough to drive all the way into D.C., knowing how much traffic we would encounter. Instead, we rode the Metro Train in every day and walked everywhere we went. It would have been nice to have had a tour guide to take us everywhere.

Thinking about our trip, I read about a tour guide who was directing visitors through a large city in his country, speaking to the group in broken English. As they went down one of the busiest streets in the city, he stopped and wanted to impress the importance of them staying close to him as they continued. Loudly he said to them, "Stick on me!"

That story made me think of John. John was not only a disciple whom Jesus loved, but he was also known as a disciple who greatly loved Jesus. Just about every time we hear of John, he is described as leaning on Jesus, as if he was 'stuck' on Jesus.

Boy, what a testimony to have that you and Jesus were so close you were inseparable! Sometimes we get so busy going about our daily duties that we allow many things to come between us and Jesus. We allow 101 things to keep us from the closeness that Jesus wants us to have with Him.

Today, beware of letting things hinder your walk with God. Don't choose the immediate over the important. Stick on Jesus, today!

When God Is Silent

*"And it came to pass after ten days, that the word of the
LORD came unto Jeremiah." (Jer. 42:7)*

What a blessing it is to pray and see the answer to that
prayer come immediately. That is not always the case,
though. Jeremiah prayed and it was *"ten days"* before God
answered him. Sometimes we pray and there seems to be
NO immediate answer; it is as if God is silent. What should
you do when this happens?

FIRST—Remember your prayer has been heard.
Just because there is not an immediate response doesn't
mean your prayer wasn't heard. God heard you the first
time you prayed.

SECOND—Don't stop praying. Don't get
discouraged and quit praying just because you don't see the
answer right away. God may be testing you to see how
serious you are about your request. When a child asks for a
certain toy every day, multiple times a day, you know that
is a true desire of their heart. God may be waiting to see if
your prayer is a true desire of your heart.

**THIRD—Sometimes the answer isn't denied, only
delayed.** God may be delaying the answer in order to grow
your faith, or to grow some character quality in you that
may be lacking.

**FOURTH—Remember, there is a spiritual warfare
going on.** Often, prayers are not denied by God but they
may be hindered by Satan. Daniel prayed a prayer that took
21 days to get answered because Satan withstood the angel
of God from delivering an answer to him. Sometimes the
silence in your prayer life is because of a spiritual warfare
taking place. So, don't give up! Don't get discouraged!
Soon the answer will come!

Forgiving The Fallen

"And in those days Peter stood up in the midst of the disciples..." (Acts 1:15)

You wouldn't think it by looking at it, but this verse is one of the best examples of forgiveness we find in the New Testament. That's right! An amazing thing happened here that you just might miss if you're not careful.

Peter is standing up to preach on the day of Pentecost and the Holy Spirit moved with such power that it produced one of the greatest responses recorded in Scripture! Acts 2:41 says that those that *"gladly received his word"* and were baptized were *"about three thousand souls"*! WOW! What a response!

But...wait a minute. Who did God use to preach this powerful message and see such an amazing response? Peter? Wasn't this the same Peter who, only forty days before had denied even knowing Jesus Christ? How was Peter able to do this? How were the disciples able to get over his denial of Jesus and not only let him attend the meeting but actually be the keynote speaker?

The answer is found in verse 14 where it says that among those who were gathered in the upper room, praying with the disciples (which included Peter) were *"Mary the mother of Jesus, and...his brethren."*

Mary and Jesus' brethren were present in this gathering in the upper room where Peter took charge. Mary could have easily held a grudge against Peter for denying and abandoning her son when it mattered most.

Don't miss this...Pentecost (and all those who were saved as a result of it) may not have happened had they not forgiven Peter! Here's a question...what blessings might YOU be missing because of your unforgiving spirit? Repent. Grant and give forgiveness, today.

A Three-Day Getaway!

"We will go three days' journey into the wilderness, and sacrifice to the LORD our God, as he shall command us."
(Ex. 8:27)

When Moses and Aaron petitioned Pharaoh to let the people of Israel go out of the land of bondage in order to sacrifice to the Lord, Pharaoh tried to give them other options instead. His ultimate goal was to prevent their complete deliverance from him. No doubt his objections were masterminded by Satan, himself, who desires to keep every soul in bondage.

The first suggestion Pharaoh gave to Moses in (v.25) was *"sacrifice to your God in the land."* In other words, "Do what you must, just don't go too far with it. Stay right here in Egypt." Moses, however, was not deceived by this proposal. They had to leave Egypt because Egypt was a type of the world. He knew that separation from the world is the first rule of service. You cannot truly worship God while still living in the world!

So, Moses tells Pharaoh that his suggestion was unacceptable. Moses said, *"We will go three days' journey into the wilderness, and sacrifice to the LORD our God, as he shall command us."*

What a lesson for us, today. Satan will do whatever is necessary to keep us in the world. He wants us to stay in bondage to our sin. But God has called us to come out of this world and live a separated life unto Him.

A *"three days' journey"* would put such a sufficient gap between Israel and Egypt so as to make it plain to anyone who saw them that they had left Egypt behind! Some are content to stay in Egypt. Others are content with only a few miles' journey. What is even better? A *"three days' journey"*!

How To Get The Most Out Of Sunday's Sermon

"So then faith cometh by hearing, and hearing by the word of God." (Rom. 10:17)

God intends for us to grow in our walk with Him each day. He wants our faith in Him to increase, but that only comes from hearing His Word. Here are five ways you can increase your faith and get the most out of each Sunday's sermon.

Prepare your heart beforehand. You will not get anything out of the sermon if your heart is not ready to receive it. Therefore, prepare your heart before you ever get to church. Ask God to speak to you through His Word.

Pray for your pastor. Your pastor needs wisdom to know what message to preach and the sensitivity to follow the leading of the Holy Spirit in the service. Pray for God to guide his mind and guard his thoughts as he preaches.

Don't be distracted. During the sermon, Satan will do 1001 things to distract you from God's Word. And the further back in the church you sit, the more distracted you will become with babies crying, toddlers playing, and with people in general. One great way to stay focused is by taking notes of the sermon.

Apply it to your life. There is a message in each sermon for you. Look for it. What is the take-a-way from your pastor's message? What lesson is there that applies to your life? Ask God to reveal it to you.

Meditate on it during the week. Don't let the sermon die once you leave the service. Take it with you! Use the notes you took as a start to your weekly daily devotions. This will plant the seeds of God's Word further down in your soul.

Who Is With You?

"But the LORD is with me...therefore my persecutors shall stumble, and they shall not prevail:" (Jer. 20:11)

A 13-year-old boy and his brother were taken to a professional baseball game by their grandmother. On the way to the game, they stopped to pick up an elderly friend of their grandmother. They were not sure how exciting it would be, going to a ballgame with two elderly ladies. But then something happened that changed everything.

The boys knew something was different when, instead of parking in the regular parking lot, they drove up to the curb of the stadium and a man in a uniform opened the car doors and greeted them. They were then given the royal treatment. The man ushered them past the long line of people to a special elevator which then led to a private box.

They could not believe how they were able to get such great seats at the ballgame. They had never watched a ballgame from their own private box before. It was later that the boys learned that their grandmother's elderly friend was actually the mother of the General Manager for the ball team!

All of the special treatment they received was not because of who *they* were, but because of who was *with* them!

One of these days we will take our last breath. We will be ushered by angels past the sun, moon, and stars. We will soar right past the Milky Way and every other galaxy in our universe. We will be carried even further still by our angelic guides right into the presence of God! And it won't be because of who WE are, but because of who is with us, JESUS! He is our ticket into Heaven. It is not our good works that will gain our entrance into glory. No! It will all be because of JESUS!

Evening, Morning, And At Noon

"Evening, and morning, and at noon, will I pray, and cry aloud: and he shall hear my voice." (Ps. 55:17)

Some believe David wrote this Psalm when he was forced to leave Jerusalem because of the rebellion his son Absalom led against him. It was one of the darkest times in the life of David. This verse reminds us that no matter what we are facing, the only real help comes from God. Notice the three times David mentions praying.

FIRST—He Prayed in the EVENING. The evening includes the midnight hour. It is the darkest part of the night. The darkest part of your trial can be the *easiest* and *hardest* times to pray. It can be the easiest time to pray because you are hurting and need relief. But it can also be the hardest time to pray because your heart is breaking and you don't even know what to say.

SECOND—He Prayed in the MORNING. The morning represents a fresh new day. The morning time can be a struggle for some because they are too busy preparing for the day. But the best prepared day is a day prepared in prayer! Even when I wake up with the freshness of a brand new day, I still need to pray because noontime is coming. The heat of the day and the darkness of night will soon be upon me.

THIRD—He Prayed at Noon. Noontime is the brightest part of the day. The sun is at its peak; things cannot get any brighter than at noontime. Sometimes, when things are going well, we don't see the need for prayer. Yet, David prayed.

The lesson is this: anytime is a good time to pray! You cannot pray at a wrong time, whether it is at evening, in the morning, or at noon.

How Thirsty Are You?

"My soul thirsteth for God, for the living God..."(Ps. 42:2)

There's nothing like being thirsty. Just ask Dave Buschow. He was one of eleven other hikers from various walks of life who were led into the hot Utah desert by expert guides. It was a wilderness survival adventure designed to test their physical and mental toughness.

By Day 2, in the blazing hot sun, Dave was already in bad shape. The guides noticed that his speech had become slurred and his body was wracked by cramps. This 29-year-old man was desperate for water and began hallucinating so badly that he mistook a tree for a person.

After going roughly 10 hours without a drink in the 100-degree heat, he finally dropped dead of thirst, face down in the dirt. Ironically, when he died of thirst he was less than 100 yards from the goal: a cave with a pool of water in it!

You want to know what the worst part of it all was? It was found out later that the guides were carrying emergency water the whole time! He died of thirst despite the fact that the very people there to protect him had water they could have given him.

This story made me think...how long has it been since we have been thirsty for God? Jesus said that He is the Water of Life, yet how long has it been since we said as David did, *"My soul thirsteth for God"*?

The great thing about thirsting after God is, He never runs out of cool, refreshing water! He has all we could ever want or need, if we will just come to Him.

Christian Atheism

"The fool hath said in his heart, There is no God..."
(Ps. 14:1)

I know what you're thinking: "There's no such thing as Christian atheism." And you would be right. But the Bible calls the atheist a "fool" and there are two types of atheists: the *intellectual* atheist, and the *practical* atheist.

An **intellectual** atheist is one who BELIEVES there is no God. A **practical** atheist is one who BEHAVES as if there is no God.

More foolish than the person who says there is no God, is a person who says he believes there IS a God but doesn't live like it!

I submit to you that there may not be any *intellectual* atheists in our churches, but there are multitudes of *practical* atheists in our churches! I'm talking about those who profess to know Christ as their Savior; they profess to BELIEVE in God, yet Monday through Saturday they BEHAVE as if there is no God!

In the Garden of Eden, Satan knew he could not convince Eve that there was no God. After all, they had fellowship with God every day. But by convincing her to disobey God's Word she BEHAVED as if there was no God and as if there was no commandment from God.

Friend, by the way we live our lives, we show whether or not we truly believe in God and His Word. When the world sees us living in disobedience to the very truths we claim to believe, then our lives are sending as mixed a message as if we called ourselves Christian Atheists!

The Uber Driver Who Fought Satan And Won!

"For we wrestle... against spiritual wickedness in high places." (Eph. 6:12)

It was a cold, snowy day and a group of Christians were outside an abortion clinic in the sleet/rain mixture hoping to persuade women to keep their babies. The group had been outside for three long, bone-chilling hours.

Just when they were deciding whether or not to leave, one of the volunteers stopped a car coming to the clinic. She talked with them a long time. The Uber driver was surprised he had driven the woman to an abortion clinic. She had not told him that her destination would bring about the death of her unborn child.

The woman got out of the car and walked into the abortion center. The Uber driver, who was a Christian, knew abortion was wrong and was almost in tears over having brought her to this place. He said he had even offered her $500 if only she would not abort, but she had refused.

A volunteer said to him, "Maybe if you go back into the clinic and fight for that baby, you could save a life." Satan was at work and there wasn't much time left.

All of the sudden, he got out of his car, and boldly went into the abortion center. A few moments later, the Uber driver emerged, his arm entwined in the woman's arm and they both were smiling!

The Uber driver was an ordinary man who God led to walk into a stronghold of Satan and rescue two lives headed for destruction. What if God asked YOU to fight Satan for someone, today? Would you be ready?

Open Your Hand

"That they do good, that they be rich in good works, ready to distribute, willing to communicate;" (1Tim. 6:18)

A little boy had his hand caught in a milk bottle. Try as they might, he and his mother could not get it out until she noticed his hand was closed. His mother said to him, "Open your hand, Billy." Billy said, "I can't. If I do, I'll lose the penny I am holding."

How often do we find ourselves acting like little Billy? When we get something we want, we hold on to it for dear life. What Billy didn't realize was that he didn't have a hold of that money, that money had a hold of him!

Paul told Timothy to charge those who are rich with this world's goods not to let their possessions possess them.

There is nothing wrong with having money or nice things, but God wants us to realize that they were not given to us so that we might be stingy and hold on to it all for ourselves. God wants us to be thankful for everything He has given to us and one way to show our thankfulness is by being rich in *"good works"* and being *"ready to distribute"* to others in need.

Have you been blessed? Open your hand up and pass on those blessing to others. It might just be all it takes to show them the love of Jesus and lead them to salvation in Christ.

There's A Frog In My Bed!

"And if thou refuse to let them go, behold, I will smite all thy borders with frogs: And the river shall bring forth frogs abundantly, which shall go up and come into thine house, and into thy bedchamber, and upon thy bed..." (Ex. 8:2-3)

King Pharaoh was in a mess! The Children of Israel were in bondage to Pharaoh and were his servants, so God sent Moses to tell Pharaoh to let His people go, but Pharaoh was a stubborn old king who refused to heed God's command.

As a result, God sent him a dire warning. He said that if Pharaoh did not obey, He would send frogs, that's right, FROGS, to invade the land. Well, Pharaoh didn't listen, so God kept His promise and sent thousands and thousands of frogs into Egypt. They were everywhere!

At bedtime, when Pharaoh pulled back the covers, he found frogs in his bed! He couldn't sleep at all that night because all night long all he heard was, "Ribet! Ribet! Ribet!" I'm sure he was sick of hearing all those frogs croaking.

When he woke up the next morning, he may have thought it was all a horrible dream, until he went to eat breakfast and found frogs in his cereal bowl.

The worst part of this was that Pharaoh brought it on himself. Had he obeyed God to begin with, none of it would have happened.

Sometimes, we can be like Pharaoh. We stubbornly go our own way and disobey God's Word. God warns us of the consequences, but we refuse to listen. We think we can somehow disobey and get away with it, but then suddenly we find a frog in our bed!

Don't run from God. Don't make God send frogs into your life before you will repent.

Why, God?

"Then Agrippa said unto Paul, Almost thou persuadest me to be a Christian." (Acts 26:28)

Paul found himself living in shackles as a prisoner. I'm sure he often asked the Lord why this was happening.

Have you ever found yourself asking God, "Why?" Have you ever questioned God's wisdom in why He allowed certain circumstances into your life? If so, you are not alone. In times like this we often find ourselves asking three why's.

WHY ME? I wonder how many nights in prison Paul asked God, "Why? Why am I locked up in jail when I could be out there witnessing to people?" I would have asked the same question. Why does it seem bad things happened to those who are serving God when the wicked seem to get away with their wickedness?

Maybe you are asking God the same thing about YOUR circumstances. "Why me?"

WHY THIS? Paul may have thought, "Of all the things that could happen to me, why should I have to be locked up? Why should I have to lose my freedom and become a prisoner?"

Maybe you have asked God the same thing. "Why does it have to be MY child who rebelled against God? Why does it have to be MY marriage that is falling apart? Why this?"

WHY NOW? Paul eventually realized that it was God's perfect timing for him to be in prison. God had a divine appointment scheduled between Paul and King Agrippa. God needed Paul in this prison at this time in order to give the gospel to a king no other believer had access to. Give your whys to God and trust He knows best.

A Thief's Joy Ride To Waffle House

"It is as sport to a fool to do mischief: but a man of understanding hath wisdom." (Prov. 10:23)

A woman is looking at theft charges after she stole an electric scooter from Walmart and took it on a joy ride to Waffle House.

WPTV reported that Sally Selby, 45, was pulled over by police in Crossville, Tennessee, while riding the stolen cart. She told the officers she was driving it to Waffle House for a cup of coffee.

At first, when she was pulled over, Selby told police she had built the cart. But a Walmart surveillance video showed her enter the store, shop with the cart, and then just drive the scooter out the store and keep going right on going through the parking lot.

In her defense, she at least had the decency to drive it in the slow lane. :)

The Bible says, *"It is as sport to a fool to do mischief."* In other words, there are foolish people who think it is fun to do foolish things. They are known as fools by their foolish actions.

How are YOU known by others? What do YOUR actions say about the type of person you are? Proverbs 13:20 says, *"He that walketh with wise men shall be wise: but a companion of fools shall be destroyed."*

If you don't want to be thought of as a fool, don't hang around with foolish people. Their foolishness will end up affecting you, too. Rather, hang around with those who are godly and wise. Then, maybe you can go to Waffle House for a cup of coffee without being arrested!

Saved by A String!

"Behold, when we come into the land, thou shalt bind this line of scarlet thread in the window which thou didst let us down by: and thou shalt bring thy father, and thy mother, and thy brethren, and all thy father's household, home unto thee." (Josh. 2:18)

History tells us that before a bridge was built across the Niagara Falls, several lives were lost as people attempted to ferry across the turbulent, roaring rapids. Not many people know that the first step in constructing a bridge over the Falls was made by a 10-year-old boy named Homan Walsh. In 1848, little Homan won a $10 prize for successfully flying a kite from one side of the gorge to the other.

Someone on the opposite side caught the kite and tied a little stronger string to the end of the kite string, and the new, thicker string was pulled back across the gorge. The process was repeated many times, adding a larger, stronger cord, until they were able to run a cable all the way across. Finally, they had cables going across that were strong enough to support workers, tools, and materials. Eventually, the two nations were connected by a sturdy bridge over which trucks and trains could pass. And it all started with one tiny kite string!

Ironically, we read in Joshua about a lady named Rahab who was able to save her entire family with a little red string! The two spies from Israel told her if she placed a scarlet thread in the window, then everyone in the house would be spared when they came to overthrow the city.

Thank God today for His scarlet thread. Thank Him for the blood of Jesus that forgives and cleanses our sin!

Alexa, Stop Listening!

"But I say unto you, That every idle word that men shall speak, they shall give account thereof in the day of judgment. 37 For by thy words thou shalt be justified, and by thy words thou shalt be condemned." (Matt. 12:36-37)

When Amazon created Alexa, it was an amazing thing. You could ask it any question and it would give you the answer. Some say Alexa is like having your own personal assistant that never asks for a raise.

But it was recently reported that there is a problem. A BIG problem! The problem is she's always listening—and so are thousands of Amazon workers, according to a report. Teams stationed around the world listen to and transcribe recordings, up to 1,000 audio clips per nine-hour shifts.

But it's not only Alexa. SIRI and Google Assistant also have human workers that listen to snippets of audio, as well.

One day, while riding in our car, my wife said something about getting our grandson son some cereal. But because "cereal" sounds like "SIRI," SIRI automatically came up on my wife's phone and said, "I will look that up for you."

SCARY!!!

We live in a day where just about anything you say can be heard (or recorded) by some form of technology.

So, it should not surprise us that God also hears every word we say, too. Not only does He hear them, but we will one day be judged by them!

If you think it's scary that Alexa, SIRI, and Google are listening, just remember that God even hears what they can't. Guard your words today. They are being recorded for later!

The Danger Of Raising Children To Be Popular

"To the praise of the glory of his grace, wherein he hath made us accepted in the beloved." (Eph. 1:6)

There is nothing wrong with popularity in and of itself. The danger is that when children SEEK popularity several things happen.

They will follow culture instead of developing character. The things that are popular in our culture are not things which tend to develop character in our children. Children who seek popularity will seek it through Pop culture which glorifies the wrong things. Therefore, I would rather my child be behind times as far as culture goes, but grow up to have character.

They will seek acceptance from the wrong people. Children who seek popularity will seek acceptance from those whom they perceive are already popular. Thus, they will feel pressured to act or do whatever the "popular" crowd does in order to gain their acceptance, which will lead them into risky behavior such as smoking, drinking, drug use, and sexual activity. They need to be taught that their acceptance comes from who they are in Christ, not by what others think of them.

They will become depressed trying to maintain a social status. They don't realize that once they attain popularity and are in the "popular" group, they have to work at staying there. Popularity is fickle: one day you're in and the next day you're out.

Popularity can become a god. Children who are raised to be popular don't realize that popularity becomes a god to them. So, teach your child to stand up for what is right, even if they stand alone.

Fair-Weather Followers

"And the multitudes that went before, and that followed, cried, saying, Hosanna to the Son of David..." (Matt. 21:9)

As Jesus rode into Jerusalem on the back of a donkey, the Bible says, *"a very great multitude"* paved the way for Him by laying their clothes and palms down forming a pathway for Him to ride upon.

At this point in His ministry, the crowd was for Him. The people celebrated Him. They saw Him as the up-and-coming leader who may help them overthrow Rome and free them. They saw Him as the answer to their problems.

But as with everything, the celebration was short lived. This very same crowd that cheered Him later jeered Him. Those who at one time said, "Crown Him! Crown Him!" later cried, "Crucify Him! Crucify Him!" Those who at one time said, "Hail Him! Hail Him!" later shouted "Nail Him! Nail Him!"

Matthew 26:67 says that not long after that, *"they spit in his face, and buffeted him; and others smote him with the palms of their hands,"*

Oh, what a difference a day makes!

How many people are the very same way, today? On Sunday they are singing about Jesus, but on Monday they're too embarrassed to mention His name. On Sunday they are serving God, but on Monday they are serving themselves.

The world is looking for someone that is real and who lives a consistent Christian life; someone who isn't afraid to stand for Jesus. They need to see someone who is the same every time they see them. Are you a fair-weather follower?

Crawling Before Quitting

"And of some have compassion, making a difference: And others save with fear, pulling them out of the fire..."
(Jude 1:22-23)

This year, thousands of runners finished the grueling 26.2 miles of the 123rd Boston Marathon. There were some incredible stories of people who were running, including one man who was running in memory of his fiancé who was killed after she ran the last marathon.

But amidst all of the stories, one stood out from the rest. What made this story so special wasn't about what had happened *before* the race, but what actually happened *during* the race.

Micah Herndon, a Marine, was running the Boston Marathon in honor of three fallen comrades. That was special, but that wasn't the unusual part.

For most of the race, Micah had done well, but suddenly things fell apart. Around the 22nd mile, his legs began to cramp. He fell down because his legs literally stopped working. But Micah wasn't going to let his legs locking up stop him from honoring these three men.

His three friends were killed in a bombing in Afghanistan in 2010. Micah survived and he wasn't going to give up for them in this marathon until he crossed the line. To everyone's amazement, he literally crawled the last four miles to the finish line on his hands and knees!

When I read his story, it got me to thinking. If a man is willing to run 22 miles and literally crawl another four miles for people who had already died, what are WE willing to do to reach those who ARE dying without Christ? Micah would rather crawl than quit. To what lengths are we willing to go to get the Gospel to those who need it most?

Throw It Overboard

"..the next day they lightened the ship; And...we cast out with our own hands the tackling of the ship."
(Acts 27:19-19)

The apostle Paul was on a ship bound for Rome when he got word from the Lord that it would be a very dangerous journey. Their ship encountered a severe storm. It was so bad that they were sure the ship would sink.

It soon became obvious that a decision had to be made concerning the heavy cargo onboard. It was so serious that every non-essential piece of cargo had to be thrown overboard.

As you and I go through life we will encounter storms. These storms can become so severe it may seem as though we will go under. What should we do when this happens?

FIRST—Assess your situation realistically. Paul knew that this storm was allowed by God because God could have stopped it. Don't buy into the doom and gloom Satan throws your way every time a storm comes. Just like Paul, God may have you in that storm for a reason so don't over-react, Just keep trusting God.

SECOND—Lighten your load. Sometimes God wants to make us reevaluate our priorities. They had to take a hard look at the things they felt they needed to keep and the things they could live without. It is easy to get our priorities out of line and begin living for things that have no eternal value.

THIRD—Maintain a right spirit. In the midst of a storm that was about to sink their ship, Paul said, *"I exhort you to be of good cheer..."* God wants us to maintain a right spirit because that shows we trust that He is still in control. Do you have things weighing you down, spiritually? If so, throw it overboard!

Homeless By Choice

"But made himself of no reputation, and took upon him the form of a servant, and was made in the likeness of men:"
(Phil. 2:7)

Years ago, I read about a group of men from a church who had a heart to reach the homeless in their city. They found where the homeless lived and for about three days each year, they would go live among them in order to grow in their love and compassion for them.

They would do their best to live like the homeless lived for those three days. They didn't take nice tents or sleeping bags to stay in. They didn't take any food or special warm clothing.

In fact, the only food they would buy would be from the money they would receive from begging like everyone else. They truly took on the form of the homeless.

I wonder if that isn't a small picture of what Jesus did for us. The God of all creation left the portals of Glory, came to Earth and *"took upon him the form of a servant, and was made in the likeness of men:"*

Why did He do that? So that He could understand how we live and sympathize with our temptations and suffering. He also came to destroy Satan's power over us.

Hebrews 2:14 says, *"Forasmuch then as the children are partakers of flesh and blood, he also himself likewise took part of the same; that through death he might destroy him that had the power of death, that is, the devil;"*

Ultimately, Jesus Christ became like us so that we could one day become like Him!

Ask God to help you sympathize with the lost around you, today, remembering where you were before Jesus saved you.

316

The Number Of Our Days

"So teach us to number our days, that we may apply our hearts unto wisdom." (Ps. 90:12)

Every birth in this world is the beginning of a countdown which, without fail, ends with a forced exit from this life. From the moment we take our first breath, our life begins counting down. Life begins ticking away, one second...one minute...one hour...one day at a time.

Life on Earth is a one-way, dead-end street. Every day about four hundred thousand new people arrive on this planet. Every day thousands of people leave it for eternity.

Their time ran out.

Sadly, most people live their lives completely indifferent to this undeniable fact and there is no amount fame or fortune that can add one second to that final countdown.

One night in the cold Atlantic ocean there was a grim countdown. The "unsinkable" *Titanic* hit an iceberg and plunged into the icy depths of the sea, carrying with it many of those who were on board—some drinking, some partying, and some enjoying life to its fullest, completely unaware their time was running out.

May we learn to *"number our days."* May we never forget that our planet is but a larger *Titanic,* carrying its enormous passenger list to the chilly waters of the grave.

Now is the time to ask God for wisdom to become better students and stewards of our time and opportunities. We number our years, not our days, but all of us have to live a day at a time, and we do not know how many days we have left.

Are you numbering YOUR days?

God's Eraser

*"I, even I, am he that blotteth out thy transgressions for
mine own sake, and will not remember thy sins."*
(Isa. 43:25)

In the 1700's, erasers had not yet been invented. Up
until then, crusts of bread were used to erase marks on
paper.

Then, one day, in 1770, British engineer Edward
Nairne was reaching for a piece of bread to erase a mistake
he had made on paper, but accidentally picked up a piece of
latex rubber by mistake. He found that the piece of latex
erased his error more effectively than the crust of bread,
leaving only rubberized "crumbs" he could easily sweep
away with his hand.

God tells us in Isaiah 43 that when we bring our sins to
the Lord—the Bread of Life—He can blot them out even
better than the best eraser man can make!

When WE make a mistake on paper that needs to be
erased, we still remember that mistake. But the Bible says
that when GOD blots out our sin, He *"will not remember"*
it anymore! Praise the Lord!

Often, Satan will bring up some past mistake or sin in
our lives in order to defeat us. But if that sin was confessed
and given to God, it no longer exists! It's been erased
forever!

If there is sin in your life that you have NOT repented
of, bring it to Jesus. Not only can He forgive your sin, but
He can completely blot it out, never to be remembered
again!

The Best Way To Attend Church

"I was glad when they said unto me, Let us go into the house of the LORD." (Ps. 122:1)

Have you ever thought about why you attend church? If someone were to ask you that question, how would you answer? What would you say?

People often attend church for different reasons and with different attitudes. David gives us the best way to attend the house of the Lord.

FIRST—Attend church PERSONALLY. David used the words "I" and "me" when referring to going to the house of the Lord. Sadly, many parents will send their children to church but will not attend themselves. Many husbands will send their wife and children but not attend themselves. What kind of message does that send?

SECOND—Attend church JOYFULLY. Next, David said, *"I was glad..."* The thought of attending the house of the Lord made David happy! Attending church should be a joyful occasion. Getting to sing songs of worship and fellowship with God's people, all while hearing God's Word preached, should make us eager to attend.

THIRD—Attend church EXPECTANTLY. We should expect something when we go to the house of the Lord. We should attend with a spirit of expectation; expecting God to speak to us through His Word. David was happy because he knew something good always happened at the house of the Lord.

Notice David said, *"I was glad when <u>they</u> said unto me..."* It encouraged David when someone else encouraged him to go to church. Think about these three things as you prepare for church this Sunday.

Direction From A Dolphin

"Howbeit when he, the Spirit of truth, is come, he will guide you into all truth:" (John 16:13)

Sailors tell the story that for 24 years (from 1888 to 1912), a certain dolphin would guide their ships through the French Pass, a dangerous channel near New Zealand. Up until this dolphin got involved, many ships had been shipwrecked because of the many big rocks and strong currents in that area.

This dolphin's direction was so reliable that when ships reached the channel they would literally wait for him to appear before they would proceed. The dolphin would always stay with the ship, playfully swimming alongside, until it was safely across the bay.

There are no telling how many human lives were saved by the actions of this dolphin.

Then one day a drunken passenger onboard a ship the dolphin was guiding drew a gun and shot the dolphin. When the crew saw blood coming from the dolphin, they nearly killed the drunk man. After being shot, the dolphin disappeared and ships had to navigate the treacherous waters alone.

But, to their surprise, a few weeks later the dolphin returned, apparently recovered from his wound, and resumed his work of guiding ships through the channel.

As Christians, we have something even better than a dolphin, we have the Holy Spirit to guide us through the treacherous waters of this world. And the best part is...He will NEVER leave us!

The Bible says the Holy Spirit was given to us to guide us *"into all truth."* Thank the Lord, this morning for the gift of the indwelling of the Holy Spirit, and the guidance He gives.

God Doesn't Need A Can Opener

"Marvel not at this: for the hour is coming, in the which all that are in the graves shall hear his voice, And shall come forth..." (John 5:28-29)

Most people do not know that it wasn't until 48 years after tin cans had been being produced that someone finally invented the can opener! Until then, the only way a person could open a can was with a hammer and chisel.

Finally, in 1858, Ezra Warnet invented the can opener, but it still did not become popular for another 10 years and then only because it was given away free with canned beef.

Today, when a person dies, they are sealed in a casket. Jesus told His disciples that one day *"all that are in the graves shall hear his voice, And shall come forth..."* This has already happened once before, after His resurrection.

*"Jesus, when he had cried again with a loud voice, yielded up the ghost...And **the graves were opened**; and many bodies of the saints which slept arose,"*
(Matt. 27:50,52).

But it is going to happen again at the Rapture!

"For the Lord himself shall descend from heaven with a shout, with the voice of the archangel, and with the trump of God: and the dead in Christ shall rise first:"
(1Thess. 4:16)

Although the casket and tombs of the dead will be sealed tight, God will not need a can opener or special gadget. All He will have to do is say, "Children, come forth!" And just like that, the dead in Christ will rise! Oh, what a moment! Are you ready?

Let God Do The Worrying

"Casting all your care upon Him; for He careth for you."
(1Peter 5:7)

I admit it. I am guilty as charged. Sometimes I can be a bonafide, full-fledged, card-carrying worrier!

How about you?

I don't want to be. I don't try to be. And I know it is wrong. Yet, in spite of all of that...I still find myself tempted to worry when circumstances come into my life that I have no control over.

Because I do not readily see how it will all work out, I can allow Satan to build up a stronghold of fear and doubt in my mind. And before I know it, my circumstances have become bigger than my God!

Does that sound familiar? Can you relate to that?

I recently heard someone describe worry as "emotional atheism!" Wow! How convicting is that? That may sound strong, but it really puts worry into perspective, doesn't it?

Charles Spurgeon said, "If God cares for you, why need you care too? Can you trust Him for your soul, and not for your body? He has never refused to bear your burdens, He has never fainted under their weight. Come, then, soul! Have done with fretful care, and leave all thy concerns in the hand of a gracious God."

Has a spirit of worry and doubt consumed you? Are you burdened down with the weight of worry? Are you struggling to give your cares to God?

He has, in no uncertain terms, invited you to cast *"all your care upon Him; for He careth for you."*

Shrimp Eyes

"Blessed are the pure in heart: for they shall see God."
(Matt. 5:8)

The mantis shrimp is neither a mantis nor a shrimp, but derives its name from claws similar to a praying mantis and a body similar to a shrimp. They can grow to be about 12 inches long. This sea creature likes to live a solitary life, hiding in rock formations and waiting for prey to come by, though it will chase and kill for food.

They were called "sea locust" by the ancient Assyrians, and in Australia they are referred to as "prawn killers." Unfortunately, they are also called "thumb splitters" because of the nasty gash they can inflict if not handled carefully.

Mantis shrimp have powerful claws that they use to attack prey, but the characteristic that really stands out in the mantis shrimp is its eyes. They are considered the most complex eyes in the animal kingdom. Each eye is mounted at the end of a stalk and can move independently. Not only that, but each eye is designed to have three regions, giving the mantis shrimp the ability to see three parts of an object from a slightly different angle!

In the Bible, Jesus talked about improving your eyesight. He said that our ability to see God is directly related to our hearts. We must be *"pure in heart"* if we want to see God as He is.

Is there any sin in your life that may be hindering your spiritual eyesight?

NOVEMBER 20

Gardening With God

"And the LORD God planted a garden...And out of the ground made the LORD God to grow every tree that is pleasant to the sight..." (Gen. 2:8-9)

Did you know that God is a gardener? The first thing He did after He created man was to create a garden in which to put man. God wanted man to garden with Him.

What a great picture of the Christian life, today. Your heart is the field, and God is the Gardener. There are two main actions a gardener must take in order to ensure a beautiful garden. Ironically, it is the same two things we as Christians must do to ensure we grow and mature as believers.

A good garden requires FEEDING. One of the most important steps in gardening is watering and fertilizing your plants. They need nutrients or they will not grow. Likewise, we must feed ourselves daily on God's Word if we expect to grow like we should.

Just like a plant will dry up and die if it does not get enough water, we will dry up and die, spiritually, without a daily walk with God. What are you feeding on? Is your life drying up, spiritually?

A good garden requires WEEDING. The natural enemy of a plant is weeds. If left unattended, weeds will grow faster and taller than the plants because they steal the nutrients away from the plants.

Satan loves to plant weeds into our lives; things that will try to steal away our spiritual life so that we dry up and die.

Maybe you need to spend some time *feeding* and *weeding* so that you can once again grow and be a healthy Christian.

When You're Waiting On An Answer

".. O LORD of hosts, if thou wilt indeed look on the affliction of thine handmaid, and...wilt give unto thine handmaid a man child..." (1Sam. 1:11)

Hannah was facing a hopeless situation. She desperately wanted a child, but God had shut up her womb. She decides to take her request to God. We find three things about her request that we should keep in mind.

Notice her PETITION. (v.10) says, *"And she was in bitterness of soul, and prayed unto the Lord, and wept sore."* Hannah had suffered because of her barrenness and the ridicule she endured. Because of her bitterness, it would have been easy for her to have blamed God. After all, it was God who had shut up her womb to begin with. Don't let your circumstances get you bitter.

Notice her SUBMISSION. In (v.11) Hannah prays, *"And she vowed a vow, and said, O LORD of hosts, if thou wilt...give unto thine handmaid a man child, then I will give him unto the LORD all the days of his life..."*

Oh, how we need mothers like that, today! How we need more God-fearing mothers who are fully surrendered to God. While she waited, she submitted.

Notice her CONFIRMATION. In (v.17) Eli, the Priest, answered and said, *"Go in peace: and the God of Israel grant thee thy petition that thou hast asked of him."* That was music to Hannah's ears! She was finally going to have a baby! Her **petition** and her **submission** paid off.

If you are still waiting on an answer, don't give up! The answer could come in one day, one month, or a year from now. We are not promised how soon God will answer, but rest assured, God heard your prayer!

How To Cast The Right Kind Of Shadow

"..they brought forth the sick into the streets, and laid them on beds and couches, that at the least the shadow of Peter passing by might overshadow some of them." (Acts 5:15)

The Bible says that people were bringing the sick hoping that they may even be healed by Peter's shadow as he passed by them! What power!

Every one of us have our own shadow of influence which can either help or hurt the cause of Christ. In order to cast the right shadow, you must have:

The right view of the SUN (SON). Anything and everything will cast a shadow when the sun comes out. You don't have to be beautiful, smart, or talented, to cast a shadow. All you have to be is in a direct view of the sun. Likewise, in order to have the right spiritual influence on others that we should, we need to be sure that we are in direct view of the S-O-N, Jesus.

The right view of SIN. In the first 10 verses of this chapter, Peter dealt with the sin of Annanias & Saphira. You will never cast the right shadow until sin has been dealt with in your own life.

The right view of YOURSELF. Peter wasn't even aware of his shadow. It wasn't planned or promoted. He was simply pointing people toward Jesus. Proud people will never cast the right shadow.

The right view of SINNERS. (v.16) says, *"and they were healed every one."* Unlike today's FAKE (faith) healers who only seem to heal certain ones, everyone that day got healed. Ask God to help you have the right shadow of influence on those around you today for the glory of God.

Who's Your Daddy?

"In this the children of God are manifest, and the children of the devil: whosoever doeth not righteousness is not of God, neither he that loveth not his brother" (1John 1:10)

The Bible says there are only two families in this world. You are either a child of God or a child of the devil. Some religions teach that we are ALL God's children, but that is not scriptural. We are all God's CREATION, but we are not all God's CHILDREN.

Only those who have been born again are God's children. In fact, Jesus said to the religious rulers of His day, *"Ye are of your father the devil..."* (John 8:44). So what is it that distinguishes a child of God from a child of the devil? Two things.

John said, *"whosoever doeth not righteousness is not of God, neither he that loveth not his brother" (1John 1:10).*

Johns says that LIVING RIGHT (doing righteousness) and LOVING RIGHT (God's love) is what separates the children of God from the children of the devil. In other words, if you are a child of God, it should show on the outside. People ought to be able to tell by the way you LIVE and the way you LOVE that you are a child of God.

So, let me ask you, "Who's your daddy? Jesus or the devil?"

Let the love of God shine through you today so that the world may see who your father really is!

When The Enemy Surrounds You

"And the children of Ammon came out, and put the battle in array...and...Joab saw that the front of the battle was against him before and behind..." (2Sam. 10:8-9)

Like David, we may find ourselves surrounded by the enemy. What should we do when this happens?

FIRST—Keep doing right. Ironically, this started after David had actually done something nice. David showed respect to the newly crowned king of the Ammonites, but the king rejected David's kindness. Sometimes your kindness will be rejected. Keep doing right, anyway.

SECOND—Don't lose hope. Satan wants you to believe that your situation is hopeless, but as long as there is a God, there is hope!

THIRD—Don't fight the enemy alone. David's military advisor chose his elite soldiers to defend the front and back gates. Don't try and fight the enemy alone. Surround yourself with others stronger than you are. That is why attending church is so important. It reminds you that you are not in this alone.

FOURTH—Have a plan of attack. They didn't ask for this war but they were not going surrender, either. You better have a plan when temptation surrounds you, or you will be defeated.

FIFTH—Keep your focus on God. Before dismissing the troops to their positions, Joab reminded them that the fight belonged to the LORD.

SIXTH—Give God the glory. They honored God and God delivered them. Trusting God when you have been surrounded honors Him. When it seems the enemy has surrounded you, just remember that your God is much bigger than your enemy!

They Brought Him To Jesus

"And they brought young children to him, that he should touch them..." (Mark 10:13)

These mothers in Mark 10 brought their children to Jesus for one reason: they wanted Him to TOUCH them. Hey, parents, that tells me that even children can be touched by the Lord! You may think your child isn't learning anything in church, but I promise you they pick up more than you think.

The best thing parents can do for their children is to bring them to Jesus; making sure they are constantly under the Word of God so that He can touch their young lives.

But notice it says, "THEY" brought them to Jesus, meaning it wasn't the baby-sitter, or the nanny; it was the PARENTS that brought them to Jesus. It isn't the pastor, youth pastor, Sunday School Teacher, or Junior Church leader's sole responsibility to get your child to Jesus; it's YOUR responsibility as their parent.

Evidently, the mothers had already been to Jesus, themselves. The mothers could not have brought their children to Jesus had THEY not already known where Jesus was, themselves. Meaning, you as a parent need to have a fresh encounter with Jesus yourself, first. Your child needs to see that Jesus has touched YOUR life before you expect Him to touch THEIR lives.

Is Jesus working in YOUR life, mom? Is Jesus working in YOUR life, dad? Let your child see Jesus in you, first, then bring them to Jesus so He can touch their lives, too!

A Whale Of A Prayer

"Then Jonah prayed unto the LORD his God out of the fish's belly," (Jonah 2:1)

When Jonah was thrown overboard by the sailors, the churning sea immediately pulled the prophet under water. He was struggling to survive, but survival in a stormy, turbulent sea was next to impossible.

Within minutes Jonah would have drowned if the Lord had not saved him. Once he was within the smelly black darkness of the fish's stomach, however, Jonah could tell where he was. In fact, he said in *(v.2) "out of the belly of hell cried I..."*

He prayed in spite of his PLACE. It says *"Jonah prayed unto the Lord his God out of the fish's belly..."* What a unique place to pray. Many people pray only in the confines of a church or other sacred-feeling place. But Jonah prayed from a fish's stomach. See, the **place** of prayer is not important. You can pray anywhere. What is important is the **practice** of prayer.

He prayed in spite of his PLIGHT. He said, *"I am cast out of thy sight...my soul fainted" (2:4,7)*. Jonah's plight was bad. His circumstances seemed so dark that he felt even God couldn't see where he was. That is a bad place to be!

He was in about the worst circumstances a person could find themselves in, yet he prayed. We do not have to feel well to pray. We do not have to be up on the mountaintop to pray. God hears us regardless of our situation. And this should encourage us to pray.

No matter what you are facing, it is always a good time to pray!

It's Time To Get Up

"..the LORD spake unto Joshua...Moses my servant is dead; now therefore arise," (Josh. 1:1-2)

Israel had seen some miraculous things under the courageous leadership of Moses but now there is a problem...Moses is dead! Thankfully, God already had a leader in place; it was Joshua.

The people were still mourning the death of Moses and even Joshua himself had fallen into despair. So, God had to remind him that it was time to get up!

God said, *"Moses my servant is dead; now therefore arise..."* In other words, "Joshua, mourning time is over. It's time to get up and move forward." Sure, there is a time for mourning, but at some point, it is time to rise up and go on for God.

There will be times in all of our lives where Satan will knock us down with circumstances that seem to overwhelm us. It may *slow* us down but we must not let it *keep* us down!

It was time for Joshua to get a wakeup call from God. He needed to be shaken out of his despair so God gave him this charge. God knew it would take more than this single challenge to sustain Joshua for the long haul. Therefore, He tells Joshua that if he is going to be successful in his new leadership role it would require a daily reminder from God's Word; he would have to meditate on the Word of God day and night.

The same is true for you and me. Sure, we can go to church three times a week and get encouraged from God's Word, but if we are going to have a successful walk with God, we will need a daily reminder from God's Word.

Thou Shalt Be Called Cephas

"..thou shalt be called Cephas, which is by interpretation, A stone." (John 1:42)

Out of all the apostles in the Bible, I think I can relate most to Peter. Peter was greatly used by God, but he always battled his flesh. His given name was Simon, which means listening. Which is ironic because that was something Peter did very little of. He was prone to speak first and think later.

Like us, Peter was sometimes all over the place, spiritually. One day he would soar to the highest highs and the next day he would sink to lowest of lows. One moment he could say the most spiritual things and the next minute say some of the ugliest things. He confessed Christ one moment and denied Him the next. One moment he was ready to fight, the next moment he was ready to flee.

Someone described Peter as being "consistently inconsistent." How true of him. How true of us!

But notice something unusual. One day Jesus looks at Peter, this man whose character seemed as shifty and unstable as the very sand they were walking on, and said to him, *"Thou **shalt** be called Cephas, which is by interpretation, a stone."*

In this amazing turn of events, Jesus gave him a name which was completely opposite to his nature. Jesus did not call him what he was, but what he was to become! He didn't say, "thou ART" but *"thou shalt be."* Peter never forgot the moment when Jesus said he was to be transformed from shifting sand into solid stone!

I don't know what name others call you by. The point is, it matters not what others (or even Satan) might say that you ARE. What matters is what Jesus has said that YOU CAN BE!

3 Ways To Fail Successfully

"Looking diligently lest any man fail of the grace of God..." (Heb. 12:15)

Wouldn't it be nice to succeed at everything you did in life? Well, the truth is failure is a part of life. The difference between those who have succeeded in life and those who haven't is...those who succeeded didn't let their failures define them.

Whether or not you become a success will be determined by what you do with your failures. Here are three ways to fail successfully.

1. Fail EARLY. It may sound strange to say you should fail early, but if you think about it, the sooner you fail at something the sooner you can succeed at it. See, growth comes from failure IF you are wise enough to LEARN from your failure. Don't let your failure defeat you because failure is often a big part of success.

2. Fail OFTEN. The person who never fails is a person who never tries anything. You will never have great reward without great risk. Don't be afraid to fail. Be afraid of not even trying.

Someone asked the famous inventor, Thomas Edison, why he didn't just quit trying to invent the lightbulb after he had failed so many times. Edison said, "I have not failed. I have simply found 10,000 ways that won't work!"

3. Fail FORWARD. As long as you learn from your failures you will fail forward. Let your failures teach you how to succeed. Great success is often birthed from great struggle so look at your struggle as something that is preparing you to succeed later.

No matter how many times you fail, remember this: FAILURE ISN'T FINAL!

Boy, Am I Full!

"And these things write we unto you, that your joy may be full." (1John 1:4)

Just recently we celebrated Thanksgiving. If there is one thing we all do every year on Thanksgiving, it's eat too much! It is so hard to see a table full of good food, followed by another table of sweet desserts, and not be tempted to try a little bit of everything! If you are like me, you don't WALK away from the Thanksgiving Day table after eating, you WOBBLE away.

Now, it takes a while for my body to become hungry after such a big meal, but eventually my body is depleted of that meal and I need to eat again. When you think about it, there are many things in life we constantly deplete that must be replenished. We eventually run out of gas in our car and must refill. We use up our energy throughout the day and must sleep at night. Every few seconds we use up the oxygen we breathed in and must breathe in new oxygen.

Likewise, our joy can be depleted if we are not careful. The Bible says *"these things"* were written that our joy *"may be full."* What *"things"*? The Bible! God's Word is where we find the joy of the Lord. Our problem is we try to find joy apart from Jesus. When you try to find joy in the things of this world, you will find yourself on empty pretty quickly.

So, as a helpful reminder, John says to us, *"these things write we unto you, that your joy may be full.*

God doesn't want you living on empty, He wants you living on full. Spend some time in His Word and get full again.

The Burned-Over Place

"..Jesus, which delivered us from the wrath to come."
(1Thess. 1:10)

The story is told about one of the early settlers of the western prairies. One day the people saw a cloud of smoke on the horizon and, to the people's horror, they recognized it as a prairie fire. Being fanned by a strong wind, it was quickly headed their way and would surely consume them and everything they owned.

As the flames grew larger and got closer, one man shocked everyone by quickly setting fire to the grass in front of them. His fire soon grew in size and widened its path leaving a charred and burned area behind.

As soon as the place was burned over, all of the people quickly moved to the grassless area and, standing in the midst of the burned area, saw the fire sweep down upon them until it reached the burned-over place and stopped!

There was nothing left to burn and they were safe while the fire swept around them. They were saved because they were in the "burned-over place!"

Listen, friend, the fires of God's judgment are quickly descending upon a wicked world but praise God He has provided a "burned-over place!" At Calvary, the fire of God's justice was met by Jesus Christ. There, He bore our sin and fully paid our punishment.

We are now saved when we accept Christ's payment for our sin and receive Him as our Savior. We are spared from the wrath of God by taking our stand by faith in the "burned-over place" of Calvary!

How about you? Are you standing in God's "burned-over place?" Have you trusted Him as YOUR Lord and Savior? Don't delay. Some people who plan to accept Christ at the eleventh hour die at ten-thirty!

4 Ways To Become A Stronger Christian

"But Saul increased the more in strength, and confounded the Jews which dwelt at Damascus, proving that this is very Christ." (Acts 9:22)

The Bible says that when Saul (also called Paul) got saved, he *"increased the more in strength."* As believers, we should seek to become stronger in our faith and walk with God. Here are 4 ways to become a stronger Christian.

#1—By identifying with God. (v.18) says, *"he... arose, and was baptized."* The first thing he did was identify with Jesus by being baptized. Baptism doesn't save you but it does identify us with the death, burial, and resurrection of Jesus.

The first step toward becoming a stronger Christian is being willing to publicly identify with Christ.

#2—By obeying God. (v.19) says, *"And when he had received meat, he was strengthened."* He received meat. Jesus said, *"My meat is to do the will of him that sent me" (John 4:34).* You will never become a strong Christian until you are willing to obey God's will for your life.

#3—By learning from others. (v.19) says, *"Then was Saul certain days with the disciples..."* We become stronger the more we are around stronger Christians. We learn from them how to be strong and it strengthens us. This is why attending church is so important.

#4—By telling others about Jesus. (vs.20, 29) says, *"And straightway he preached Christ in the synagogues...And he spake boldly in the name of the Lord Jesus..."* One of the best ways to become a stronger Christian is by telling others about what Jesus has done in your life.

A Reason To Blaspheme

"..by this deed thou hast given great occasion to the enemies of the LORD to blaspheme," (2Sam. 12:14)

David's sin had been found out. What he had done *privately,* God made *public!* The prophet Nathan had lovingly confronted David about his sin of adultery and murder. David was convicted and owned up to it by saying, *"I have sinned."*

Nathan told David that his sin had been forgiven, but he would still suffer consequences. Repentance and forgiveness to not eliminate God's chastisement. No one repented better of his sins than David did, yet he was severely *chastened* for his sins though he was *forgiven* of his sins.

Child of God, never think you can sin and get away with it. While you can repent of that sin you are enjoying, there will STILL be consequences to suffer for it.

One of the sad consequences of David's sin was that he had *"given great occasion to the enemies of the LORD to blaspheme,"* By the way we live our lives, we either confirm or deny God to unbelievers around us.

Those in Daniel's day watched how he lived his life and were actively looking for a reason to not believe his God, but he never gave them a reason to blaspheme God.

"Then the presidents and princes sought to find occasion against Daniel concerning the kingdom; but they could find none occasion nor fault..." (Dan. 6:4)

This story of David is a warning to all of us! Sin always dishonors God, and like David's sin with Bathsheba and Uriah, our sin can give *"great occasion to the enemies of the Lord to blaspheme."*

3 Things You'll Do When Jesus Touches You

"And we have confidence in the Lord touching you, that ye both do and will do the things which we command you."
(2Thess. 3:4)

They say we have about 17,000 tactile receptors on our hands, with around 100 on each fingertip. God created us with thousands of sensory receptors in our skin that tell us about the world around us. Some are sensitive to pressure and pain, hot and cold, and even vibration.

Touch is very important to us, but it is also important to God. Our text verse gives us three things you will do when Jesus touches you.

FIRST—You will obey God's Word. Paul said that when Jesus touches you, you will *"do the things which we command you."* You can tell someone whose life has been touched by the Lord; they are living in obedience to God's Word.

SECOND—You will have a heart for God. In (v.5) Paul said, *"And the Lord direct your hearts into the love of God..."* A person who does not have a heart and passion for God has never been touched by Him. Or, at the very least, it has been so long since they were touched that they have forgotten what it was like when Jesus touched them.

THIRD—You will live in light of Christ's return. Lastly, Paul said, *"and into the patient waiting for Christ."* When you are living for Jesus, you will be looking for His return. A person who has not been touched by Jesus does not think of His return. They are only living for themselves.

Has Jesus touched you? If not, reach out and touch Him right now in prayer. Once He touches you, you will never be the same!

The Preacher Who Had A Hitman After Him!

"And after that many days were fulfilled, the Jews took counsel to kill him:" (Acts 9:23)

Before the apostle Paul was saved, he did his best to persecute Christians in hopes of stopping Christianity. But after his conversion, God changed his heart. He went from persecuting Christians to preaching Christ! (v.29) says, *"..he spake boldly in the name of the Lord Jesus..."* As a result, he went from being the hunter, to becoming the hunted! It says they *"took counsel to kill him."* But Paul didn't quit. And neither should we.

FIRST—He continued, though he was ABUSED. (v.29) says *"..the Grecians..went about to slay him."* Paul was forced to leave town, but he didn't quit; he went on to Jerusalem. He preached in Jerusalem until the Grecians wanted to kill him...but he didn't quit. Instead, he just went on to Tarsus and began preaching Christ.

We are living in dark days. It will become increasingly more dangerous and difficult to stand for Christ. But stand for Christ we must!

SECOND—He continued, even though he was ABANDONED. In (2Tim. 4:16-17) Paul said, *"At my first answer no man stood with me, but all men forsook me...Notwithstanding the Lord stood with me, and strengthened me..."* There was a time when Paul found himself serving God all alone...but he served anyway! Paul had hitmen after him and he still took a stand for Jesus.

As we get closer to the coming of Christ, we may face more and more persecution. Ask God to give you the courage and boldness to stand even if no one will stand with you.

The Price Of Prayer (Part 1)

"And in the morning, rising up a great while before day, he went out, and departed into a solitary place, and there prayed." (Mark 1:35)

Jesus is our greatest example of how to pray. No one knew how to pray like Jesus. In fact, the disciples saw this in His life. When they heard Him pray, they knew that His prayer life was on an entirely different level than theirs was. That is why they said to Him, *"Lord, teach us to pray" (Luke 11:1).*

The prayer life of Jesus teaches us many things. But one of the biggest things we learn is that prayer will cost us something. There is a price to prayer.

For the next few days, I want you to notice three things prayer will cost you. Today, I will give you the first thing.

FIRST—Prayer will cost you TIME. The Bible says that when Jesus prayed, He got up *"a great while before day..."* He wasn't lazy. He got up and He went out early in the morning to talk to the Father in prayer.

I believe He prayed early in the morning to prepare Himself for the rest of the day. We do not know what circumstances will befall us throughout each day, but God does. Therefore, we need to get alone with Him before our day begins so that we can prepare ourselves for what may come our way.

Martin Luther said, "If I fail to spend two hours in prayer each morning, the Devil gets the victory through the day."

You don't have to spend two hours a day, but you need to have SOME time set aside to get alone with God so He can give you your marching orders for the day.

The Price Of Prayer (Part 2)

"And being in an agony he prayed more earnestly: and his sweat was as it were great drops of blood falling down to the ground." (Luke 22:44)

SECOND—Prayer will cost you EFFORT. We think we can say a little "Now I lay me down to sleep. I pray the Lord my soul to keep" type of prayer and everything is good; we've done our part. But that is not *real* praying.

Yesterday, we saw that prayer will cost you TIME, but it will also cost you EFFORT. While Jesus was **praying**, He wasn't **playing**!

It says that He was *"in an agony"* while He prayed. The word *"agony"* means struggle. If you have ever felt that you had a difficult time trying to pray, you are not alone. Jesus struggled in his praying.

In fact, it was so intense that it says *"his sweat was as it were great drops of blood falling down to the ground."* Wow! That is some intense praying, right there!

His disciples had already given up on praying because (v.45) says, *"And when he rose up from prayer, and was come to his disciples, he found them sleeping..."* Can you relate to that? I sure can!

Why is it such a struggle to pray? Because Satan fights prayer! Guy King said, "No one's a firmer believer in the power of prayer than the devil; not that he practices it, but he suffers from it." Therefore, he fights us when we try to pray.

Jesus struggled; He fought back Satan in His prayer time. Maybe we wouldn't struggle as much in LIFE, if we learned to struggle more in our PRAYER CLOSET!

The Price Of Prayer (Part 3)

Prayer is the most crucial element to the success of a believer. You cannot be a successful Christian without prayer. Edwin Harvey said, "A day without prayer is a day without blessing, and a life without prayer is a life without power."

So far we have seen that real prayer will cost you TIME and EFFORT. But there is one last price we must pay to really pray.

THIRD—Prayer will cost you TEARS. *"He that goeth forth and weepeth, bearing precious seed, shall doubtless come again with rejoicing, bringing his sheaves with him." (Ps. 126:6)*

First, we see *the PRIORITY* of this kind of praying. For there to be weeping, there must be a burdened heart behind those tears. When one begins to weep in their prayers, you know this need is not a little matter to them; it is a high priority.

Next, we see *the PRODUCT* of this kind of prayer. It says this person will be, *"bearing precious seed."* This reminds us again of the effort required on our part. We must pay the price if we expect an answer. God cannot answer a prayer not prayed.

Finally, we see *the PROMISE.* It says that the person who weeps and bears precious seed *"shall doubtless come again with rejoicing, bringing his sheaves with him."* What a promise! If you sow *"weeping"* you will reap *"rejoicing"*! You sow seeds and you reap sheaves!

In other words, God says you will reap MORE than you sow when you pray. What an encouragement that should be to us.

The next time Satan tries to discourage you from praying, just remember the reward of prayer is far greater than the price of prayer!

Satan's Stink Bomb

"No weapon that is formed against thee shall prosper;"
(Isaiah 54:17)

Not everything works as planned. For example, a woman devised a seemingly sure-fire way to rob a bank and decided to build a "stink bomb" as her weapon of choice. The day of the robbery came. She loaded her "stink bomb" into a bag and walked into the bank. As she approached the cashier, she told him she had explosives in her bag that she would use unless he gave her all the money he had in his drawer. That's when her plan took a turn for the worse!

When she dropped her bag on the counter, she accidentally triggered the stink bomb. As the nasty smell began to fill the air, the woman took off running out of the building with the bank security following after her. As you would imagine, the police had no trouble finding the "stinky" suspect.

Reading that story reminded me of what God told Isaiah about any weapons Satan may try to use against His people. He said, *"No weapon that is formed against thee shall prosper..."*

Satan is wise. He has been doing a lot of surveillance and has been studying the weaknesses of humans for thousands of years. You can be sure that he has a host of diabolical plans and weapons at his disposal. He has plenty of "stink bombs" ready and waiting for us.

But we serve a God Who is bigger and more powerful than Satan. And He has promised to protect us from Satan's weapons if only we will *"Put on the whole armor of God..."* (Eph. 6:11). Are you wearing the armor of God, this morning? Put it on before Satan detonates his "stink bomb" in your life.

Taming Your Tongue

"But the tongue can no man tame; it is an unruly evil, full of deadly poison." (James 3:8)

It is amazing the power that words have. Words may be harmless by themselves but when put together with other words can become extremely harmful to others. Words like: "I hate you," "You are worthless," "You will never amount to anything," can scar a person for life!

ANGRY words can HURT others. (Prov. 14:17) says, *"He that is soon angry dealeth foolishly..."* Many marriages have been permanently destroyed because someone spoke something foolishly out of anger. They didn't really mean what they said, but it didn't matter because the damage was already done. Be careful of your words during a disagreement because they can do more harm than you intend.

CRITICAL words can DISCOURAGE others. Some parents don't realize how they are harming the spirit of their child by always being critical of them. Nothing they do is ever good enough. Therefore, their child feels as if there is no need to even try because they can never please their parents. Critical words can also destroy the spirit of your spouse as well.

ENCOURAGING Words Can BUILD UP Others. You never go wrong by encouraging others. Try to find some way to encourage your children and spouse every day and just watch their countenance light up! Everyone loves encouragement.

So, how can we tame our tongue? *First—surrender your tongue to God.* Let God control your tongue and not your emotions. *Second—think before you speak!*

Do these two simple things and you'll be surprised how your relationships change.

Living Between The Plow And The Altar

"I beseech you therefore, brethren, by the mercies of God,
that ye present your bodies a living sacrifice..."
(Rom. 12:1)

What do you think of when you think of a sacrifice? Maybe you think of the sacrifices in the Old Testament where a perfect lamb was offered up. Today, we usually think of dead sacrifices, not living ones.

I once read that in China, Olympic athletes are chosen as young as 6 years old. Once they are chosen, they attend special schools and begin training intensively. They will be so busy training that they will rarely even see their parents. Everything about their lives revolves around training for the Olympics. They will live in total surrender to Communist China. They are living sacrifices to their country.

As Christians, God has called us to be living sacrifices, too! If these children can commit their lives to work for a gold medal, how much more should we commit our lives to CHRIST?

Presenting your body as a living sacrifice to Jesus is the key to victory and joy. (2 Cor. 8:5) says the Christians *"first gave their own selves to the Lord..."* God wants 100% commitment from us.

On one of the old Roman coins was the figure of an ox standing between a plow and an altar with the inscription, "Ready for either." That is to be the attitude we should have as a sold-out Christian. We should be living between the PLOW and the ALTAR, ready for **service** and **sacrifice**.

4 Ways To Respond To Being Attacked

"And when king David came to Bahurim, behold, thence came out a man of the family of the house of Saul...and cursed still as he came...And he cast stones at David..."
(2Sam. 16:5-6)

While passing the city of Bahurim, David encountered a relative of King Saul who came running out of the city cursing and abusing David. How should WE respond when being attacked by someone?

FIRST—Act, don't react. Usually, what the attacker is trying to do is provoke you into reacting out of anger, and thereof make you look foolish. David did not retaliate. He did respond, but it was a controlled response.

SECOND—See if there is any truth to the accusation. He accused David of being a bloodthirsty murderer and a man of Belial. He also shouted that God was now judging David for his sins.

David realized God was using him to unwittingly pronounce judgment on his REAL sin of adultery with Bathsheba and the murder of her husband, Uriah. That is why David said in (v.11), *"let him alone, and let him curse; for the LORD hath bidden him."*

THIRD—Leave It In God's Hands. In (v.12) David said, *"the LORD will requite me good for his cursing this day."* In other words, "God knows the truth. If I am being falsely accused, God will reward me in the end."

LASTLY—Refresh Yourself In The Lord. (v.14) *"And the king, and all the people...refreshed themselves there."* The best way to overcome an attack and not let it make you bitter is by staying close to the Lord and letting Him refresh your spirit.

Something Sweeter Than Honey

"How sweet are thy words unto my taste! yea, sweeter than honey to my mouth!" (Ps. 119:103)

From the earliest post-Flood times, ancient cultures believed that honey was a gift from God because it was so beneficial. David likened the Word of God to honey. Notice three characteristics that honey and God's Word have in common.

FIRST—Honey Doesn't Make Itself. Honey doesn't grow naturally. It must be produced by honeybees. Honeybees visit as many as 1500 flowers in order to fill their honey stomachs. On the way back to the hive, they add enzymes to the nectar which begins its conversion to honey.

As miraculous as the production of honey is, even more miraculous is how the Bible was given to us. (2Pet. 1:21) says that, just like honey, the Bible wasn't made by man. Rather, *"..holy men of God spake as they were moved by the Holy Ghost."*

SECOND—Honey Kills Harmful Germs. Records show how the ancient Egyptians used honey to prevent and cure various diseases, and heal wounds.

Likewise, when we read and study God's Word, it has the power to kill the harmful sin that Satan is constantly trying to tempt us with. That is why David said, *"Thy word have I hid in mine heart, that I might not sin against thee"* (Ps. 119:11).

THIRD—Honey will sustain you. John the Baptist actually survived for years on honey as a part of his daily diet. Matthew 3:4 says that *"his meat was locusts and wild honey."* Honey has many nutrients that that are good for your body. Likewise, the Bible will sustain you in life when nothing else will!

3 Characteristics Of Godly Parents

"And they were both righteous before God..." (Luke 1:6)

You cannot find a better example in all the Bible of godly parents than Zacharias and Elizabeth, John the Baptist's parents. Let see what made them such a godly example.

1. They had a godly heritage. (v.5) says Zacharias was a priest *"Of the course of Abia"* which started in the time of David. And his wife Elizabeth *"was of the daughters of Aaron"* and of the tribe of Levi. My, what a godly heritage they gave John the Baptist!

You may not have come from a godly heritage, but you can make sure you give *your* children one.

2. They had a godly testimony. Not everyone with a godly heritage has a godly testimony. But the Bible says *"They were both righteous."* We all have different gifts and abilities, but we can ALL be righteous.

Next, it says that their righteousness was not just a show before man but it was *"before God."* You may appear righteous to others, but God sees the real you!

You will never be the parents God wants you to be without the righteousness of God in your life. Zacharias and Elizabeth had a godly testimony because (v.6) says they were *"..walking in all the commandments and ordinances of the Lord blameless."*

Where do you think John the Baptist learned to walk with God like he did? From his parents! They taught him by example.

3. They had a servant's heart. (v.8) says it was while Zacharias did his duty that he heard the good news that he would have a son. If you want special blessings from God, be faithful to your duty. Let your children see you faithfully serving the Lord.

The Enigma Of Prayer

"But verily God hath heard me; he hath attended to the voice of my prayer." (Ps. 66:19)

An enigma is something that is mysterious or puzzling. It is something that is difficult to understand. Prayer is somewhat of an enigma; it is something mysterious and sometimes puzzling.

"How so," you ask?

While prayer is the most inexpensive thing in the world (because it is free), it is also the costliest; and while it is the easiest thing in the world, it is also the most difficult. And while even an innocent child can do it, some of the godliest Christians can struggle with it.

Prayer is mysterious in that though we may be alone in our prayer closet, physically, we are NOT alone spiritually. There is an unseen spiritual warfare going on when we pray.

While we may never leave our prayer closet, *physically*, while praying, we ARE transported *spiritually* past the sun, moon, and stars to the very throne of God!

Yet, while we have an open invitation to call on God, such as: *"Call unto me, and I will answer thee, and shew thee great and mighty things, which thou knowest not"* (Jer. 33:3) and *"Ask and it shall be given you" (Mat. 7:7),* there can be hindrances to our prayer.

Praying with sin in our heart will prevent God from hearing our prayer (Ps. 76:18). Asking for something that we will consume on our own lusts will keep our prayers from being heard (James 4:8).

Prayer is not a RIGHT; it is a PRIVILEGE! Prayer is an investment given to us by God, not to be used for selfish purposes but for His glory.

Watching Where You're Walking

"Thy word is a lamp unto my feet, and a light unto my path." (Ps. 119:105)

Believers have a tremendous advantage over the unsaved. As believers, we know where we are going as we journey through life and we know how to get there. We have God to help us and the Bible to show us the way.

However, the ancient world did not have flashlights like we have today that can light up our pathway ahead of us. The people back then carried little clay dishes containing oil, and the light illuminated their path only one step ahead.

Likewise, we do not see the entire path God has for us at one time. We are walking by faith when we follow the Word of God. Each act of obedience shows us the next step, and eventually we arrive at the appointed destination.

You might not want to admit it, but if you don't know where you are going, you are lost. And that is the condition of every unsaved man and woman on earth. The Bible does not use the word "unsaved" to describe the condition of those without Christ; it uses the word "lost."

Praise God, if you know Jesus as your personal Savior, you are no longer LOST! You have found the way! You are on the right path which leads to life everlasting!

Once we are on the right path, obedience to the Word keeps us walking in the light. And when we walk in the light we are cleansed from our sin. John said in (1John 1:7) *"But if we walk in the light, as he is in the light, we have fellowship one with another, and the blood of Jesus Christ his Son cleanseth us from all sin."*

Take the light of God's Word with you, today, so you can be watching where you're walking!

5 Things To Stop Praying For

"And this is the confidence that we have in him, that, if we ask any thing according to his will, he heareth us:"
(1John 5:14)

God gives us a wonderful promise that if we pray according to His will He hears our prayer! But there are some things we should NOT pray for.

STOP praying for anything that goes against God's will. God's will is in God's Word. Therefore, we should not pray for that which goes against the will and Word of God. Jesus said we are to pray, *"Thy will be done"* not "MY will be done."

STOP praying for anything that feeds our flesh. (Gal. 5:16) says we are to *"Walk in the Spirit"* and not *"fulfil the lust of the flesh."* Therefore, God will not answer a prayer that feeds our flesh.

STOP praying for anything that costs nothing. God expects us to do OUR part in the Christian life. He will not do for us what we could and should do for ourselves. For example, don't ask God to heal your marriage if you are not willing to do your part to work on it, yourself.

STOP praying for things we already have. How many times does God bless us with something and we quickly get dissatisfied with it and ask Him for another one even better? Instead of learning contentment, we are always wanting the newer, better version of what God has already given to us.

STOP praying for things other people have. "I wish I had his job." "I wish I had her good looks." "I wish I had her boyfriend." All of these statements reveal a heart of covetousness, which the Bible condemns.

Stop praying these prayers and start praying prayers that honor and glorify God.

I Need Help!

"God is our refuge and strength, a very present help in trouble." (Ps. 46:1)

Some people have the mistaken assumption that once a person gets saved they will no longer have any problems. Anyone who tells you that the Christian life is a problem-free life is promoting a false version of Christianity. In fact, when a person gets saved, they have a NEW problem they didn't have before....Satan is now after them!

The truth is, real Christianity isn't a PROBLEM-FREE life but it is a PROMISE-FILLED life! Sure we face problems, but unlike unbelievers, when we go through trials we have God's presence to comfort us, God's truth to guide us, and God's promises to carry us.

The psalmist reminds us of God's promises.

FIRST—It is a PERSONAL promise. In (v.1a) He said, *"God is **our** refuge..."* I am glad that God is MY refuge and strength. I am glad He knows what I am going through.

SECOND—It is a POWERFUL promise. Next, he said, *"God is our **refuge** and **strength**..."* The word *"refuge"* means shelter. God is our shelter when the storms of life come our way. He is also the strength we need to endure the storms.

THIRD—It is a PERMANENT promise. In (v.2-3) He says, *"Therefore will not we fear, though the earth be removed, and though the mountains be carried into the midst of the sea..."*

Traumatic events will come in life. The question is, will you allow them to **flatten** you or **fortify** you? If you need help, call on Jesus right now! He is *"a very present help in trouble."*

5 Words That Will Change Your Day

"..he that is greatest among you, let him be as the younger; and he that is chief, as he that doth serve." (Luke 22:26)

In Luke 22, we see that the disciples were having a bad day. There was strife between them because they were arguing. What were they arguing about? (v.24) says they were arguing over *"which of them should be accounted the greatest."*

They were men just like us; prone to the same temptation of pride that we are prone to. They were fighting over who should be the greatest disciple in the kingdom! They wanted to know who would have the most power and rule over the others.

Can you believe that? How silly. How childish. How...like us!

So, how did Jesus respond to this childish behavior? What was His solution? Jesus reminded them that that is a worldly focus. The world is concerned about ruling over others but that is not how a Christian is to live. Jesus said, *"But **ye** shall not be so: but he that is **greatest** among you, let him be as the younger; and he that is chief, as he that doth **serve**."*

So, what are the five words that will completely change your day? Here they are: **WHO CAN I SERVE, TODAY?**

That's it!

See, your day begins going downhill when the focus is all about YOU and what YOU want. Jesus said you need to focus on others and how you can serve them.

Is your morning already starting off badly? Then stop and ask yourself, "Who can I serve today?"

353

Wherever You Go, He's There!

"Whither shall I go from thy spirit? or whither shall I flee from thy presence?" (Ps. 139:7)

One of Satan's favorites tactics is to make us think that we are all alone. Not only does he tell us that friends and family have forsaken us, but he wants us to believe that even God has forsaken us, too. But there are too many examples in the Bible that say otherwise.

For example: Adam and Eve could not hide from God in the Garden. Jonah could not hide from God in a boat, and Shadrach, Meshach, and Abednego could not escape God's presence in the fiery furnace. In our text verse this morning, even the psalmist said, *"Whither shall I go from thy spirit? or whither shall I flee from thy presence?"*

Why? The Bible gives us many different names for God. He is called **Jehovah-Jireh,** which means "the God who provides." He is called **Jehovah-Shalom,** which means "the God of peace." He is called **Jehovah-Rophe,** which means "Jehovah heals." But He is also called **Jehovah-Shammah**, which means the LORD is there!

What a name: "The LORD is there!" How encouraging it should be to know that you cannot escape the presence of God for He is everywhere! In that fiery furnace, with the three Hebrew children, He was there. Among the thick, green, trees of the Garden of Eden with Adam and Eve, He was there. Even way down in the depths of the ocean, inside the belly of a whale with Jonah, HE WAS THERE!

In fact, that is what Christmas is all about—the fact that God, Who is everywhere, took on flesh and came to us! As you celebrate the birth of Jesus, be ENCOURAGED because there is not a place you can go, today, where God is not at. Give Him praise and glory this morning because wherever you go, He's there!

How To Survive A Marriage Earthquake

"What therefore God hath joined together, let not man put asunder." (Mark 10:9)

I Googled, "How To Survive An Earthquake" and found that the advice given would also work for a marriage earthquake too! So, how can your marriage survive?

1. Drop to your knees. The first thing they say to do during an earthquake is to drop to your knees before the earthquake knocks you down. Likewise, the best way for your marriage to survive is for you to drop to your knees in prayer. Take your earth-shattering trial to God.

2. Take cover immediately. Whether it is under a table or a sturdy desk, cover yourself immediately. The same is true, spiritually. In order to survive your marriage earthquake, you must cover your head (mind). Protect your thoughts by reading and meditating on God's Word.

3. Hold on tight. During an earthquake, it is wise to stay put and hold on until the shaking stops. Likewise, a marriage earthquake is the time to hold on tighter to your spouse and to your commitment to the marriage.

4. Render Aid. After an earthquake has ended, render aid to those who have been injured. A marriage earthquake can devastate a marriage, leaving both parties injured emotionally and spiritually. The best way for your marriage to survive is by taking time to heal together.

5. Prepare ahead of time for the next earthquake. Many do not survive a marriage earthquake because they simply have not prepared themselves ahead of time. God's Word gives us the tools we need to survive the earth-shattering trials that come our way. Stay close to Him and you will make it through.

I Don't Know Why I'm Telling You This

"And of some have compassion, making a difference:"
(Jude 1:22)

One day a man was doing some work at our house. During our conversation, it came that I was a pastor and also the Chaplain for the Sheriff's Office.

Later, as I was in another room with him, he stopped working for a moment and began pouring out his troubles. Some of the things he told me about were very personal struggles he was trying to deal with but that were overwhelming him.

After he got through telling me his story, he looked at me and said, "I don't why I'm telling you this. I haven't told anyone about these things except my wife." Then he said, "I guess I just need someone to pray for me."

Before he left, I asked him about his salvation and he assured me he was saved but wasn't living like he knew he should. So I said, "Can I have a word of prayer with you before you leave?" He said, "I would like that."

It got me to thinking. We never know what struggles someone we encounter might be facing. That seemingly rude waitress, that quiet cashier, that co-worker no one gets along with may all be facing struggles they are trying to deal with in their lives. They don't need our impatience or angry reply. What they need is compassion!

Ask yourself, "Who can I be a blessing to, today? Whose heart can I touch for Jesus, today?" You might just find yourself listening to someone's overwhelmed heart, when all of the sudden they stop and say, "I don't know why I'm telling you this." And you will say to yourself, "I do!"

You've Got A Friend In Me

"A man that hath friends must shew himself friendly: and there is a friend that sticketh closer than a brother."
(Prov. 18:24)

It has been said that if you have three true friends you have something special. There is one sure way to tell who your "true" friends really are...just go through a trial! A true friend is one who walks in when everyone else walks out.

We all want friends, but what makes a good friend? What qualities do you look for in a true friend? Trustworthiness? Honesty? Dependability? Well, I've got some good news for you...you already have a friend who matches all those characteristics—Jesus!

Jesus is a TRUSTWORTHY friend. Others may betray you or stab you in the back. Has that ever happened to you? But there is one friend whom you can completely trust. He will NEVER let you down. And that friend is Jesus. Jesus is so trustworthy that not only can you trust Him with your LIFE, but also with your ETERNITY!

Jesus is a DEPENDABLE friend. Some so-called friends are there as long as they need you. But when you really need them, they are gone! Not so with Jesus.

Some friends will be with you through thick or thin; Jesus will stick with you through thick and *thicker!* He is 100% dependable.

Jesus is a FAITHFUL friend. You will never find a more faithful friend than Jesus because He has promised to *"never leave thee, nor forsake thee" (Heb. 13:5).*

Anyone who has watched the Toy Story movie instantly recognizes the title to my devotion as being a song in the movie. But is it more than a song. With Jesus, it is a reality. You really do have a friend in Him!

Leftover Ham And A Second-Hand Sweater

"and when they had opened their treasures, they presented unto him gifts; gold, and frankincense, and myrrh."
(Matt. 2:11)

What if all you got for Christmas was a worn out sweater someone was tired of wearing? These wise men didn't bring second-hand trinkets. These wise men gave their *treasures* to Jesus. What are YOU giving to Jesus for all He has done for you?

FIRST—Give Him the treasure of your TIME. There were many other things these wise men could have busied themselves with; many other places they could have gone, but there was nothing more important to them than finding Jesus. Do you spend most of your time on worldly things and only give Jesus your leftover time?

SECOND—Give Him the Treasure of Your TALENTS. Their *"gold, and frankincense, and myrrh"* could have been given to an earthly king, but they gave them to Jesus. It is sad that the average church struggles to have good musicians and singers because many Christians are using their talents in the world and not for the Lord.

THIRD—*(and most importantly)* **Give Him the Treasure of Your HEART?** On this Christmas Eve, what better present to give Jesus, than to give Him your heart! Truth is…if He doesn't have your heart, nothing else you give Him really matters.

Jesus deserves our best. He deserves more than just leftover ham and a second-hand sweater. Stop giving Jesus your leftovers. He gave His best for you. Give your best for Him!

It's All About Jesus

"And when they were come into the house, they saw the young child with Mary his mother, and fell down, and worshipped him..." (Matt. 2:11)

The Bible says that God led the wise men by a star to where Jesus was. It says that by the time they arrived, Mary, Joseph, and baby Jesus were already living in a house. But there are a couple of truths I want to focus on this morning.

They were wise men for SEEKING Jesus. Not every man in that day sought Jesus. These were wise men indeed who saw the importance of following God's star to the place where Jesus was. And can I say, wise men STILL seek Jesus! Man doesn't need to seek Jesus because **Jesus** is lost. No. Man must seek Jesus because **man** is lost! If you do not know Christ as Lord and Savior, seek Him today.

They were wise men for WORSHIPPING Jesus. It says that when the wise men finally found Jesus, they *"fell down, and worshipped him..."* A lot of false religions would be put out of business if they only understood this verse correctly. There are religions who worship and pray to Mary. There are religions which worship and pray to angels. But there was no worship of Mary, here. There was no worship of Joseph, here. There was no worship of angels, here. No, my friend, the only worship that was going on was directed solely and completely toward JESUS! Why? Because He ALONE is worthy of worship!

This is Christmas morning. You are probably opening gifts and enjoying time with your family, celebrating Christmas. Enjoy this day. Enjoy the gifts. Enjoy your family. Just don't forget it's all about Jesus.

Not So, Lord!

*"And there came a voice to him, Rise, Peter; kill, and eat.
But Peter said, Not so, Lord..." (Acts 10:13-14)*

What do we do when we don't *want* to do what God
has *told* us to do? That's a tongue twister, isn't it? What do
we do when God has told us something but we aren't really
sure about it?

This happens often. God calls a man to be a missionary
to a foreign field but this man says, "Not so, Lord. I can't
go there. I don't know what to do. I have never been a
missionary before. Besides, I have my family here. I have
my friends here. I have a good paying job here. I have
indoor plumbing here!"

Or maybe God has called a man to preach and his first
response is, "Not so, Lord. I could never preach. Surely
you've made a mistake. You really meant this call for
someone else; someone who knows more Bible than I do;
someone who has been to Bible college; someone who isn't
terrified to stand up and speak in front of people."

Then there are times when God tells us something that,
quite frankly, we just don't want to do. This was the case
with Peter. The Jews had no dealing with the Gentiles, yet
God was now telling him to go minister to the Gentiles.
Peter's first response was, "Not so, Lord."

Finally, after repeated attempts to convince him this
message was from God, Peter submits himself to God's
Word and obeys.

So, what is it that God may be trying to get you to do?
Is there some area in which God has been dealing with you
but you keep saying, "Not so, Lord"?

Do like Peter and submit yourself to Him. The happiest
Christian is one who responds to Jesus like Samuel did
when he said, *"Speak Lord, for thy servant heareth."*

Andrew's Courage

"One of the two which heard John speak, and followed him, was Andrew, Simon Peter's brother." (John 1:40)

Andrew was the first of two men who followed Jesus. He didn't do it because everybody else was following Him. He, along with John, were the first ones to do it. Most people will wait until they see if something is going to be popular before they decide to do it. After they see what the "in crowd" is doing THEN they gladly jump on the bandwagon.

But it takes real courage to step out on faith, especially when you are the first to do it. It took courage for Andrew to say, "Nobody else is following this Jesus, and I'm not even 100% sure where this will take me or how it will turn out. But I believe Jesus is the Messiah and I am willing to put everything on the line for Him."

He did not care about what others thought. What they would say about what he did made no difference to him. He was a man who could think for himself, and he made up his mind to follow Christ, even if he was the only one to do it.

He wasted no time in making his decision to follow Christ. He was familiar with the words of Isaiah, *"Seek ye the Lord while he may be found, call ye upon him while he is near" (Isa. 55:6).* So Andrew made haste to go with Jesus.

Are you a disciple of Christ? Will you have the courage like Andrew to stand up for God even if no one else does? Will you have the boldness follow Jesus and not be ashamed?

We need more with the courage of Andrew!

I Can...Through Christ

"I can do all things through Christ which strengtheneth me." (Phil. 4:13)

This verse is a popular verse to many. The problem is, we often focus on the wrong words in this verse.

Some focus on *"I."* They think everything is about them. I've got news for you, the universe doesn't revolve around you. While you do have a part in His great plan, His plan includes everyone, not just you.

Some like to focus on the words: *"I can do all things."* They love the idea that no matter what THEY want to accomplish in life, they should be able to do it, even if it is not God's will. That is not what those words mean. God is not some magical Genie in a bottle forced to grant your every wish just so you can live your life YOUR way and not His way.

The correct words to focus on in this verse are *"through Christ."* We try to do more through the flesh than through Christ. All of the power we need in life comes from Christ. Therefore, if Jesus is not a part of your life, this verse does not apply to you.

There is power to OVERCOME. God has given every believer the power to overcome the trials we may face in this world. Jesus said in *(John 16:33) "In the world ye shall have tribulation: but be of good cheer; I have overcome the world."*

There is power to ENDURE. Sometimes it isn't God's will for us to overcome our trial but for us to endure our trial. God never removed Paul's thorn in the flesh, but rather said to Paul *"My grace is sufficient for thee:" (2Cor. 12:9).* Don't try to live without Jesus, because it is only THROUGH CHRIST that you can live the victorious life.

Healing From The Hurt

"The LORD is nigh unto them that are of a broken heart; and saveth such as be of a contrite spirit." (Ps. 34:18)

Have you been hurt by someone you love? Maybe it was a close friend or family member who betrayed you or broke your trust. Maybe you were hurt by a church member. No matter who it was, it can be a painful experience when someone you care about has stabbed you in the back and hurt you.

King David knew what it was like to be betrayed. He said, *"..it was not an enemy that reproached me; then I could have borne it...But it was thou, a man mine equal, my guide, and mine acquaintance" (Ps. 55:12-13).*

When you have been hurt deeply, Satan wants you to isolate yourself and withdraw from everyone, including God. He will tell you that you have been hurt too deeply to go on any further. He will say that you will NEVER be happy again.

Well, when the devil comes around telling you that, you remind him that he is a liar and that the Bible says that in the presence of Jesus there *"is fulness of JOY; at thy right hand there are PLEASURES for evermore" (Ps.16:11).*

The best thing to do when you've been hurt deeply is to get as close to the Lord as possible. HE is the one who loves you and cares for you and has promised that He would never leave nor forsake you! Satan wants you to focus on your hurt and on the one who hurt you. By doing this, the hurt and pain stay fresh in your mind and it keeps you from moving forward.

So, if you have been hurt, the best way to get over the one who HURT you is by focusing on the one who can HEAL you!

Avoiding A Spiritual Blister

John Wooden was the head coach at the University of California, Los Angeles. Nicknamed the "Wizard of Westwood," he won ten NCAA national championships in a 12-year period as head coach. He was known for teaching his players practical things that ensured top-level performance.

For one thing, he taught them how to put on their socks! No kidding. Each season Coach Wooden showed his players how to prevent sock-wrinkles around the little toe and heel, and how to lace up their shoes with a double-knot. This helped his players avoid blisters. In the closing minutes of a close game, the player without blisters on his feet will perform better. This simple, basic detail contributed to a series of National Championships.

Wooden never had to resort to pep talks or tirades. He just helped his players excel at the basics because, as Coach Wooden said, "Excelling at the basics wins ball games."

The same is true of the Christian life. Learning to excel at the basics is what will help a believer be a successful Christian. There are no tricks and no short-cuts to this process. The only way to excel in the Christian life is to do the basics: daily prayer, daily Bible study, daily worship…in other words, daily walking with God.

Spending time in prayer, memorizing a Bible verse, or visiting a shut-in to encourage them may sometimes seem about as exciting as putting on your socks! But when you do it right, that is what prevents spiritual blisters that can eventually hurt your walk with God if you are not careful.

Have you gotten away from the basics?

Discounted Jesus: 50% Off!

"Having a form of godliness, but denying the power thereof." (2Tim. 3:5)

Years ago, one of America's biggest department stores tried marketing a doll in the form of Baby Jesus. The advertisements described it as being "washable, cuddly, and unbreakable" and it was packaged in straw, satin, and plastic. To the department store executives, it looked like a surefire winner; a real moneymaker. But they were wrong. It didn't sell. In a last-ditch effort to get rid of the dolls, one of the store managers placed a huge sign in the store window that read:

JESUS CHRIST:
Marked Down 50%
Get Him While You Can!

Sadly, that same marketing strategy is being used today by many popular TV and radio hucksters! They have watered down the Gospel in hopes of drawing a crowd and are offering nothing more than a "Marked Down, 50% Off, Get Him While You Can" type of Jesus.

But the truth is…Christianity costs! To be a true follower of Jesus Christ you must pay the price! Jesus said, *"If any man will come after me, let him deny himself, and take up his cross, and follow me" (Mark 16:24).*

The world is tired of seeing fakes and phonies. What they need to see is something real! How you live, today, will say a lot about who God is. Will you show the world there is a God who is alive and well, or you will give them nothing more than a water-down version of a discounted Jesus?

ATTENTION!

If you enjoyed this book, would you consider leaving an honest book review for this book on Amazon.com?

Amazon does not require that you purchase the book online in order to leave a review. Simply go to www.Amazon.com and search for "Mark Agan." Select this book and leave a review.

Why is a review important?

Reviews are important because the more reviews a book has, the more visibility it gets. Good book reviews are what help others determine whether or not to purchase the book. Especially if they are not familiar with the author.

Thank you, in advance, for taking the time to leave an honest review and helping make sure more books like these get noticed!

Made in the USA
Lexington, KY
11 November 2019

56850461R00203